Mobil Travel Guide®

Get the inside scoop with Mobil's new City Guide series.

- Written for busy travelers who are always on the hunt for the best places to visit during a short jaunt to destination cities

- Anonymous _____ _____ tels, restaurants an _____ al writers provide the m _____ a city

- Available Ja _____ e sold

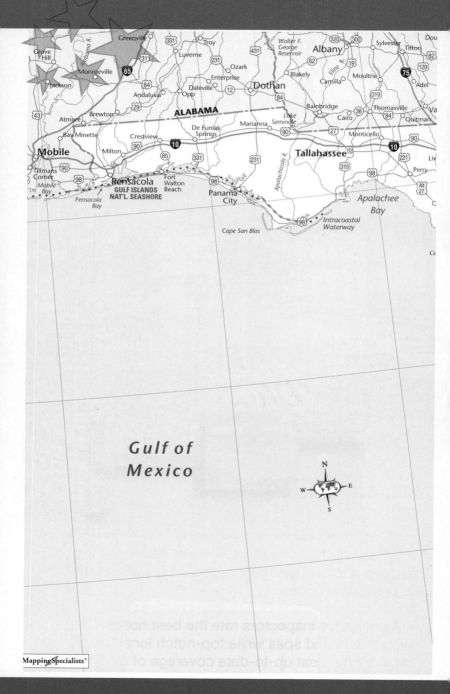

The Center for Hospitality Research

Hospitality Leadership Through Learning

The Cornell School of Hotel Administration's
world-class faculty explores new ways
to refine the practice of hospitality
management.

Our research drives better results.
Better strategy.
Better management.
Better operations.

See our work at:
www.chr.cornell.edu

537 Statler Hall • hosp_research@cornell.edu • 607.255.9780

Cornell University
School of Hotel Administration

FLORIDA

ACKNOWLEDGMENTS

We gratefully acknowledge the help of our representatives for their efficient and perceptive inspections of the lodging and dining establishments listed, the establishments' proprietors for their cooperation in showing their facilities and providing information about them, and the many users of previous editions who have taken the time to share their experiences. Mobil Travel Guide is also grateful to all the talented writers who contributed entries to this book.

Front and back cover images: ©iStockPhoto.com

All maps: created by Mapping Specialists

The information contained herein is derived from a variety of third-party sources. Although every effort has been made to verify the information obtained from such sources, the publisher assumes no responsibility for inconsistencies or inaccuracies in the data or liability for any damages of any type arising from errors or omissions.

Neither the editors nor the publisher assume responsibility for the services provided by any business listed in this guide or for any loss, damage or disruption in your travel for any reason.

ISBN: 9-780841-60857-3   Manufactured in Canada

10 9 8 7 6 5 4 3 2 1

2

FLORIDA

★
★
★
★

TABLE OF CONTENTS

3

FLORIDA

★
★
★
★
★

WRITTEN IN THE STARS

Because time is precious and the travel industry is ever-changing, having accurate, reliable travel information at your fingertips has never been more important. With this in mind, Mobil Travel Guide has provided invaluable insight to travelers through its Star Rating system for more than 50 years.

The Mobil Corporation (known as Exxon Mobil Corporation since a 1999 merger) began producing the Mobil Travel Guide books in 1958 following the introduction of the U.S.-interstate highway system in 1956. The first edition covered only five Southwestern states. Since then, our books have become the premier travel guides in North America, covering all 50 states and Canada, and beginning in 2008, international destinations such as Hong Kong and Beijing.

Today, the concept of a "five-star" experience is one that permeates the collective conciousness, but few people realize it's one that originated with Mobil. We created our star rating system to give travelers an easy-to-recognize quality scale for choosing where to stay, dine and spa. Based on an objective process, we make recommendations to our readers that we believe will enhance the quality and value of their travel experiences. Our trusted Mobil One- to Five-Star rating system is the oldest and most respected lodging and restaurant inspection and rating program in North America. Most hoteliers, restaurateurs and industry observers favorably regard the rigor of our inspection program and understand the prestige and benefits that come with receiving a Mobil Star rating.

The Mobil Travel Guide process of rating each establishment includes unannounced inspections, incognito evaluations and a review of unsolicted comments from the general public. We inspect more than 500 attributes at each property we visit, from cleanliness to the condition of the rooms and public spaces, to employee attitude and courtesy. It's a system that rewards those properties that strive for and achieve excellence each year. And the very best properties raise the bar for those that wish to compete with them.

Only facilities that meet Mobil Travel Guide's standards earn the privilege of being listed in the guide. Properties are continuously updated, and deteriorating, poorly managed establishments are removed. We wouldn't recommend that you visit a hotel, restaurant or spa that we wouldn't want to visit ourselves.

★★★★★ The Mobil Five-Star Award indicates that a property is one of the very best in the country and consistently provides gracious and courteous service, superlative quality in its facility and a unique ambience. The lodgings and restaurants at the Mobil Five-Star level consistently continue their commitment to excellence, doing so with grace and perseverance.

★★★★ The Mobil Four-Star Award honors properties for outstanding achievement in overall facility and for providing very strong service levels in all areas. These award winners provide a distinctive experience for the ever-demanding and sophisticated consumer.

★★★ The Mobil Three-Star Award recognizes an excellent property that provides full services and amenities. This category ranges from exceptional hotels with limited services to elegant restaurants with a less formal atmosphere.

★★ The Mobil Two-Star property is a clean and comfortable establishment that has expanded amenities or a distinctive environment. These properties are an excellent place to stay or dine.

★ The Mobil One-Star property is limited in its amenities and services but provides a value experience while meeting travelers' expectations. The properties should be clean, comfortable and convenient.

We do not charge establishments for inclusion in our guides. We have no relationship with any of the businesses and attractions we list and act only as a consumer advocate. We do the investigative legwork so that you won't have to.

Restaurants and hotels—particularly small chains and stand-alone establishments—change management or even go out of business with surprising quickness. Although we make every effort to continuously update information, we recommend that you call ahead to make sure the place you've selected is still open.

5

FLORIDA

STAR RATINGS

MOBIL RATED HOTELS

Whether you're looking for the ultimate in luxury or the best bang for your travel buck, we have a hotel recommendation for you. To help you pinpoint properties that meet your needs, Mobil Travel Guide classifies each lodging by type according to the following characteristics.

★★★★★The Mobil Five-Star hotel provides consistently superlative service in an exceptionally distinctive luxury environment. Attention to detail is evident throughout the hotel, resort or inn, from bed linens to staff uniforms.

★★★★The Mobil Four-Star hotel provides a luxury experience with expanded amenities in a distinctive environment. Services may include automatic turndown service, 24-hour room service and valet parking.

★★★The Mobil Three-Star hotel is well appointed, with a full-service restaurant and expanded amenities, such as a fitness center, golf course, tennis courts, 24-hour room service and optional turndown service.

★★The Mobil Two-Star hotel is considered a clean, comfortable and reliable establishment that has expanded amenities, such as a full-service restaurant.

★The Mobil One-Star lodging is a limited-service hotel, motel or inn that is considered a clean, comfortable and reliable establishment.

For every property, we also provide pricing information. The pricing categories break down as follows:

$ = Up to $150

$$ = $151-$250

$$$ = $251-$350

$$$$ = $351 and up

All prices quoted are accurate at the time of publication; however, prices cannot be guaranteed.

MOBIL RATED RESTAURANTS

Every restaurant in this book has been visited by Mobil Travel Guide's team of experts and comes highly recommended as an outstanding dining experience.

★★★★★The Mobil Five-Star restaurant offers one of few flawless dining experiences in the country. These establishments consistently provide their guests with exceptional food, superlative service, elegant décor and exquisite presentations of each detail surrounding a meal.

★★★★The Mobil Four-Star restaurant provides professional service, distinctive presentations and wonderful food.

★★★The Mobil Three-Star restaurant has good food, warm and skillful service and enjoyable décor.

★★The Mobil Two-Star restaurant serves fresh food in a clean setting with efficient service. Value is considered in this category, as is family friendliness.

★The Mobil One-Star restaurant provides a distinctive experience through culinary specialty, local flair or individual atmosphere.

Because menu prices can fluctuate, we list a pricing category rather than specific prices. The pricing categories are defined as follows, per diner, and assume that you order an appetizer or dessert, an entrée and one drink:

FLORIDA

★
★
★
★
★

$ = $15 and under

$$ = $16-$35

$$$ = $36-$85

$$$$ = $86 and up

MOBIL RATED SPAS

Mobil Travel Guide's spa ratings are based on objective evaluations of hundreds of attributes. About half of these criteria assess basic expectations, such as staff courtesy, the technical proficiency and skill of the employees and whether the facility is clean and maintained properly. Several standards address issues that impact a guest's physical comfort and convenience, as well as the staff's ability to impart a sense of personalized service. Additional criteria measure the spa's ability to create a completely calming ambience.

★★★★★The Mobil Five-Star spa provides consistently superlative service in an exceptionally distinctive luxury environment with extensive amenities. The staff at a Mobil Five-Star spa provides extraordinary service beyond the traditional spa experience, allowing guests to achieve the highest level of relaxation and pampering. These spas offer an extensive array of treatments, often incorporating international themes and products. Attention to detail is evident throughout the spa, from arrival to departure.

★★★★The Mobil Four-Star spa provides a luxurious experience with expanded amenities in an elegant and serene environment. Throughout the spa facility, guests experience personalized service. Amenities might include, but are not limited to, single-sex relaxation rooms where guests wait for their treatments, plunge pools and whirlpools in both men's and women's locker rooms, and an array of treatments, including a selection of massages, body therapies, facials and a variety of salon services.

★★★The Mobil Three-Star spa is physically well appointed and has a full complement of staff.

INTRODUCTION

If you've been a reader of Mobil Travel Guides, you may have noticed a new look and style in our guidebooks. Since 1958, Mobil Travel Guide has assisted travelers in making smart decisions about where to stay and dine. Fifty-one years later, our mission has not changed: We are committed to our rigorous inspections of hotels, restaurants and, now, spas, to help you cut through all the clutter, and make easy and informed decisions on where you should spend your time and budget. Our team of anonymous inspectors are constantly on the road, sleeping in hotels, eating in restaurants and making spa appointments, evaluating hundreds of standards to determine a property's star rating.

As you read these pages, we hope you get a flavor of the places included in the guides and that you will feel even more inspired to visit and take it all in. We hope you'll experience what it's like to stay in a guest room in the hotels we've rated, taste the food in a restaurant or feel the excitement at an outdoor music venue. We understand the importance of finding the best value when you travel, and making the most of your time. That's why for more than 50 years, Mobil Travel Guide has been the most trusted name in travel.

If any aspect of your accommodation, dining, spa or sightseeing experience motivates you to comment, please contact us at Mobil Travel Guide, 200 W. Madison St., Suite 3950, Chicago, IL 60606, or send an email to info@mobiltravelguide.com Happy travels.

FLORIDA

★
★
★
★

FLORIDA

THERE'S A REASON VACATIONERS HEAD SOUTH TO FLORIDA—BALMY WATERS, TOWERING palm trees and a delightfully tropical climate make it an obvious destination for rest and relaxation. Especially appealing to winter-weary Northerners, Florida provides a place where beachgoing is not only a favorite recreational activity, but something that's possible year-round.

Florida is a 450-mile-long and 150-mile-wide peninsula and from the border of Georgia to its southernmost coast, Florida's landscape is unlike any other. The pines near the Georgia border give way to palms and sea grape, then to bougainvillea and hibiscus, and finally to saw grass and mangrove down in the Everglades. With 8,426 miles of coastline (including that of the panhandle), Florida has the largest tidal coastline in the United States. The Gulf Stream flows through the Florida straits between Florida and Cuba and north up the Atlantic coast influencing the tropical climate that exists there.

When Ponce de Leon first discovered Florida, he stepped ashore near St. Augustine and mapped the entire coast, but failed to establish a colony. In 1539, Hernando de Soto and his army marched through the tropical land and started what is now the Tampa Bay area. Spanish settlements became rooted in St. Augustine and Pensacola in the 17th century, but in the 18th century, Florida was taken as a British province. Following the defeat of the British in the American Revolution, Spain resumed control, but in 1812, the Americans took over and in 1819 took formal possession of Florida. During the Civil War, Tallahassee was the only Confederate capital east of the Mississippi River to escape capture by Union forces.

Henry Morrison Flagler, a colorful tycoon with a passion for railroads and hotels, transformed Florida from a remote and swampy outpost to a resort destination. Flagler pushed his Florida East Coast Railroad from Jacksonville to Key West, opening one area after another along the coast to tourist and commercial development. On the west coast Henry Plant, another millionaire railroader, competed with Flagler on a somewhat more modest scale.

Florida is now one of the top 10 most populated states in the country. More people migrate to Florida to retire than to any other state. Florida's major industry is tourism—it brings in about $41 billion per year. Kennedy Space Center, the launch facility for the Apollo Moon Mission in 1961, brings in more than three million visitors each year. Walt Disney World has welcomed untold millions since its opening in 1971. With so many

FUN FACTS

St. Augustine, established in 1565, is Florida's oldest city.

The process of making artificial ice was patented in Apalachicola in 1851.

Major League Baseball teams (currently 18) that hold spring training in Florida play each other in what's called the Grapefruit League.

Florida is one of nine states that do not impose a personal income tax.

things to do and see, Florida is an ideal location to visit—and a place to keep coming back to.

Information: www.flausa.com

ALTAMONTE SPRINGS

This city is a growing northern suburb of Orlando. The town is surrounded by lakes.

Information: Seminole County Regional Chamber of Commerce, 1055 AAA Drive, Heathrow, 407-333-4748; www.seminolebusiness.org

WHAT TO SEE AND DO

WEKIWA SPRINGS STATE PARK

1800 Wekiwa Circle, Apopka, 407-884-2008; www.floridastateparks.com

At 7,000 acres, Wekiwa Springs State Park, located at the headwaters of the Wekiva River, is a popular spot to cool off in the bubbling spring. Waters move at a rate of 42 million gallons per day. Its Indian name literally means "spring of water" or "bubbling water." Swimming, camping, canoeing, fishing and hiking are popular activities. If volleyball and horseshoes are more to your liking, those activities are also available. Daily 8 a.m.-sundown.

HOTELS

★★EMBASSY SUITES

225 Shorecrest Drive, Altamonte Springs, 407-834-2400, 800-362-2779; www.embassysuites.com/es/orlando-north

277 rooms, all suites. Pets accepted; fee. Full complimentary breakfast. Wireless Internet access. Restaurant, bar. Fitness room. Indoor pool, whirlpool. Business center. $

★★★HILTON ORLANDO/ALTAMONTE SPRINGS

350 N. Lake Blvd., Altamonte Springs, 407-830-1985, 800-445-8667; www.orlandoaltamontesprings.hilton.com

Located in an upscale suburban area, this hotel is a leading convention and business center just eight miles from downtown Orlando. 322 rooms. Wireless Internet access. Restaurant, bar. Fitness room. Outdoor pool, whirlpool. Airport transportation available. Business center. $

★★HOLIDAY INN

230 W. Highway 436, Altamonte Springs, 407-862-4455, 407-862-4455; www.hotelaltamontesprings.com

262 rooms. Pets accepted, some restrictions; fee. Complimentary continental breakfast. Lunch and dinner. Complimentary wireless Internet access. Café. Restaurant, bars. Outdoor pool. Business center. $

RESTAURANTS

★★★ENZO'S RESTAURANT ON THE LAKE

1130 S. Highway 17-92, Longwood, 407-834-9872, 800-765-8608; www.enzos.com

Located on Lake Fairy, this authentic, upscale Italian trattoria in a restored lakeside house is a local favorite for special occasions. Owner Enzo Perlini oversees the dining room and the kitchen. Italian menu. Lunch, dinner. Closed Sunday. Bar. Children's menu. $$$

★
★
★
★
★

★★KOBE JAPANESE STEAK HOUSE

468 W. Highway 436, Altamonte Springs, 407-862-2888; www.kobesteakhouse.com
Japanese menu, sushi, steak. Dinner. Bar. Children's menu. Casual attire. Reservations recommended. **$$$**

★★★MAISON & JARDIN

430 S. Wymore Road, Altamonte Springs, 407-862-4410; www.maisonjardin.com
Step back in time at this neo-classical, museumlike restaurant. The Swiss chef creates classic European dishes and the restaurant has an award-winning, 1,200-bottle wine cellar. Continental menu. Dinner. Bar. Children's menu. Business casual attire. Reservations recommended. Outdoor seating. **$$$**

★★STRAUB'S FINE SEAFOOD

512 E. Altamonte Drive, Altamonte Springs, 407-831-2250; www.straubsseafood.com
Seafood menu. Lunch, dinner. Bar. Children's menu. Casual attire. Reservations recommended. **$$**

AMELIA ISLAND

Catch views of Cumberland Island and the Georgia coast from Amelia Island, separated from the mainland by St. Mary's River on the north, the Amelia River Intracoastal Waterway on the west, and Nassau Sound on the south.
Information: Amelia Island Welcome Center, 102 Centre St., Fernandina Beach, 904-261-5841, 800-226-3542; www.ameliaisland.com

WHAT TO SEE AND DO
AMELIA ISLAND PLANTATION

6800 First Coast Highway, Amelia Island, 904-261-6161, 888-261-6161; www.aipfl.com
Features 54 championship holes. Tom Fazio designed the par-72 Long Point course (6,775 yards); Pete Dye designed the par-72 Oak Marsh course (6,502 yards) and Bobby Weed and Pete Dye designed the par-70 Ocean Links course (6,200 yards).

HOTELS
★★★AMELIA ISLAND PLANTATION INN

6800 First Coast Highway, Amelia Island, 904-261-6161, 800-874-6878; www.aipfl.com
This sprawling, 1,300-acre resort boasts panoramic views of the Atlantic Ocean. Kids and parents will appreciate the extensive recreation program that can be tailored to individual interests. 905 rooms. Pets accepted, some restrictions; fee. Wireless Internet access. Seven restaurants, three bars. Children's activity center. Fitness room, fitness classes available, spa. Beach. 23 indoor and outdoor pools, children's pool, whirlpool. Golf, 54 holes. Tennis. Business center. **$$**

★★★ELIZABETH POINTE LODGE

98 S. Fletcher Ave., Amelia Island, 904-277-4851, 800-772-3359;
www.elizabethpointelodge.com
The main house at this lodge, perched on the Amelia Island sand, is 1890s "Nantucket Shingle" style with a wraparound porch and plenty of rocking chairs. A maritime theme is prominent throughout the house, and the cozy living room features floor-to-ceiling bookcases, an old stone fireplace and window seats with a view of the porch. This property is located just minutes from historic Fernandina Beach and its

AMELIA ISLAND

Amelia Island is best known for its bluff-height dunes and white, wide beaches. The best way to get there is to travel north via Route A1A, which involves taking a car ferry across the mouth of the St. Johns River at the naval town of Mayport.

Before you reach Mayport, stop at Kathryn Abbey Hanna Park, where you can play in the ocean, picnic, kayak, go lake fishing and camp. Past Mayport about two miles on Route A1A, turn off at Fort George Island to see Kingsley Plantation Historic Site. Learn how cotton was farmed and tabby homes were built. Little Talbot Island State Park lies a few miles to the north if you are looking for a place on the beach away from the crowds and hiking trails previously traveled by early explorers and colonists.

Up A1A about six miles, cross the bridge to Amelia Island. Fort Clinch State Park, at the Island's north end along Route A1A, is a good place to visit the beach and experience some of the island's history. Civil War soldier re-enactors bring history to life and weekend candlelight tours are a hit with kids and couples. From the fort's embankments you can see long sweeps of beach and Georgia's Cumberland Island. This is also a great spot for collecting seashells, fishing from a pier, camping and picnicking. To reach downtown Fernandina Beach, head west a few miles on Atlantic Avenue, which turns into Centre Street, the heart of the historic district. This well-preserved pirate seaport and former playground of the rich showcases its Victorian influence and is known for its wonderful bed and breakfast inns. Learn the history on a visit or specialty tour from Amelia Island Museum of History in the old jail. Check out the Palace Saloon, shop in the unique boutiques and fill up on white shrimp, a local specialty. Hook up with a local kayak tour of the salt marshes on the islands leeward side or hire a fishing captain and see what you can catch. Approximately 55 miles.

★
★ ★
★
★

quaint shops and restaurants. After indulging in the delicious complimentary breakfast, enjoy a walk to the barrier island sand dunes. 20 rooms. Complimentary full breakfast. Wireless Internet access. Beach. $$$

★★★FLORIDA HOUSE INN

20-22 S. Third St., Fernandia Beach, 904-261-3300, 800-258-3301;
www.floridahouseinn.com

This inn is Florida's oldest surviving hotel and located in the historic Fernandia Beach district. Open since 1857, the inn features rooms decorated with antiques and updated with crisp white linens or colorful quilts. Cocktails are served in the small pub, and breakfast is served in the restaurant. 25 rooms. Restaurant. Boating, golf, tennis, horseback riding. $$$

★★★★THE RITZ-CARLTON, AMELIA ISLAND

4750 Amelia Island Parkway, Amelia Island, 904-277-1100, 800-241-3333;
www.ritzcarlton.com

Located on a barrier island off Florida's northeastern coast, this resort captures the essence of this magical place, where time seems to stand still. The guest rooms are decorated with floral prints and pastel colors and all offer coastal or ocean views. Spend the day by the beach or try tennis, golf, horseback riding or sailing. For young guests, there are Ritz Kids activity programs, a playground and a nanny service. Fernandina Beach, a quaint Victorian area with specialty boutiques, is just down the road. The resort's numerous restaurants and lounges serve up a variety of specialties with a focus on seafood. 444 rooms. Wireless Internet access. Four restaurants including one outdoor, four bars. Children's activity center. Fitness room, fitness classes available, spa. Beach. Indoor pool, outdoor pool, children's pool, whirlpool. Golf, 18 holes. Tennis. Business center. $$

SPECIALTY LODGINGS

AMELIA ISLAND WILLIAMS HOUSE

103 S. Ninth St., Amelia Island, 904-277-2328, 800-414-9258; www.williamshouse.com
This national historic inn is a 149-year-old mansion and offers a courtyard and English gardens that make it one of the island's most charming places to stay. 11 rooms. Children over 12 years only. Complimentary full breakfast. Whirlpools. $$

FAIRBANKS HOUSE

227 S. Seventh St., Amelia Island, 904-277-0500, 888-891-9882; www.fairbankshouse.com
Canopied and four-poster beds, fireplaces and balconies are only a few of the amenities found in this 1885 Italian-style villa. Listed on the National Register of Historic Places, it's located just minutes from the beach, excellent restaurants and the center of the quaint, historic town of Fernandina Beach. 12 rooms. Children over 12 years only. Complimentary full breakfast. Outdoor pool. Wireless Internet access. $$

RESTAURANTS

★★BRETT'S WATERWAY CAFÉ

1 S. Front St., Amelia Island, 904-261-2660; www.brettswaterwaycafe.com
Seafood, steak menu. Lunch, dinner. Closed holidays. Bar. Children's menu (dinner). $$

★★★SALT: THE GRILL AT THE RITZ-CARLTON

4750 Amelia Island Parkway, Amelia Island, 904-277-1028, 800-241-3333;
www.ritzcarlton.com
A restaurant with the word "grill" in its name may sound like a local joint where burgers, fries and perhaps a cold pint of beer are the specialties. The food at Salt, however, is decidedly more refined. The menu of seasonal, regional American fare is tinged with global flavors with plenty of grilled fish, meat and vegetarian options. The formal dining room has views of the Atlantic, which makes a seat at a window table in the dining room a worthwhile choice. The wine list features approximately 500 selections to match any taste. Regional American menu. Dinner, Sunday brunch. Closed Monday. Bar. Children's menu. Business casual attire. Reservations recommended. Valet parking. $$$

SPA

★★★★THE RITZ-CARLTON SPA, AMELIA ISLAND

The Ritz-Carlton, Amelia Island, 4750 Amelia Island Parkway, Amelia Island,
904-277-1087; www.ritzcarlton.com/ameliaisland
Tranquility is inevitable at this custom-designed facility. The 27,500-square-foot space utilizes the private sanctuary that is Amelia Island and the ocean breezes that

encircle it to award guests with the ultimate in luxury and relaxation. Every detail is meticulously accounted for, from a new plunge pool with underwater music to spa butlers on hand. If you're in the mood for a rubdown but hesitate to give up your beachfront perch, why not try the Heaven in a Hammock massage ($200), which combines the rhythmic rocking of a hammock swing with deep tissue massage to create a sense of weightlessness? Or unwind in one of the 26 inviting treatment rooms and console sunburned skin with a soothing Ocean Breeze Wrap ($145) using the natural properties of noni gel.

APALACHICOLA

Apalachicola (formerly known as West Point) is a Native American word that means "people on the other side." At one time, the town was a leading cotton-shipping port, but today its major crop is oysters—nearly 90 percent of Florida's oysters are harvested from nearby St. George Sound. Local history goes back to 1528, when the Spanish conquistador Narváez stopped here to build boats to sail to Mexico. Trinity Church on Gorrie Square was brought in sections on a schooner from New York in 1839, and its original bell was melted down to make a Confederate cannon.

Information: Chamber Office and Visitor Center, 122 Commerce St., 850-653-9419; www.apalachicolabay.org

HISTORIC APALACHICOLA

Once a thriving antebellum cotton port, river city Apalachicola offers visitors a glimpse of the past with more than 50 historic sites, including the largest collection of pre-Civil War architecture in Florida. While there, sample the Apalachicola Bay oysters, farmed and harvested locally where the river meets the sea. The drive across the bridge over the Apalachicola River provides a glimpse of what there is to see by foot.

Begin at the Apalachicola Bay Chamber of Commerce (99 Market Street) for a walking tour brochure and map. Like most of the nearby shops, antique stores and galleries, the chamber office occupies a lovely brick historic storefront. The Apalachicola Maritime Museum lies across the street at 71 Market Street. Nearby, you can't help but notice the town's centerpiece, the Gibson Inn. Built in 1907 and restored in 1983, the inn is reminiscent of Old Florida with its wraparound verandas and Victorian style. It is a good place to stop for lunch or dinner, but if you're looking for a place where the locals go, head to Boss Oyster at 123 Water Street, just a few blocks to the east. This is seafood-processing headquarters, and bobbing boats and huge mounds of empty oyster shells attest to Apalachicola's reputation as provider of 10 percent of the nation's oyster meat. To the northwest, along Water Street at Avenue J, you'll find the Greek Revival-style Orman House. The view alone is worth the visit. Other highlights of the town's historic district include the Chestnut Street Cemetery on Avenue E between Sixth and Seventh streets, 1838 Trinity Episcopal Church at 79 Sixth Street, and the John Gorrie State Museum at Sixth Street and Avenue D.

FORT GADSDEN
Highway 65, north of Bucks Siding, 850-670-8616
In 1814, the British built a fort on this 75-acre area as a base for recruitment during the War of 1812. The fort was later destroyed by U.S. forces, but in 1818 Andrew Jackson ordered another to be built as a supply base. It was occupied by Confederate forces from 1862 to 1863, and evidence of this remains visible. An open-sided kiosk has a miniature replica of Fort Gadsden with interpretive exhibits. Fishing, hiking trails, an interpretive trail and a picnicking pavilion are all available here. Monday-Friday.

JOHN GORRIE MUSEUM STATE PARK
Sixth St., Apalachicola, 850-653-9347; www.floridastateparks.org/johngorriemuseum
This park serves as a memorial to Dr. John Gorrie, a physician who built the first ice-making machine in 1845 to cool the rooms of yellow fever victims. The museum contains a replica of the first ice machine and scenes of early local history. Thursday-Monday 9 a.m.-5 p.m.

ST. GEORGE ISLAND
Highway G1A
Swimming beaches, surf fishing. Also here is St. George Island State Park. This park is more than 1,800 acres and features miles of undeveloped beaches, dunes, forest and marshes. Swimming, saltwater fishing, hiking, picnicking, backwoods and improved camping can be found here as well. Vehicles prohibited in dune areas. Daily 8 a.m.-sundown.

16

FLORIDA

★
★★
★★
★

ATLANTIC BEACH

This Northeastern Florida town, part of the sprawl of Jacksonville, began as a resort area developed after Henry Flagler's railroad was built through the area.
Information: Jacksonville & the Beaches Convention and Visitors Bureau, 550 Water St., Jacksonville, 904-798-9111, 800-733-2668; www.visitjacksonville.com

WHAT TO SEE AND DO
HANNA PARK
500 Wonderwood Drive, Atlantic Beach, 904-249-4700; www.coj.net
This 450-acre recreation area includes a plaza overlooking the ocean. Saltwater and freshwater fishing, nature and bicycle trails, picnicking and camping. Daily. A mile and a half of beach access. 60-acre lake. 293 campsites. Open daily 8 a.m.-8 p.m., April-October and 8 a.m.-6 p.m., November-March.

HOTEL
★COMFORT INN
2401 Mayport Road, Atlantic Beach, 904-249-0313, 877-424-6423;
www.comfortinn.com
108 rooms. Wireless Internet access. Exercise room. Complimentary continental breakfast. Outdoor pool. $

RESTAURANT

★★RAGTIME

207 Atlantic Blvd., Atlantic Beach, 904-241-7877; www.ragtimetavern.com

Seafood menu. Lunch, dinner. Sunday brunch. Bar. Children's menu. **$$**

AVENTURA

This Miami suburb began as a resort area dotted with high-rise condominiums. It's now known for its upscale shopping and beachfront location.

19200 W. Country Club Drive, Aventura, 305-466-8900; www.cityofaventura.com

WHAT TO SEE AND DO

AVENTURA MALL

19501 Biscayne Blvd., Aventura, 305-935-1110; www.shopaventuramall.com

This multilevel indoor mall, anchored by Bloomingdales, JCPenney, Macys and Sears, caters to an upscale crowd in North Miami, as well as to out-of-town visitors looking for a shopping excursion. You'll find more than 250 specialty shops, restaurants and a 24-screen movie theater. Kids love Adventurer's Cove, the large indoor play area. Monday-Saturday 10 a.m.-9:30 p.m., Sunday noon-8 p.m.

HOTELS

★★★ACQUALINA

17875 Collins Ave., Sunny Isles Beach, 305-918-8000; www.acqualina.com

Located on a stretch of sand just north of Miami Beach, this sprawling Mediterranean-style resort offers a quiet and luxurious retreat. Rooms are swathed in crisp white tones and filled with elegant furnishings. Amenities include flatscreen TVs, whirlpool tubs and private terraces. Spend some time lazing by the oceanfront pool or relaxing in the full-service spa. The resort has an outpost of famed New York eatery Il Mulino, which serves heaping portions of sophisticated Italian cooking. 188 rooms. Pool. Fitness center. Beach. Spa. Restaurant, bar. **$$$$**

★★COURTYARD BY MARRIOTT

2825 N.E. 191st St., Aventura, 305-937-0805, 800-321-2211; www.courtyard.com

166 rooms. High-speed Internet access. Restaurant. Fitness room. Outdoor pool. Whirlpool. Pets not accepted. Service animals allowed for persons with disabilities. **$$**

★★★★THE FAIRMONT TURNBERRY ISLE RESORT & CLUB

19999 W. Country Club Drive, Aventura, 305-932-6200, 866-840-8069;
www.fairmont.com

Located near Fort Lauderdale in Aventura, Turnberry Isle underwent a $100 million renovation in 2006. The hotel, set on the Atlantic Ocean, is reminiscent of a palatial private estate featuring terra-cotta tiles and pastel color schemes in its rooms. Four restaurants and five lounges serve delectable seafood and continental dishes. Two Robert Trent Jones, Sr. golf courses provide a challenge, while the famous Island Green 18th hole continues to be one of the more difficult holes. Turnberry's two tennis centers are often counted among the country's best. 392 rooms. Four restaurants, three bars. Wireless Internet access. Fitness room, spa. Indoor pool. Golf. Tennis. Business center. Pets accepted, some restrictions; fee. **$$$$**

★HAMPTON INN

1000 S. Federal Highway, Hallandale Beach, 954-874-1111, 800-426-7866;
www.hamptoninnaventura.com

151 rooms. Wireless Internet access. Complimentary breakfast. Restaurant. Fitness room. Outdoor heated pool. **$**

★★★★TRUMP INTERNATIONAL SONESTA BEACH RESORT

18001 Collins Ave., Sunny Isles Beach, 305-692-5600, 800-461-8501;
www.trumpsonesta.com

Standing 32 stories above the white, sandy beaches of Sunny Isles, the Trump International Sonesta Beach Resort is a distinctive tower of luxury near tony Bal Harbour. Guests here have everything at their fingertips, from three nearby golf courses to access to jet skis, catamarans and kayaks. The comfortably sized, contemporary guest rooms are equipped with wet bars, microwaves, refrigerators and CD players. For complete rejuvenation, head to the 8,000-square-foot Aquanox Spa. The resort's signature restaurant, Neomi's, offers contemporary American cuisine with a tropical flair. 249 rooms. Pets accepted, some restrictions; fee. High-speed Internet access. Restaurant, two bars. Children's activity center. Fitness room, spa. Beach. Outdoor pool, whirlpool. Tennis. Airport transportation available. Business center.

RESTAURANT
★★★CHEF ALLEN'S

19088 N.E. 29th Ave., Aventura, 305-935-2900; www.chefallens.com

Chef Allen Susser, the man behind chef Allen's, is one of Florida's wildest, most passionate cooks. Susser mixes ingredients from the Mediterranean with those from Asia and the Caribbean. With his gutsy menu of new-world cuisine, Susser proves that taking risks in the kitchen can pay off. While the room could use refreshing, the dining experience offers dishes such as pistachio-crusted black grouper served with a feisty fricassee of rock shrimp with mango, leeks and coconut rum. New World menu. Dinner. Bar. Children's menu. Casual attire. Reservations recommended. Valet parking. **$$$**

SPA
★★★AQUANOX SPA

18001 Collins Ave., Sunny Isles Beach, 305-692-5600; www.trumpmiami.com

What doesn't Aquanox Spa have going for it? It's located on miles of white sandy beaches in Sunny Isles Beach (just north of Miami) in the Trump International Sonesta Beach Resort. The signature Trump style of unparalleled luxury is found at this oasis of tranquility, where guests are thoroughly pampered with an array of treatments like purifying facial and skin care, energizing body treatments and relaxing massage therapy. Aquanox Spa reinvents classic treatments such as facials, massages and body wraps with a cutting-edge approach. The Sea-Champagne Oxygen facial is designed to purify and detoxify, while the Tattered Tootsie Footsie treatment hydrates, exfoliates and massages neglected feet. For some post-treatment bliss, the eucalyptus steam room offers a soothing transition back to reality. Daily.

★★★★ESPA AT ACQUALINA RESORT & SPA
17875 Collins Ave., Sunny Isles, 305-918-6844; www.acqualinaresort.com

Drawing traditional beauty and wellness treatments from every corner of the Earth, the internationally renowned ESPA makes its American home in Miami Beach with an upscale pampering paradise at Acqualina. Your day at ESPA is designed to be a holistic journey, complete with essential oils and products crafted from organic ingredients. From Chakra Balancing with Hot Stones, to Holistic Foot and Nail treatments, a few hours here promise to be as much for the soul as they are for the body.

★★★★WILLOW STREAM, THE SPA AT THE FAIRMONT TURNBERRY ISLE RESORT & CLUB
19999 W. Country Club Drive, Aventura, 305-933-6930, 866-840-8069; www.fairmont.com

The spa has it all, from massages and facials to body therapies and exotic rituals. It features 13 different kinds of massages inspired by techniques from around the world, including lomi lomi and reflexology. The facials include classic European and deep-pore cleansing treatments as well as aromatherapy, revitalizing and oxygenating options. Experience Balinese cultural traditions like a royal Javanese lulur ritual, originally created for brides from regal families, or aboriginal Australian customs such as mala mayi and lowanna, both of which offer a blend of nourishing body treatments to restore energy. Enjoy Thai relaxation techniques with a coconut scrub, or a body glow mud wrap or a Dead Sea water bath.

BAL HARBOUR

This neighborhood north of Miami Beach is known for its luxury shopping. The Bal Harbour shops include Gucci, Pucci, Armani and more.
Information: www.balharbourflorida.com

FLORIDA

★
★
★
★
★

HOTEL
★★★THE REGENT BAL HARBOUR
10295 Collins Ave., Bal Harbour, 305-455-5400, 800-545-4000; www.regentbalharbour.com

There's nowhere better to be in Miami Beach but oceanside, and thankfully that's *every* side of the Regent Bal Harbour, whether you're taking a dip in the Atlantic Ocean, enjoying water sports in Baker's Haulover Inlet, or sipping piña coladas in the pool's private cabanas. Land lovers can relax with a trip to the Guerlain Spa, followed with an exquisite meal at 1 Bleu and drinks at The View Bar. At night, everyone can rejuvenate in one of the hotel's super chic rooms (atop a cushy bed outfitted with luxe Anichini bedding, each with a terrace overlooking the water—in case you started to miss it. 124 rooms, 62 suites. Wireless Internet access. Restaurants, bar. Fitness center. Pool. Spa. Business center. **$$$$**

RESTAURANTS
★★AL CARBON
9701 Collins Ave., Bal Harbour, 305-865-7511

Mediterranean menu. Dinner. Bar. Children's menu. Business casual attire. Reservations recommended. Valet parking. Outdoor seating. **$$$**

★★CARPACCIO
9700 Collins Ave., Bal Harbour, 305-867-7777
Italian menu. Lunch, dinner. Bar. Casual attire. Valet parking. Outdoor seating. **$$**

SPA
★★★★GUERLAIN SPA AT THE REGENT BAL HARBOUR
The Regent Bal Harbour, 10295 Collins Ave., Bal Harbour, 305-455-5411;
www.regentbalharbour.com
Bathed in a neutral beige-and-white palate, the 10,000-square-foot Guerlain Spa is its own calming getaway within the already blissful Regent Bal Harbour. And you can forget about those spas that try to soothe you with sounds of the ocean—Guerlain is the real deal, thanks to its views of the water from the treatment suites. Ease your jet lag with a specially tailored jet-lag regimen ($600) or with a foot rubdown in the serene, white-curtain-clad Foot Therapy Lounge, and follow it up with a makeup application ($165) to get you ready for Miami Beach nightlife. If your body needs a little love the next morning, detox with a facial or a "Harmonising" massage—our favorite is the 4-Hand Impériale Massage ($330-495), which includes two therapists and a whole lot of relaxation.

BAY HARBOR ISLANDS
This greater Miami town is sandwiched between tiny Bal Harbour and Miami Beach. High-rise condominiums dot the town's stretch of beach.
Information: www.bayharborislands.org

RESTAURANTS
★★CAFFE DA VINCI
1009 Kane Concourse, Bay Harbor Island, 305-861-8166; www.caffedavinci.com
Italian menu. Lunch, dinner. Bar. Business casual attire. Reservations recommended. Valet parking. Outdoor seating. **$$**

★★★THE PALM
9650 E. Bay Harbor Drive, Bay Harbor Island, 305-868-7256; www.thepalm.com
Caricatures of celebrities hang on the walls of the Palm, the counterpart to the famous New York City restaurant. The menu is filled with steakhouse classics. Seafood, steak menu. Dinner. Bar. Business casual attire. Reservations recommended. Valet parking. **$$$**

BOCA RATON
Florida architect Addison Mizner bought several thousand acres of farmland so that he could build his dream city, Boca Raton. Unfortunately, his plans were foiled by the bust that followed the Florida land boom of the 1920s. For three decades, Boca Raton was a small resort town with little more than the architecture of Mizner's Boca Raton Resort and Club to show for it. In recent years, however, the town has been at the forefront of Palm Beach County's explosive growth. Throughout this period, Boca Raton has retained its resort atmosphere while becoming an educational, technical and cultural center for Florida.
Information: Greater Boca Raton Chamber of Commerce, 1800 N. Dixie Highway,
Boca Raton, 561-395-4433; www.bocaratonchamber.com

WHAT TO SEE AND DO

BOCA RATON MUSEUM OF ART

Mizner Park, 501 Plaza Real, Boca Raton, 561-392-2500; www.bocamuseum.org
Exhibits include paintings, photography, sculpture and glass. Lectures, tours. Tuesday, Thursday-Friday 10 a.m.-5 p.m.; Wednesday 10 a.m.-9 p.m.; Saturday-Sunday noon-5 p.m.

GUMBO LIMBO ENVIRONMENTAL COMPLEX

1801 N. Ocean Blvd., Boca Raton, 561-338-1473; www.gumbolimbo.org
Offering a complete nature experience, families are able to view four 20-foot-diameter saltwater sea tanks, stroll a 1,628-foot boardwalk through a dense tropical forest and climb a 40-foot tower to overlook the tree canopy. The forest holds several different tropical species growing north of the tropics. The center's staff leads guided turtle walks to the beach to see nesting females come ashore and lay their eggs. Monday-Saturday 9 a.m.-4 p.m., Sunday from noon; closed holidays.

MIZNER PARK

433 Plaza Real, Boca Raton, 561-362-0606; www.miznerpark.org
This is a 30-acre shopping village with gardenlike spaces that makes for a unique shopping experience. There are more than 50 retail stores to choose from; restaurants with sidewalk cafés; an amphitheater that offers outdoor concerts; and an art museum and a movie theater.

HOTELS

★★★BOCA RATON RESORT & CLUB

501 E. Camino Real, Boca Raton, 561-447-3000, 888-491-2622; www.bocaresort.com
Since opening in 1926, this classic resort has been a top destination on Southern Florida's Gold Coast. Occupying 356 acres fronting the Atlantic Ocean, the resort has a private stretch of beach, two 18-hole golf courses, 30 tennis courts, 7 pools, and a 32-slip marina. A wide variety of restaurants and lounges can be found here, and the Spa Palazzo offers signature treatments such as the Honey-Cocoa-Mango body scrub. 1,041 rooms. High-speed Internet access. 13 restaurants. Five Bars. Children's activity center. Fitness room, fitness classes available, spa. Beach. Five outdoor pools, children's pool, whirlpool. Golf, 36 holes. Tennis. Business center. **$$$$**

★★DOUBLETREE GUEST SUITES

701 N.W. 53rd St., Boca Raton, 561-997-9500, 800-222-8733; www.doubletree.com
198 rooms, all suites. Pets not accepted. High-speed Internet access. Restaurant, bar. Business center. Golf. Casual attire. Outdoor pool, whirlpool. **$**

★HAMPTON INN BOCA RATON

1455 Yamato Road, Boca Raton, 561-988-0200, 800-426-7866; www.hamptoninn.com
94 rooms. Complimentary full breakfast. Wireless Internet access. Outdoor pool. Restaurant. Bar. Fitness center. Business center. Pets not accepted. **$**

★★★HILTON SUITES BOCA RATON

7920 Glades Road, Boca Raton, 561-483-3600, 800-445-8667; www.hilton.com
Located in a lakeside complex in the heart of Boca Raton, this hotel is surrounded by shopping and dining. It is also just minutes away from Gold Coast Atlantic beaches.

Each suite features a separate bedroom and living room, a balcony, a microwave and a coffeemaker. Guests can mingle at the complimentary manager's reception. A full breakfast is served each morning and an outdoor pool, whirlpool, fitness center and complimentary local shuttle are all available. 200 rooms, all suites. Complimentary full breakfast. Wireless Internet access. Restaurant, bar. Fitness room. Outdoor pool, whirlpool. Airport transportation available. Business center. Pets accepted. **$$**

★★★RENAISSANCE BOCA RATON HOTEL
2000 N.W. 19th St., Boca Raton, 561-368-5252, 888-236-2427;
www.renaissancehotels.com

This Mediterranean-style hotel is located five miles east of downtown Boca Raton in an area of businesses and restaurants. Some amenities include the outdoor pool with waterfall, whirlpool, restaurant and two bars, a fitness room and a business center. The property offers one floor designated for female travelers and each of these rooms includes a basket with magazines, an extra throw blanket and an aromatherapy candle. 189 rooms. Wireless Internet access. Restaurant, two bars. Fitness room. Outdoor pool, whirlpool. Business center. **$$**

SPA

★★★★SPA PALAZZO AT BOCA RATON RESORT & CLUB
501 E. Camino Real, Boca Raton, 561-347-4772, 888-491-2622; www.spapalazzo.com

Spa Palazzo reflects the beauty of the Mediterranean in its architecture and seductive design. Modeled after Spain's Alhambra palace, this spa offers services in which nature is the inspiration. From eucalyptus and chamomile to honey-coconut-mango, the body scrubs pay tribute to the natural ingredients. Body wraps use grapefruit, peppermint, moor mud and algae. Facials cleanse and soothe with botanical extracts, Florida citrus and aromatherapy oils. Signature treatments include Thai massage, aromatherapy massage, Palazzo stone therapy, the double oxygen facial and the Florida citrus scrub and wrap. 44 treatment rooms. Fitness center. Pool.

RESTAURANTS

★★★ARTURO'S
6750 N. Highway 1, Boca Raton, 561-997-7373; www.arturosrestaurant.com

This elegant and formal family-owned Italian restaurant located in an Italian villa-style building has maintained its commitment to excellent service and fine cuisine. Fresh roses are on each table and in large vases around the restaurant. Live piano music sets the mood, as do the tuxedoed waiters and candlelit tables. Italian menu. Lunch Monday-Friday, dinner daily. Closed three weeks in July. Bar. Business casual attire. Reservations recommended. Valet parking. **$$$**

★★BASIL GARDEN
5837 N. Federal Highway, Boca Raton, 561-994-2554

Italian menu. Dinner. Closed Sunday; Bar. Casual attire. Reservations recommended. Valet parking. **$**

★★GIGI'S
346 Plaza Real, Mizner Park, Boca Raton, 561-368-4488; www.gigis.com

American bistro menu. Lunch, dinner, late-night. Bar. Children's menu. Business casual attire. Reservations recommended. Valet parking. Outdoor seating. **$$$**

★★KATHY'S GAZEBO CAFÉ

4199 N. Federal Highway, Boca Raton, 561-395-6033; www.kathysgazebo.com

French menu. Lunch Monday-Friday, dinner daily. Closed Sunday. Outdoor seating. Reservations recommended. **$$$**

★★LA VILLETTA

4351 N. Federal Highway, Boca Raton, 561-362-8403

Italian menu. Dinner. Closed Monday. Four bars. Casual attire. Valet parking. **$$$**

★★★LINDA B OF BOCA

41 E. Palmetto Park Road, Boca Raton, 561-367-0200

"Geo-classical" is how chef Reto Demarmels describes his continental restaurant. An exceptional experience, from the service and geographically rotating menu to the black-and-white photographs of 1910 Boca Raton on the walls. Regulars recommend the clams in roasted walnut sauce. Continental menu. Dinner. Bar. Business casual attire. Reservations recommended. Valet parking. Outdoor seating. **$$$**

★★★LUCCA

501 E. Camino Real, Boca Raton, 561-447-5822, 888-491-2622; www.bocaresort.com

Located on the ground floor of the Boca Raton Resort & Club, Lucca is an understated, elegant Tuscan-style restaurant that was opened under the care of consultant Drew Nieporent, the visionary restaurateur who brought Tribeca Grill, Montrachet and Nobu to New York City. The restaurant features an open kitchen, floor-to-ceiling windows, a wood-burning oven and an open hearth, and offers a simple, stunning menu of seasonal dishes inspired by various regions of Italy. Italian menu. Lunch, Dinner. Bar. Children's menu. Business casual attire. Reservations recommended. Valet parking. **$$$**

★★MARK'S MIZNER PARK

344 Plaza Real, Boca Raton, 561-395-0770; www.chefmark.com

American menu. Lunch, dinner. Bar. Business casual attire. Reservations recommended. Valet parking. Outdoor seating. **$$$**

★★★MAX'S GRILLE

404 Plaza Real, Boca Raton, 561-368-0080; www.maxsgrille.com

This modern restaurant in Mizner Park, an area lined with brick streets, colorful Spanish-tiled buildings and manicured landscaping, offers New American comfort food in an energetic atmosphere. The open kitchen allows diners to watch their meals being prepared. The outdoor patio is a popular dining spot. American menu. Lunch, dinner. Bar. Children's menu. Business casual attire. Reservations recommended. Valet parking. Outdoor seating. **$$**

★★★MORTON'S, THE STEAKHOUSE

5050 Town Center Circle, Boca Raton, 561-392-7724; www.mortons.com

This branch of the popular national steakhouse chain serves consistently well-prepared steaks, seafood and standard steakhouse sides such as Caesar salad and crisp onion rings. Steak menu. Dinner. Bar. Business casual attire. **$$$**

★★PADRINO'S
20455 State Road 7, Boca Raton, 561-451-1070
Cuban menu. Lunch, dinner. Casual attire. **$$**

★UNCLE TAI'S
5250 Town Center Circle, Boca Raton, 561-368-8806; www.uncle-tais.com
Chinese menu. Lunch, dinner. Four bars. Casual attire. Outdoor seating. **$**

BONITA SPRINGS

Located directly on the Gulf of Mexico, Bonita Springs has several popular boat and nature tours, especially with the Imperial River flowing through the city.
Information: Bonita Springs Area Chamber of Commerce,
25071 Chamber of Commerce Drive, Bonita Springs, 239-992-2943, 800-226-2943;
www.bonitaspringschamber.com

WHAT TO SEE AND DO
EVERGLADES WONDER GARDENS
27180 Old Highway 41, Bonita Springs, 239-992-2591
Native reptiles, birds and animals in an Everglades setting. Natural history museum. Guided tours. Daily 9 a.m.-5 p.m.

HOTELS
★COMFORT INN
9800 Bonita Beach Road, Bonita Springs, 239-992-5001, 877-424-6423;
www.comfortinn.com
69 rooms. Complimentary continental breakfast. Wireless Internet access. Restaurant. Outdoor pool, whirlpool. **$**

★★★HYATT REGENCY COCONUT POINT RESORT & SPA
5001 Coconut Road, Bonita Springs, 239-444-1234, 800-233-1234; www.hyatt.com
Keep the whole family entertained at this tropical resort on Estero Bay. From relaxing on the secluded beach to sliding down the 140-foot water slide into the lagoon-style pool to being pampered at the Stillwater Spa, there is something for everyone. Comfortable guest rooms feature Floridian décor in tropical shades of peach and sage, a desk and armchair, marble-topped vanities and balconies with views. The property is located between Fort Myers and Naples and close to the Southwest International Airport. 454 rooms. Restaurant, bar. Fitness room. Two outdoor pools, children's pool, whirlpool. Airport transportation available. Stillwater spa. Golf course. Tennis. Business center. **$$$**

BOYNTON BEACH

Fishing docks and two marinas make Boynton Beach a gateway to Sailfish Alley. Boynton Beach Inlet connects the Intracoastal Waterway and Lake Worth with the Atlantic Ocean.
Information: Greater Boynton Beach Chamber of Commerce,
Boynton Beach, 639 E. Ocean Ave., 561-732-9501; www.boyntonbeach.org

WHAT TO SEE AND DO
ARTHUR R. MARSHALL LOXAHATCHEE NATIONAL WILDLIFE REFUGE
10216 Lee Road, Boynton Beach, 561-734-8303; www.loxahatchee.fws.gov
More than 145,000 acres of freshwater marsh and swamp in the Everglades. Fishing, nature trails, canoe trail, bike trail, visitor center. Daily.

HOTELS
★HAMPTON INN & SUITES BOYNTON BEACH
1475 W. Gateway Blvd., Boynton Beach, 561-369-0018, 800-426-7866;
www.hamptoninn.com
161 rooms. Complimentary continental breakfast. Pool. Fitness center. Business center. Wireless Internet access. Pets not accepted. **$**

★★HOLIDAY INN
1601 N. Congress Ave., Boynton Beach, 561-737-4600, 866-733-8554;
www.holiday-inn.com
170 rooms. Restaurant, bar. Wireless Internet access. Fitness room. Outdoor pool, whirlpool. Business center. Pets not accepted. Reservations recommended. **$**

RESTAURANTS
★★BANANA BOAT
739 E. Ocean Ave., Boynton Beach, 561-732-9400; www.bananaboatboynton.com
Seafood menu. Lunch, dinner. Two bars. Casual attire. Outdoor seating. Valet Parking. **$$**

★TWO GEORGES HARBOR HUT
728 Casa Loma Blvd., Boynton Beach, 561-736-2717; www.twogeorgesrestaurant.com
Seafood menu. Lunch, dinner. Bar. Children's menu. Casual attire. Outdoor seating. Valet parking. Live music every Saturday and Sunday 2-5 p.m. **$$**

BRADENTON
Located on the Manatee River, Bradenton provides access to river, bay and Gulf fishing, as well as 20 miles of white-sand beaches. The city took the name of Dr. Joseph Braden, whose nearby fortlike house was a refuge for early settlers during Native American attacks.
Information: Bradenton Area Convention and Visitors Bureau, 1 Haben Blvd.,
Palmetto, 941-729-9177, 800-822-2017; www.floridaislandbeaches.org

WHAT TO SEE AND DO
DE SOTO NATIONAL MEMORIAL
Highway 64, Bradenton, 941-792-0458; www.nps.gov/deso
At a spot believed to be somewhere near this memorial, Don Hernando de Soto landed on May 30, 1539, with more than 600 conquistadors to begin the first European expedition into the interior of what is now the Southeastern United States. In a 4,000-mile, four-year wilderness odyssey, de Soto and his army explored beyond the Mississippi, staking out claims to a vast empire for Spain. The visitor center has weapons and armor of the de Soto era and a movie depicting the de Soto expedition. The living history area depicts aspects of 16th-century Spanish life. Daily 9 a.m.-5 p.m.

★
★
★
★
★

GAMBLE PLANTATION HISTORIC STATE PARK

3708 Patten Ave., Ellenton, 941-723-4536; www.floridastateparks.org/gambleplantation
This park is a Confederate memorial and the only surviving antebellum house in South Florida. Major Robert Gamble ran a 3,500-acre sugar plantation and refinery here with 190 slaves. In May 1865, Judah P. Benjamin, secretary of state to the Confederacy, fled to the plantation to hide from Union troops. Avoiding a surprise raid by Union forces, Benjamin escaped to Bimini and then to Nassau and England. The restored mansion, which you can tour, is furnished with period pieces. Visitor center with displays; picnicking. Monday, Thursday-Sunday. 8 a.m.-sundown.

MANATEE VILLAGE HISTORICAL PARK

1404 Manatee Ave. E., Bradenton, 941-741-4075;
www.manateeclerk.com/clerkservices/hisvill/mchvillage.htm
This park contains renovated historic buildings from the 1800 and early 1900s. First Court House; Old Church; Wiggins Store Museum; a one-room schoolhouse; a potter barn; smokehouse; sugar mill; Fogarty's Boat Works and the Stephens House, built in a style known as Cracker Gothic that is an excellent example of a Florida rural farm house in the period between the 1870s and World War I. Tour guides are available in winter. Monday-Friday 9 a.m.-4:30 p.m., second and fourth Saturday of each month.

SPECIAL EVENT
PITTSBURGH PIRATES SPRING TRAINING

McKechnie Field, 1611 Ninth St. West, Bradenton, 941-748-4610;
www.pittsburgh.pirates.mlb.com
Watch the Pittsburgh Pirates baseball spring training and exhibition games. Early March-early April.

HOTEL
★★HOLIDAY INN

100 Riverfront Drive, Bradenton, 941-747-3727, 800-465-4329;
www.holiday-inn.com/bradentonfl
153 rooms. Two restaurants, bar. Wireless Internet access. Fitness room. Outdoor pool, whirlpool. Pets not accepted. $

★RAMADA LIMITED ELLENTON

5218 17th St. East, Ellenton, 941-729-8505, 888-298-2054; www.ramada.com
73 rooms. Wireless Internet access. Complimentary continental breakfast. Outdoor pool, whirlpool. Pets accepted; fee. $

SPECIALTY LODGING
HARRINGTON HOUSE BEACH FRONT BED & BREAKFAST INN

5626 Gulf Drive North, Holmes Beach, 941-778-5444, 888-828-5566;
www.harringtonhouse.com
19 rooms. Children over 12 years only. Complimentary full breakfast. Outdoor pool. $$$

RESTAURANTS
★★★BEACH BISTRO

6600 Gulf Drive, Holmes Beach, 941-778-6444; www.beachbistro.com
American menu. Dinner. Bar. Reservations Recommended. $$$

★GULF DRIVE CAFÉ
900 N. Gulf Drive, Bradenton, 941-778-1919
American menu. Breakfast, lunch, dinner. Children's menu. Casual attire. Outdoor seating. **$**

★★LEE'S CRAB TRAP II
4815 17th St. E., Ellenton, 941-729-7777; www.leescrabtrap.com
American Seafood menu. Lunch, dinner. Bar. Children's menu. Outdoor seating. Casual attire. **$$$**

★MILLER'S DUTCH KITCH'N
3401 14th St. W., Bradenton, 941-746-8253; www.millersdutchkitchen.com
American menu. Lunch, dinner. Closed Sunday. Children's menu. Casual attire. **$**

★★SANDBAR
100 Spring Ave., Anna Maria, 941-778-0444; www.groupersandwich.com
Seafood menu. Lunch, dinner. Bar. Children's menu. Outdoor seating. **$$**

BROOKSVILLE

Located in a hilly stretch of countryside unusual in Florida, Brooksville is best known for being the home of the wonderfully kitschy Weeki Wachee Spring and its more than 60-year-old underwater mermaid shows.

Information: Greater Hernando County Chamber of Commerce, 101 E. Fort Dade Ave., Brooksville, 352-796-0697; www.hernandochamber.com

WHAT TO SEE AND DO
WEEKI WACHEE SPRING, THE CITY OF MERMAIDS
6131 Commercial Way, Brooksville, 352-596-2062, 800-469-3354; www.weekiwachee.com
An underwater amphitheater combines nature and engineering to showcase underwater mermaid shows. Producing more than 168 million gallons of water daily, the spring has a measured depth of 250 feet, but goes deeper. In 1947, after a former Navy frogman developed underwater breathing techniques at Weeki Wachee, he built an auditorium 6 feet below the surface. The first underwater show was so successful that a second, million-dollar auditorium seating 500 was built 16 feet below the surface. Today's visitors watch underwater performances through 19 plate-glass windows nearly three inches thick. Each performance lasts approximately 30 minutes, with three performances daily. Other attractions include the Wilderness River Cruise down the Weeki Wachee River. Daily. Closed Monday-Wednesday during October-December.

HOTEL
★★QUALITY INN WEEKI WACHEE
6172 Commercial Way, Spring Hill, 352-596-2007; www.qualityinn.com
116 rooms. Pets accepted; fee. Complimentary continental breakfast. Restaurant, bar. Outdoor pool, children's pool. Wireless Internet access. **$**

CAPE CORAL

Settled only in 1958, Cape Coral has grown rapidly over the past several decades and has the second-largest area of Florida's cities. Water-related activities on the Caloosahatchee River and golfing are popular.

Information: Chamber of Commerce, 2051 Cape Coral Parkway, Cape Coral,
239-549-6900, 800-226-9609; www.capecoralchamber.com

HOTEL
★QUALITY HOTEL NAUTILUS
1538 Cape Coral Parkway E., Cape Coral, 239-542-2121, 800-228-5151;
www.qualityinn.com
142 rooms. Pets accepted, some restrictions; fee. Bar. Wireless Internet access. Valet parking. Free Continental breakfast. Fitness room. Outdoor pool. $

RESTAURANT
★ARIANI
1529 S.E. 15th Terrace, Cape Coral, 239-772-8000; www.chefdario.com
Italian menu. Dinner. Closed Sunday. Bar. Children's menu. Business casual attire. Reservations recommended. $$

CLEARWATER

Clearwater is a tourist destination that has retained its quiet feel despite the rapid population growth.

Information: Clearwater Regional Chamber of Commerce, 1130 Cleveland St.,
Clearwater, 727-461-0011; www.clearwaterflorida.org

WHAT TO SEE AND DO
MOCCASIN LAKE NATURE PARK
2750 Park Trail Lane, Clearwater, 727-462-6024; www.myclearwater.com
An environmental and energy education center consisting of a 51-acre wilderness preserve; 5-acre lake; bird walks; nature trails and boardwalks (1 ½ miles); native wildlife and plant exhibits; alternative energy displays. Guided tours by appointment. Tuesday-Friday 9 a.m.-5 p.m., Saturday 10 a.m.-6 p.m., Sunday and Monday: closed except for special programming.

ORIGINAL DOLPHIN ENCOUNTER CRUISE
25 Causeway Blvd., Clearwater, 727-442-7433; www.dolphinencounter.org
Reservations recommended. Daily. Cruises aboard double-deck, 25-passenger *Clearwater Express*. Dolphin watching, bird feeding. $$$

SPECIAL EVENTS
FLORIDA ORCHESTRA
Ruth Eckerd Hall and Tampa Bay Performing Arts Center, 1111 N. McMullen Booth Road,
Clearwater, 813-286-2403, 800-662-7286
Classical and pop performances. September-late May.

PHILADELPHIA PHILLIES SPRING TRAINING

Bright House Networks Field, 601 N. Old Coachman Road, Clearwater, 727-441-8638; www.philadelphia.phillies.mlb.com

Philadelphia Phillies baseball spring training, exhibition games. Early March-early April.

HOTELS

★★★BELLEVIEW BILTMORE GOLF RESORT & SPA

25 Belleview Blvd., Clearwater, 727-373-3000, 800-237-8947; www.belleviewbiltmore.com

Since 1897, this Victorian-style resort on the Intracoastal Waterway has entertained everyone from corporate groups to brides-to-be. The woodwork and stained glass have been carefully preserved, and wide corridors and wood floors add to the charm. Red-clay tennis courts, a Donald Ross-designed golf course and a 14,000-square-foot spa are just a few of the onsite activities. Although the resort is basically on the Gulf, there is no beach on the property, but guests can be shuttled to the resort's private beach. 246 rooms. High-speed Internet access. Three restaurants, three bars. Pub. Ice-cream parlor. Fitness room, fitness classes available, spa. Indoor pool, outdoor pool, whirlpool. Golf, 18 holes. Tennis. Business center. $$

★★COURTYARD ST. PETERSBURG CLEARWATER

3131 Executive Drive, Clearwater, 727-572-8484, 800-321-2211; www.courtyard.com

149 rooms. High-speed Internet access. Restaurant, bar. Fitness room. Outdoor pool, whirlpool. Pets not accepted. $

★★HOLIDAY INN

3535 Ulmerton Road, Clearwater, 727-577-9100, 800-465-4329; www.holiday-inn.com

173 rooms. Wireless Internet access. Complimentary continental breakfast. Restaurant, bar. Fitness room. Outdoor pool, whirlpool. Tennis. Airport transportation available. Business center. Pets not allowed. Complimentary airport shuttle. $

★KNIGHTS INN

34106 Highway 19, Palm Harbor, 727-789-2002, 800-843-5644; www.knightsinn.com

114 rooms. Pets accepted; fee. Free Continental breakfast. Wireless Internet access. Outdoor pool. $

★★RADISSON HOTEL CLEARWATER CENTRAL

20967 Highway 19 N., Clearwater, 727-799-1181, 800-333-3333; www.radisson.com

148 rooms. Pets accepted, some restrictions; fee. Complimentary full breakfast. High-speed Internet access. Restaurant, bar. Fitness room. Outdoor pool, children's pool, whirlpool. Business center. $

★★★SAFETY HARBOR RESORT AND SPA

105 N. Bayshore Drive, Safety Harbor, 727-726-1161, 888-237-8772; www.safetyharborspa.com

This retreat on Tampa Bay offers extensive spa treatments and salon services, including five natural mineral springs. Lounge along the 28 miles of white sand on the Gulf or catch a show in the 300-seat theater. 189 rooms. Pets accepted, some restrictions; fee. High-speed Internet access. Restaurant, bar. Fitness room, fitness classes available, spa. Indoor pool, two outdoor pools, whirlpool. Tennis. Business center. $$$

RESTAURANTS

★★★ALFANO'S

1702 Clearwater/Largo Road, Clearwater, 727-584-2125; www.alfanosrestaurant.com

A local favorite since 1984, this family-owned restaurant features classic Italian fare, available à la carte or as a three-course prix fixe meal, as well as a number of selections to suit everyone from vegetarians to meat-lovers and seafood eaters. Entrées such as filet mignon, manicotti and striped Maine lobster ravioli are nicely complemented by the award-winning wine list. Don't miss the chocolate truffle cake and cannoli for dessert. Live jazz is offered on Wednesday nights in the lounge, and a pianist performs on Friday and Saturday nights. Italian menu. Lunch, dinner. Closed Sunday from Mother's Day through November. Bar. Children's menu. Business casual attire. Reservations recommended. Outdoor seating. $$

★★E & E STAKEOUT GRILL

100 N. Indian Rocks Road, Belleair Bluffs, 727-585-6399; www.3bestchefs.com

Southwestern menu. Lunch, dinner. Bar. Children's menu. Reservations recommended. $$

★★MEZZA

2325 Ulmerton Road, Clearwater, 727-571-3400

Mediterranean menu. Lunch, dinner. Bar. Business casual attire. Reservations recommended. Outdoor seating. $$

★PANDA CHINESE RESTAURANT

1201 Cleveland St., Clearwater, 727-447-3830

Carved entrance archway of Chinese cypress. Chinese menu. Lunch, dinner. Bar. $

CLEARWATER BEACH

This four-mile-long island of white-sand beaches is connected to the mainland by Memorial Causeway. The beach extends the full length of the island and is between 350 and 1,700 feet wide. There is a fishing pier, and the marina has slips, docks, boat rentals, sailing and a sport-fishing fleet. Skin diving and shelling are also popular activities. The beach is also near the city of Clearwater, which is a perfect jumping-off point for exploring the western Florida and other cities, such as St. Petersburg and Tampa. Folks flock to the latter two to check out major attractions such as Busch Gardens, Tampa Bay, the Florida Aquarium, the Clearwater Marine Aquarium, Big Cat Rescue and Adventure Island.

Information: Clearwater Regional Chamber of Commerce, 1130 Cleveland St., Clearwater, 727-461-0011; www.clearwaterflorida.org

WHAT TO SEE AND DO

CLEARWATER MARINE AQUARIUM

249 Windward Passage, Clearwater Beach, 727-441-1790, 888-239-9414; www.cmaquarium.org

This is one of only three facilities on Florida's expansive west coast equipped for the rescue and treatment of marine mammals and sea turtles. Visitors watch the progress and feeding of recuperating dolphins, otters and sea turtles. The aquarium also has research laboratories and educational programs. Check the Web site for upcoming programming. Monday-Thursday 9 a.m.-5 p.m., Friday and Saturday 9 a.m.-8 p.m., Sunday 10 a.m.-5 p.m.

SUNSETS AT PIER 60

Pier 60 Park, Clearwater Beach, 727-449-1036; www.sunsetsatpier60.com

Artists, crafters, performers and musicians come out to celebrate the setting of the sun two hours before and after sunset. Nightly.

HOTELS

★★★HILTON CLEARWATER BEACH RESORT

400 Mandalay Ave., Clearwater Beach, 727-461-3222, 877-461-3222;
www.hiltonclearwaterbeachresort.com

Overlooking the Clearwater Pier, this family-friendly hotel is situated on sandy white beaches and is right in the center of all the action—the beach, shopping, and dining are just steps away. Guest rooms have a contemporary feel and provide balconies, which offer views of the Gulf of Mexico. 416 rooms. Wireless Internet access. Two restaurants, two bars. Children's activity center. Fitness room. Beach. Outdoor pool, children's pool, whirlpool. Business center. $$$

★★MARRIOTT SUITES CLEARWATER BEACH ON SAND KEY

1201 Gulf Blvd., Clearwater Beach, 727-596-1100, 800-228-9290;
www.clearwaterbeachmarriottsuites.com

220 rooms, all suites. Wireless Internet access. Three restaurants, two bars. Children's activity center. Fitness room, fitness classes available, spa. Outdoor pool, children's pool, whirlpool. Business center. Valet parking. $$$

★★★SHERATON SAND KEY RESORT

1160 Gulf Blvd., Clearwater Beach, 727-595-1611, 800-456-7263;
www.sheratonsandkey.com

The Sheraton Sand Key Resort is located in a quiet setting, just slightly off the main area of Clearwater Beach. Overlooking Clearwater Bay, the well-landscaped beach-front property offers 10 acres to roam and is adjacent to Sand Key Park and Preserve. Guest rooms feature balconies or ground-floor patios, wicker furniture, and high-quality linens in which you can relax after a long day at the beach. The attractive outdoor pool leads to the beach, and guests can rent wave runners and other water sports equipment.

375 rooms. Pets accepted, some restrictions. High-speed Internet access. Four restaurants, two bars. Fitness room; fee. Beach. Outdoor pool, children's pool, whirlpool. Tennis. Business center. $$

RESTAURANT

★★BOB HEILMAN'S BEACHCOMBER

447 Mandalay Ave., Clearwater Beach, 727-442-4144; www.heilmansbeachcomber.com

American menu. Lunch, dinner. Bar. Children's menu. Business casual attire. Reservations recommended. Valet parking. Outdoor seating. $$

COCOA

When the name "Indian River City" was rejected in 1882 by the U.S. postal authorities because it was too long for a postmark, the boys in the general store chose the town's present name from a box of Baker's cocoa. The city was swept into the space age due to its proximity to both Cape Canaveral and Kennedy Space Center.

Information: Cocoa Beach Area Chamber of Commerce, 400 Fortenberry Road, Merritt Island, 321-459-2200; www.cocoabeachchamber.com

WHAT TO SEE AND DO

BREVARD MUSEUM OF HISTORY AND NATURAL SCIENCE

2201 Michigan Ave., Cocoa, 321-632-1830; www.brevardmuseum.org

Exhibits include native artifacts, a hands-on Discovery Room, mollusk collection, nature center, an archaeological dig of the 7000-plus-year-old Windover burial site and 22 acres of nature preserves and trails through three different ecosystems. Butterfly garden, Covered pavilion with picnic tables. Tuesday-Saturday 10 a.m.-4 p.m.

HISTORIC COCOA VILLAGE

430 Delannoy Ave., Cocoa, 321-631-9075; www.cocoavillage.com

Self-guided tour of four-block historic area, including Cocoa Village Playhouse, Porcher House, Gothic church and 11 other sites, plus unique shops and restaurants. Advance reservations required.

HOTELS

★BEST WESTERN COCOA INN

4225 W. King St., Cocoa, 321-632-1065, 866-262-6229; www.bestwestern.com

120 rooms. Pets not allowed. Complimentary continental breakfast. Bar. Outdoor pool. Free parking. Business center. Wireless Internet access. $

★★CLARION HOTEL

260 E. Merritt Island Causeway, Merritt Island, 321-452-7711, 800-584-1482; www.clarionspacecoast.com

128 rooms. Complimentary continental breakfast. Wireless Internet access. Restaurant, bar. Fitness room. Outdoor pool. Tennis. Business center. $

RESTAURANTS

★★BLACK TULIP

207 Brevard Ave., Cocoa, 321-631-1133

American menu. Lunch, dinner. Closed Sunday. $$

★★★CAFE MARGAUX

220 Brevard Ave., Cocoa, 321-639-8343; www.margaux.com

This classic French restaurant serves dishes such as pork loin stuffed with pear, brie, walnut and beef tenderloin with cabernet herb demiglace sauce. The wine list is extensive and features bottles from around the world. French, seafood menu. Lunch, dinner. Closed Sunday. Outdoor seating. $$

COCOA BEACH

Inaccessible except by boat until 1923 when a bridge was built to Merritt Island, Cocoa Beach remained a sparsely populated hamlet until about 1940. Located south of the city is Patrick Air Force Base. This facility includes the Logistical and Administrative Center of the Air Force Eastern Test Range. Cape Canaveral and the Kennedy Space Center are north of the city.

Information: Cocoa Beach Area Chamber of Commerce, 400 Fortenberry Road, Merritt Island, 321-459-2200; www.cocoabeachchamber.com

SPECIAL EVENTS

RON JON EASTER SURFING FESTIVAL

Cocoa Beach Pier, Cocoa Beach, 321-799-8888; www.eastersurffest.com

More than 100,000 visitors flock to Cocoa Beach every year to witness this surfing spectacular that includes both professional and amateur surfing events, some of which are used to determine the National Longboard Championship. Thursday-Sunday of Easter weekend.

SPACE COAST ART FESTIVAL

Downtown, Cocoa Beach, 321-784-3322; www.spacecoastartfestival.com

More than 230 artists display and sell their works, student artists participate in a judged show, and budding artists up to six years old enjoy hands-on activities at this outdoor family festival. 5K run. Thanksgiving weekend November 29-30.

FLORIDA

★
★
★
★

KENNEDY SPACE CENTER

Visit the Kennedy Space Center and see the inner workings of America's space program firsthand. The public extension of NASA, the Kennedy Space Center Visitor Complex tells the story of space exploration and has spacecraft, rockets and displays situated on 70 acres of NASA's launch headquarters. The information and exhibits change constantly, reflecting the evolution of the space program. Daily 9 a.m.-7 p.m.; closed December 25 and on certain launch days.

The Astronaut Hall of Fame is located just a few miles down the road and is home to the world's largest collection of astronaut memorabilia, as well as displays, exhibits and tributes to the heroes of Mercury, Gemini and Apollo.

The Kennedy Space Center Tour, which lasts 2 to 2½ hours, includes stops near the space shuttle launch pads and the launch complex's 39 Observation Gantry, where visitors may take photographs. Also included on the tour is the Apollo/Saturn V Center, which features multimedia shows and numerous hands-on displays that provide visitors a look into America's quest for the moon and an actual 363-foot *Saturn V*. The tour is included in the price of admission. Buses depart every 15 minutes between 10 a.m. and 2:15 p.m. Information: Kennedy Space Center, Highway 405, 321-449-4400, 800-572-4636; www.kennedyspacecenter.com

HOTELS

★COMFORT INN

3901 N. Atlantic Ave., Cocoa Beach, 321-783-2221, 800-247-2221;
www.comfortinncocoabeach.com
170 rooms. Wireless Internet access. Bar. Outdoor pool, whirlpool. Airport transportation available. Business center. **$**

★★DOUBLETREE HOTEL

2080 N. Atlantic Ave., Cocoa Beach, 321-783-9222, 800-222-8733;
www.cocoabeachoceanfront.doubletree.com
148 rooms. Complimentary continental breakfast. Restaurant, two bars. Fitness room. Beach. Outdoor pool, children's pool. Business center. Wireless Internet access. **$$**

★★★HILTON COCOA BEACH OCEANFRONT

1550 N. Atlantic Ave., Cocoa Beach, 321-799-0003, 800-445-8667;
www.cocoabeachhilton.com
This oceanfront hotel is located 10 minutes from Port Canaveral, home to luxury cruise liners and deep-sea fishing charters. The hotel claims to have the largest sun deck on the Florida space coast. 296 rooms. Beach, Outdoor pool. Restaurant, bar. Fitness center. Whirlpool, surfing, water sports, outdoor dining, valet parking. Wireless Internet access. Business center.

★THE INN AT COCOA BEACH

4300 Ocean Beach Blvd., Cocoa Beach, 321-799-3460, 800-343-5307;
www.theinnatcocoabeach.com
50 rooms. Bar. Fitness room. Beach. Outdoor pool. **$**

★★RADISSON RESORT AT THE PORT

8701 Astronaut Blvd., Cape Canaveral, 321-784-0000, 888-201-1718; www.radisson.com
200 rooms. Restaurant, bar. Fitness room. Outdoor pool, children's pool, whirlpool. Tennis. Pets accepted. Business center. Wireless Internet access. **$**

SPECIALTY LODGING

LUNA SEA BED AND BREAKFAST MOTEL

3185 N. Atlantic Ave., Cocoa Beach, 321-783-0500, 800-586-2732;
www.lunaseacocoabeach.com
44 rooms. Complimentary continental breakfast. Outdoor pool. **$**

RESTAURANTS

★★GREGORY'S STEAK & SEAFOOD GRILL

900 N. Atlantic Ave., Cocoa Beach., 321-799-2557; www.gregorysonthebeach.com
Steak, seafood menu. Dinner. Bar. Children's menu. Casual attire. Outdoor seating. Closed on Sunday. Reservations recommended. **$$**

★★★HEIDELBERG

7 N. Orlando Ave., Cocoa Beach, 321-783-6806
A fine selection of German beers and wines complements the traditional menu at this quaint restaurant. German menu. Lunch, dinner. Bar. Wednesday-Saturday 11 a.m.-10 p.m. Sunday 5-10 p.m. Closed on Monday and Tuesday. **$$$**

★★JACK BAKER'S LOBSTER SHANTY

2200 S. Orlando Ave., Cocoa Beach, 321-783-1350;
www.jackbakerslobstershanty.com
Seafood menu. Lunch, dinner. Bar. Children's menu. Outdoor seating. **$$**

★★★MANGO TREE

118 N. Atlantic Ave., Cocoa Beach, 321-799-0513; www.themangotreerestaurant.com
Set in an elaborate tropical garden, this colorful, casual restaurant serves dishes such
as scallops in puff pastry with lobster beurre blanc and Indian river crab cakes. American menu. Dinner. Bar. Closed Monday. **$$$**

CORAL GABLES

As one of the 29 separate municipalities that make up metropolitan Miami-Dade
County, Coral Gables was designed by George Merrick, the son of a Massachusetts
minister. Merrick laid out the entire city, but relied on slightly sensational techniques
to populate it. To lure prospective buyers from the north, Merrick offered steamship
and bus service to Coral Gables, with transportation expenses reimbursed for anyone who purchased land. He hired William Jennings Bryan to lecture on the merits
of Coral Gables' investments and engaged Paul Whiteman and the chorus of Earl
Carroll's *Vanities* to entertain buyers. Houses were designed in Mediterranean-Florida
style, with sections in French, Italian, Dutch South African and Chinese styles to provide contrast. Today, Coral Gables requires that its board of architects approve every
new building. The city includes eight planned entrances, two with arched gateways
constructed of carved native rock, and 14 planned plazas.
Information: Chamber of Commerce, 224 Catalonia Ave., Coral Gables,
305-446-1657; www.gableschamber.org

★
★
★
★
★

WHAT TO SEE AND DO
CORAL GABLES MERRICK HOUSE

907 Coral Way, Coral Gables, 305-460-5361; www.coralgables.com
Built in 1899, this "Coral-rock" plantation house was the boyhood home of the city's
founder, George Merrick. Made out of oolitic limerock and Dade County pine, it
reflects the New England roots of the family while adapting to the southern climate.
The grounds feature original furnishings, historic pieces and gardens. Wednesday,
Sunday 1-4 p.m.; also by appointment.

FAIRCHILD TROPICAL BOTANIC GARDEN

10901 Old Cutler Road, Coral Gables, 305-667-1651; www.fairchildgarden.org
This 83-acre tropical paradise showcases rare plants from all over the world including many different kinds of palms, orchids, cycads and flowering trees. Fairchild
Tropical Gardens was created in the 1940s by Colonel Robert H. Montgomery, who
named it after his friend David Fairchild. A small museum in the garden is dedicated
to Fairchild, considered to be one of the United States' foremost horticulturalists.
For more than 35 years, he traveled around the world collecting new species, and
he is credited with introducing many plants to the United States, including mangos,
nectarines, bamboo and flowering cherries. Daily 9:30 a.m.-4:30 p.m. Closed on
December 25.

LOWE ART MUSEUM

1301 Stanford Drive, Coral Gables, 305-284-3535; www.lowemuseum.org

Located on the campus of the University of Miami, the Lowe started as a teaching facility and has expanded into a public art museum featuring some 10,000 pieces of art from the Renaissance and Baroque periods in addition to American, Native American, pre-Columbian and Asian art. Tuesday-Wednesday, Friday-Saturday 10 a.m.-5 p.m., Thursday noon-7 p.m., Sunday noon-5 p.m. Closed on Monday.

MIRACLE MILE

224 Miracle Mile, Coral Gables, 305-569-0311; www.shopcoralgables.com

The Miracle Mile shopping district is best known for its many bridal shops and jewelry stores. If you're planning a wedding and want the latest in gowns and bridesmaid dresses, this is the place to visit. You can also shop for men's suits and tuxedos and find a variety of high-end specialty and boutique shops. Miracle Mile is home to some of the best restaurants in the area as well as several art galleries and specialty furniture stores throughout the downtown area. The two award-winning theaters found here, Actors Playhouse and the Miracle Theatre, are known for unusual contemporary and off-Broadway plays.

UNIVERSITY OF MIAMI

5050 Brunson Drive, Coral Gables, 305-284-2211; www.miami.edu

This is the largest independent university in the Southeast, with campuses covering 287 acres and more than 153 buildings. Gusman Concert Hall and Jerry Herman Ring Theatre present various programs throughout the year.

SPECIAL EVENTS

JUNIOR ORANGE BOWL FESTIVAL

1390 S. Dixie Highway, Coral Gables, 305-662-1210; www.jrorangebowl.com

20 events from October to January, including the world-famous Junior Orange Bowl Parade. Events include a 5K run, prestigious juniors' golf, gymnastics and tennis tournaments, soccer, queen's pageant and ball, gala evening parade and much more.

SUN DAY ON THE MILE

Downtown, Coral Gables

Sun Day on the Mile features some of the best Latin jazz in the world in the historic district of downtown Coral Gables. The event takes place in the street, and the food is catered by some of the best-known restaurants in the Miami area. Peruse art exhibits and booths while you enjoy the music. This one-day event is usually held in the first Sunday in March.

HOTELS

★★★BILTMORE HOTEL CORAL GABLES

1200 Anastasia Ave., Coral Gables, 305-445-1926, 800-727-1926;
www.biltmorehotel.com

The Biltmore Hotel is a South Florida institution. Located in the exclusive residential community of Coral Gables, this resort has welcomed Hollywood luminaries and royalty since it opened in 1925. Home to the largest swimming pool at any hotel in the United States, the Biltmore staged incredible aquatic shows. The refined accommodations are fitted with modern luxuries, while an 18-hole golf course, fitness and tennis centers and spa provide numerous recreational opportunities. The resort has four restaurants, including the much-praised La Palme d'Or. 275 rooms. Four restaurants, two bars. Fitness room, spa. Outdoor pool. Golf, 18 holes. Tennis. Business center. $$$

★★★HOTEL PLACE ST. MICHEL

162 Alcazar Ave., Coral Gables, 305-444-1666, 800-848-4683; www.hotelstmichel.com
Built in 1926, this small European-style hotel was once the Sevilla Hotel, a destination for society's upper crust. It offers rooms uniquely decorated with fine antiques and artwork, and room service presents perfectly prepared dishes. The interior is Mediterranean with Spanish accents, and the lace-curtained restaurant is an impressive romantic hideaway. 28 rooms. Complimentary continental breakfast. Restaurant, bar. Wireless Internet access. $$

★★★HYATT REGENCY CORAL GABLES

50 Alhambra Plaza, Coral Gables, 305-441-1234, 800-233-1234; www.hyatt.com
Located in the center of Coral Gables, the Hyatt Regency is the perfect spot to enjoy nearby shopping, dining, entertainment, beaches and golf. Onsite amenities include a lap pool, jogging paths and a health club. Business travelers will appreciate the relaxing environment, where business rooms provide copying, faxing and printing capabilities. 242 rooms. Two restaurants, bar. Children's activity center. Fitness room. Beach. Outdoor pool, children's pool, whirlpool. Business center. Wireless Internet access. $$$

★★★WESTIN COLONNADE HOTEL

180 Aragon Ave., Coral Gables, 305-441-2600, 800-228-3000; www.westin.com
With its European design and mahogany furnishings, the Colonnade is charming and luxurious. Built in 1926, the rooms are generously sized and feature rich upholstery, marble bathrooms and views of the surrounding Coral Gables area. While the hotel caters to business travelers with complimentary wireless Internet access in each room and a full business center, kids also receive special treatment. Upon check-in, children are given a bag that includes an activity book, crayons, a deck of cards and sunglasses. 157 rooms. Pets accepted, some restrictions; fee. Restaurant, bar. Fitness room. Outdoor pool, whirlpool. Wireless Internet access. Business center. $$$

FLORIDA

★
★
★
★
★

RESTAURANTS

★★BANGKOK BANGKOK II

157 Giralda Ave., Coral Gables, 305-444-2397
Thai menu. Lunch, dinner. Casual attire. Valet parking. $

★★★CHEF INNOCENT AT ST. MICHEL

162 Alcazar Ave., Coral Gables, 305-446-6572; www.chefinnocent.com
Located in the romantic Hotel Place St. Michel, this restaurant is the perfect spot for intimate conversation and innovative, sophisticated French-American fare. The Art Deco dining room boasts hardwood floors, magnificent plate-glass windows and soft lighting, making it a smart choice for special occasions. Seafood and steak menu. Breakfast, lunch, dinner, Sunday brunch. Bar. Business casual attire. Reservations recommended. Valet parking. Outdoor seating. $$$

★★DIEGO'S

65 Alhambra Plaza, Coral Gables, 305-448-2498; www.diegorestaurant.com

Spanish menu. Lunch, dinner. Bar. Casual attire. Reservations recommended. Closed Sunday. $$$

★JOHN MARTIN'S

253 Miracle Mile, Coral Gables, 305-445-3777; www.johnmartins.com

American, Irish menu. Lunch, dinner, Sunday brunch. Bar. Children's menu. Casual attire. Reservations recommended. Sunday-Thursday 11:30 a.m.-midnight, Friday-Saturday until 2 a.m. $$

★★★LA DORADA

177 Giralda Ave., Coral Gables, 305-446-2002

Authentic Spanish seafood, much of it flown in directly from Spain, is the specialty at this formal Spanish eatery. Mediterranean, seafood menu. Lunch, dinner. Bar. Casual attire. Reservations recommended. Valet parking. $$

★★★★LA PALME D'OR

1200 Anastasia Ave., Coral Gables, 305-913-3201; www.biltmorehotel.com

Located inside the Biltmore Hotel in Coral Gables, La Palme d'Or is a 1920s-era dining room decked out in flowers and tropical foliage, with mirrored columns, ornate light fixtures, and a view of the hotel's beautiful, oversized swimming pool. Besides a long list of inspired à la carte choices, the chef offers a six-course prix fixe experience and a nine-course tasting menu. Each menu can be paired with wine for an additional fee. The food here is varied in influence, with many contemporary French choices and several dishes inspired by Spain, Italy and Morocco. Plates are artfully presented by servers who practice their craft with care and professionalism. French menu. Dinner. Bar. Business casual attire. Valet parking. Closed Sunday-Monday. $$$$

★★★ORTANIQUE ON THE MILE

278 Miracle Mile, Coral Gables, 305-446-7710; www.cindyhutsoncuisine.com

The menu at this elegant restaurant echoes the Caribbean, offering authentic island fare marked by tropical fruits, spices, herbs and marinades. Ceviche del Mar, West Indian curried crab cakes, and jerk-rubbed Sonoma foie gras are some of the kitchen's most eagerly devoured signature dishes. Caribbean menu. Lunch: Monday-Friday, dinner: daily. Bar. Casual attire. Reservations recommended. Valet parking. Outdoor seating. $$$

★★PUCHETTA RESTAURANT

160 Giralda Ave., Coral Gables, 305-444-4553; www.puchettarestaurant.com

Italian menu. Lunch, dinner. Closed Sunday. Bar. Casual attire. Valet Parking. $$

★★★SHIBUI

7101 S.W. 72nd St., 305-274-5578; www.shibuimiami.com

Though fans rave about the freshness of the fish, this restaurant's real claim to fame is the menu: If you can get past the 45 different sushi rolls, you'll find a vast array of appetizers, combos, and entrées. Japanese menu. Dinner. Children's menu. Reservation suggested. $$$

CRYSTAL RIVER

Favored by Florida residents as a bountiful fishing ground, the area around Crystal River is also a prime diving area. The town stands where the Crystal River meets King's Bay, and both saltwater and freshwater fish are abundant. The river is a designated manatee sanctuary where the endangered species spends the winter months from mid-November through March.

Information: Citrus County Chamber, 401 Tompkins St., Inverness, 352-726-2801; www.citruscountychamber.com

HOTELS

★★BEST WESTERN CRYSTAL RIVER RESORT

614 N.W. Highway 19, Crystal River, 352-795-3171, 800-435-4409; www.seawake.com
114 rooms. Pets accepted; some restrictions; fee. Restaurant. Bar. Outdoor pool, whirlpool. High-speed Internet access. **$**

★COMFORT INN

4486 N. Suncoast Blvd., Crystal River, 352-563-1500, 800-424-6423; www.choicehotels.com
60 rooms. Pets not accepted. Complimentary continental breakfast. Outdoor pool. Whirlpool. Tennis. Free wireless Internet access. **$**

★★PLANTATION GOLF RESORT & SPA

9301 W. Fort Island Trail, Crystal River, 352-795-4211, 800-632-6262; www.plantationinn.com
202 rooms. Two restaurants, two bars. Two outdoor pools, whirlpool. Golf, 27 holes. Tennis. Spa. Boating. Fishing. Swim with manatees. **$**

DAYTONA BEACH

One of the oldest Floridian resort areas, Daytona Beach achieved international fame in the early days of the automobile due to its 23-mile, 500-foot-wide beach, which offered a natural speedway. In 1903, Alexander Winton set the world record of 68 miles per hour at Daytona Beach. Autos are still allowed on certain sections of the beach (daylight hours only February-early November), but the speed limit is 10 miles per hour. The city, with a three-sided waterfront (the Atlantic Ocean and two sides of the Halifax River), has developed as a year-round vacation spot, especially popular in spring and summer with vacationing students and families. Deep-sea fishing from charter boats at offshore reefs is enjoyed as well as river fishing on the inland waters and from the six bridges spanning the Halifax River. Supplementing tourism is Bethune-Cookman College, Embry-Riddle Aeronautical University, and a branch campus of the University of Central Florida, Orlando.

Information: Daytona Beach Area Convention and Visitors Bureau, 126 E. Orange Ave., 386-255-0415, 800-854-1234; www.daytonabeach.com

WHAT TO SEE AND DO

DAYTONA INTERNATIONAL SPEEDWAY

1801 W. International Speedway Blvd., Daytona Beach, 386-254-2700; www.daytonaintlspeedway.com
This 2½-mile, high-speed, banked track with grandstand seating for 167,860 is a testing ground for car and accessory manufacturers. Track (daily); tours except during

SPEED WEEKS

There's something about the energy, the noise, the excitement—every year, thousands flood into Daytona Beach for the Daytona 500 NASCAR stock car racing. The big race takes place mid-February, but Speed Weeks kicks off the beginning of the month with the Rolex 24 sports-car race. If you want to stay close to the speedway, you'll need to make hotel reservations a year in advance. Accommodations are available within 10 minutes of the track, beachside, usually through December. Beginning the last week of December, the Daytona Beach Area Convention and Visitors Bureau (800-854-1234) posts a daily list of Speed Weeks' room availability. You can view it via the Web site (www.daytonabeach.com). If you miss the big event, a film at the interactive attraction Daytona USA re-creates the thunder. You can also tour the track when races are not in session. To purchase Speed Weeks tickets, contact Daytona International Speedway at 386-254-2700 or www.daytonaintlspeedway.com

races and special tests. Most racing events are held February, March, July, October and December.

DAYTONA USA

1801 W. International Speedway Blvd., Daytona Beach, 386-947-6800

Located just outside the speedway's Turn 4, this theme park is like a racing fan's Disney World featuring track tours, loads of memorabilia, racing simulator rides, the car of the latest Daytona 500 winner and two films in the IMAX Theatre (NASCAR 3D: The IMAX Experience and Daytona 500: The Movie). In addition, Daytona USA regularly hosts appearances by drivers and other celebrities. Daily 9 a.m.-7 p.m.

LIVING LEGENDS OF AUTO RACING MUSEUM

Sunshine Park Mall, 2400 S. Ridgewood Ave., South Daytona, 386-763-4483;
www.livinglegendsofautoracing.com

If you can't get enough of NASCAR's early history, visit this museum owned by a local group whose president, Ray Fox, is a Hall of Fame car builder credited with helping Junior Johnson win the 1960 Daytona 500. Employees offer interesting stories about past drivers, owners and pit crews. Monday-Saturday 10 a.m.-5 p.m.

MARINE SCIENCE CENTER

100 Lighthouse Drive, Ponce Inlet, 386-304-5545; www.marinesciencecenter.com

The Marine Science Center is just around the corner from the Ponce de Leon Inlet Lighthouse. The facility may be small, but inside you'll find small alligators, snakes, a moray eel, aquariums and environmental exhibits. In the classroom lab, kids can make craft projects such as sea turtle paper plates and paper-bag pelicans. Outside, stroll Turtle Terrace to observe the sea turtle rehabilitation area. The sea bird rehabilitation center is on the other end of the parking lot, and a nature trail is located across the street. Tuesday-Saturday 10 a.m.-4 p.m., Sunday noon-4 p.m.

OCEAN WALK SHOPPES @ THE VILLAGE

250 N. Atlantic Ave., Daytona Beach, 386-258-9544, 877-845-9255;
www.oceanwalkshoppes.com

Located between the Hilton Daytona Beach Oceanfront Resort and the Ocean Walk Resort, this colorful dining, shopping and entertainment complex offers specialty shops and restaurants, a 10-screen movie theater, live entertainment and more. To the east, find the historic oceanfront Bandshell. Built in 1937 of coquina shells, the Bandshell hosts concerts and events throughout the year. The Daytona Lagoon (www.daytonalagoon.com), with a water park, arcade and go-karts, is across the street from the Shoppes.

PONCE DE LEON INLET LIGHTHOUSE AND MUSEUM

4931 S. Peninsula Drive, Ponce Inlet, 386-761-1821; www.ponceinlet.org

The scenic town of Ponce Inlet features the country's second-tallest lighthouse, located at the southern tip of the Daytona area's barrier island. At the top is an incredible view of both the Intracoastal Waterway and the ocean. Once back on solid ground, explore the original homes and buildings that surround the lighthouse. Each is filled with exhibits on lighthouse, maritime and area history, including a continuously running black-and-white video of beach races from the 1940s. Daily 10 a.m.-6 p.m.

SUGAR MILL GARDENS

950 Old Sugar Mill Road, Daytona Beach, 386-767-1735; www.echotourism.com

Twelve acres of botanical gardens on grounds of ruined sugar mill; flowering trees include magnolia; other flora. Daily dawn-dusk.

HOTELS

★ACAPULCO HOTEL & RESORT

2505 S. Atlantic Ave., Daytona Beach Shores, 386-761-2210, 800-245-3580;
www.acapulcoinn.com

133 rooms. Restaurant, bar. Beach. Outdoor pool, children's pool, two whirlpools. High-speed Internet access. Pets not accepted. **$**

★★BEST WESTERN AKU TIKI INN

2225 S. Atlantic Ave., Daytona Beach, 386-252-9631, 800-258-8454;
www.bestwestern.com

132 rooms. Restaurant, bar. Beach. Outdoor pool, children's pool. Game room for kids. Pets not accepted. **$**

★HAMPTON INN

1715 W. International Speedway Blvd., Daytona Beach, 386-257-4030, 800-593-0344;
www.hoteldaytona.com

122 rooms. Complimentary continental breakfast. Fitness room. Outdoor pool, whirlpool. High-Speed Internet access. **$**

★★★HILTON GARDEN INN DAYTONA BEACH AIRPORT

189 Midway Ave., Daytona Beach, 386-944-4000, 800-445-8667; www.hiltongardeninn.com

156 rooms. Restaurant. High-speed Internet access. Fitness room. Outdoor pool, whirlpool. Business center. Wireless Internet access. Pets not allowed. **$**

FLORIDA

★
★
★
★
☆

★★HOLIDAY INN EXPRESS

2620 W. International Speedway Blvd., Daytona Beach, 386-258-6333, 800-465-4329; www.hiexpress.com

151 rooms. Complementary breakfast. Fitness room. Outdoor pool, children's pool. Golf. Tennis. Airport transportation available. Wireless Internet access. Business center. Pets not accepted. **$**

★★LA PLAYA RESORT & SUITES

2500 N. Atlantic Ave., Daytona Beach, 386-672-0990, 800-874-6996; www.staydaytona.com

238 rooms. Restaurant only for breakfast, bar. Fitness room. Beach. Indoor pool, outdoor pool, children's pool, whirlpool. **$**

★★MAYAN INN

103 S. Ocean Ave., Daytona Beach, 386-252-2378, 800-448-2286; www.themayaninn.com

110 rooms. Complimentary continental breakfast. Laundry services. Bar. Children's activity center. Beach. Outdoor pool, children's pool, Pets not accepted. **$**

★★PLAZA RESORT AND SPA

600 N. Atlantic Ave., Daytona Beach Shores, 386-255-4471, 800-329-8663; www.plazaresortandspa.com

320 rooms. Three restaurants, bar. Children's activity center. Fitness room. Spa. Beach. Outdoor pool. High-speed Internet access. **$**

★QUALITY INN

2323 S. Atlantic Ave., Daytona Beach Shores, 386-255-0476, 800-874-7517; www.qualityinn.com

110 rooms. Pets accepted; fee. Complimentary continental breakfast. Beach. Outdoor pool, children's pool, whirlpool. Wireless Internet access. **$**

★★★THE SHORES RESORT & SPA

2637 S. Atlantic Ave., Daytona Beach Shores, 386-767-7350, 866-396-2217; www.shoresresort.com

This oceanfront resort has a beach-cottage feel to it with its wicker-and-terra-cotta filled lobby. Visit nearby attractions, including historic St. Augustine and Kennedy Space Center. 212 rooms. Pets accepted, some restrictions; fee. Restaurant, bar. Spa. Fitness room. Beach. Outdoor pool, children's pool, whirlpool. Wireless Internet access. Business center. **$**

★★SUN VIKING LODGE

2411 S. Atlantic Ave., Daytona Beach, 386-252-6252, 800-815-2846; www.sunviking.com

91 rooms. Restaurant. Children's activity center. Fitness room. Beach. Indoor pool, outdoor pool, children's pool, whirlpool. Golf course. **$**

SPECIALTY LODGING

COQUINA INN BED & BREAKFAST

544 S. Palmetto Ave., Daytona Beach, 386-254-4969, 800-805-7533; www.coquinainn.com

Built in 1912, this hotel served as a parsonage for many years. Four rooms. Children over 16 years only. Whirlpool. Wireless Internet access. Pets accepted. **$**

RESTAURANTS

★AUNT CATFISH'S ON THE RIVER
4009 Halifax Drive, Port Orange, 386-767-4768; www.auntcatfishontheriver.com
Seafood, steak menu. Lunch, dinner, Sunday brunch. Bar. Children's menu. Casual attire. Outdoor seating. **$$**

★★CHART HOUSE
1100 Marina Point Drive, Daytona Beach, 386-255-9022; www.chart-house.com
Seafood, steak menu. Dinner. Bar. Children's menu. Casual attire. Reservations recommended. Outdoor seating. **$$$**

★MARIA BONITA
1784 S. Ridgewood Ave., South Daytona, 386-767-9512
Cuban menu, Mexican menu. Lunch: Monday-Friday, dinner. Bar. Children's menu. Casual attire. Outdoor seating. **$$**

DEERFIELD BEACH

Established in 1898, the town of Deerfield Beach is a popular tourist destination due to the excellent fishing and beautiful beaches. When discovered, the Hillsboro River formed the northern boundary of Deerfield, but this was later dredged into a canal that linked the town with Lake Okeechobee, 45 miles to the northwest. Although primarily an agricultural area until the late 1940s, the Hillsboro Canal was an unloading site for rumrunners during Prohibition—federal agents occasionally captured a boatload of liquor.

Information: Greater Deerfield Beach Chamber of Commerce, 1601 E. Hillsboro Blvd., 954-427-1050; www.deerfieldchamber.com

WHAT TO SEE AND DO

QUIET WATERS PARK
401 S. Powerline Road, Deerfield Beach, 954-360-1315; www.broward.org/parks
A 431-acre county park with swimming, cable waterskiing, fishing, boating (marina, rentals); children's water playground, picnicking, concessions, playground, tent camping. Daily.

HOTELS

★★★COMFORT SUITES DEERFIELD BEACH
1040 E. Newport Center Drive, Deerfield Beach, 954-570-8887; www.comfortinn.com
101 rooms, all suites. Pets accepted, some restrictions; fee. Restaurant. Complimentary continental breakfast. Wireless Internet access. Outdoor pool, whirlpool. Airport transportation available. **$**

★★★HILTON DEERFIELD BEACH/BOCA RATON
100 Fairway Drive, Deerfield Beach, 954-427-7700, 800-445-8667; www.deerfieldbeach.hilton.com
Beaches, golf courses, the Boca Raton Town Center Mall and businesses are all within easy reach of this hotel, thanks to a complimentary shuttle service offered to guests traveling within a five-mile radius of the hotel. Spacious rooms feature work desks, coffeemakers, granite and marble bathrooms with Crabtree & Evelyn bath amenities.

FLORIDA

★
★
★
★
★

There's a palm tree-lined pool, where poolside service is offered, and a fitness center. Bobby Bahia's, the hotel's restaurant, serves up breakfast, lunch, and dinner in a casual setting. 221 rooms. Restaurant. Bar. Fitness room. Outdoor pool, whirlpool. Business center. Wireless Internet access. Pets accepted. **$$**

RESTAURANT
★★★BROOKS
500 S. Federal Highway, Deerfield Beach, 954-427-9302; www.brooks-restaurant.com
A flute of champagne welcomes diners to this classic and elegant restaurant. Housed in a stucco building with businesses and shops nearby, it boasts four distinctive dining rooms. The menu focuses on international cuisine, and opera is performed once per month. This restaurant is a top choice for special occasion meals or group parties. International continental menu. Dinner. Closed Monday; also Tuesday from Mother's Day to November. Bar. Children's menu. Business casual attire. Reservations recommended. Valet parking. **$$$**

DELAND
New York manufacturer Henry A. DeLand had a dream of establishing an "Athens of Florida" and chose this site as the place to do it. After planting water oaks 50 feet apart along prospective streets, he encouraged the building of a schoolhouse, a venture subsidized by hat manufacturer John B. Stetson. The school, first known as DeLand Academy, continues to thrive as Stetson University.
Information: DeLand Area Chamber of Commerce, 336 N. Woodland Blvd., 386-734-4331, 800-749-4350; www.delandchamber.org

WHAT TO SEE AND DO
BLUE SPRING STATE PARK
2100 W. French Ave., Orange City, 386-775-3663; www.floridastateparks.org/bluespring
The water at this park stays a delightful 72 degrees year-round and is a favorite spot for snorkelers and divers. Scuba divers must register at the entrance station between 8 a.m. and 3 p.m. with an up-to-date certification card and a partner. Manatees do frequent the area, but swimming or diving with the gentle giants is not permitted. You'll also find a historic house, as well as ample opportunities for fishing, canoeing, boating and hiking. Picnicking, playground equipment, camping facilities and cabins are also available. Daily 8 a.m.-sundown.

DELEON SPRINGS STATE PARK
601 Ponce deLeon Blvd., DeLeon Springs, 386-985-4212;
www.floridastateparks.org/deleonsprings
Old sugar mill (early 1800s); 50 acres of gardens. Swimming in "fountain of youth," bathhouse, snorkeling, fishing, paddleboats, canoe rentals; hiking and nature trail, picnicking, concession. Daily 8 a.m.-sundown.

HONTOON ISLAND STATE PARK
2309 River Ridge Road, DeLand, 386-736-5309; www.floridastateparks.org/hontoonisland
This 1,650-acre island in the St. Johns River contains a 300-foot-long Timucuan Indian ceremonial mound. Recreational opportunities in the park include fishing, nature trails and picnicking. Tent camping is allowed, and cabins are available for rent.

Overnight docking; fee. No vehicles; accessible only by ferry boat from the parking lot across the river. Daily 8 a.m.-sundown.

HOTEL

★★HOLIDAY INN

350 E. International Speedway Blvd., DeLand, 386-738-5200, 800-465-4329; www.holiday-inn.com

148 rooms. Complimentary continental breakfast. Restaurant, bar. Fitness room. Outdoor pool, whirlpool. Pets accepted; fee. Wireless Internet access. $

DELRAY BEACH

This placid resort town boasts beautiful beaches, championship golfing and fishing opportunities and a historic downtown district. Many noteworthy restaurants and bistros help give Delray Beach a cosmopolitan air.

Information: Delray Beach Chamber of Commerce, 64A S.E. Fifth Ave., Delray Beach, 561-278-0424; www.delraybeach.com

WHAT TO SEE AND DO

THE MORIKAMI MUSEUM AND JAPANESE GARDENS

4000 Morikami Park Road, Delray Beach, 561-495-0233; www.morikami.org

Includes a gallery, tea ceremony house, theater, bonsai collection, and surrounding gardens. Tuesday-Sunday 10 a.m.-5 p.m. Closed on Monday.

MORIKAMI PARK

4000 Morikami Park Road, Delray Beach, 561-495-0233; www.morikami.org

Park includes a one-mile, self-guided nature trail. Picnicking.

SPECIAL EVENT

BON FESTIVAL

Morikami Park, 4000 Morikami Park Road, Delray Beach, 561-495-0233; www.morikami.org

Japanese summer festival features Japanese folk dancing and music, games, food, special displays. Mid-August.

HOTELS

★★HOLIDAY INN

2809 S. Ocean Blvd., Highland Beach, 561-278-6241, 800-465-4329; www.holiday-inn.com

115 rooms. Restaurant, bar. Fitness room. Beach. Spa. Outdoor pool, children's pool, whirlpool. Tennis. Pets not allowed. High-speed Internet access. $

★★★MARRIOTT DELRAY BEACH

10 N. Ocean Blvd., Delray Beach, 561-274-3200, 877-389-0169; www.delraybeachmarriott.com

The boutiques, cafes and shops of Atlantic Avenue are all within walking distance of this Mediterranean-style hotel located on North Ocean Boulevard. Each of the guest rooms provides a coffeemaker and minibar, and some rooms offer ocean views and private balconies. Take a dip in one of the heated pools (one pool is adults only), or bask in the sun on the beach. 268 rooms. Restaurants, bars. Fitness room. Outdoor pool, whirlpool. Business center. Wireless Internet access. $$

★
★★
★★
★

RESTAURANTS

★★BOSTON'S UPPER DECK

40 S. Ocean Blvd., Delray Beach, 561-278-3364; www.bostonsonthebeach.com

American, seafood menu. Lunch Friday-Sunday, dinner Monday-Thursday. Bar. Children's menu. Casual attire. Outdoor seating. Valet Parking. **$$**

★★PINEAPPLE GRILLE

800 Palm Trail, Delray Beach, 561-265-1368; www.pineapplegrille.com

Caribbean menu. Lunch, dinner. Sunday brunch. Bar. Children's menu. Casual attire. Outdoor seating. **$$**

DESTIN

Perched on a narrow strip of land between Choctawhatchee Bay and the Gulf of Mexico, Destin is a beach community visited for its outstanding fishing. The waters of the Gulf are full of king mackerel, cobia, marlin, wahoo and sailfish. Party boats bring in red snapper and grouper. Destin retains the atmosphere of the New England birthplace of its founder, Captain Leonard Destin, who pioneered the snapper fishing industry more than 100 years ago.

Information: Chamber of Commerce, 4484 Legendary Drive, Destin, 850-837-6241; www.destin-fwb.com

WHAT TO SEE AND DO

STATE GARDENS

181 Eden Gardens Road, Point Washington, 850-231-4214; www.floridastateparks.org/edengardens

Overlooking Choctawhatchee Bay, this was once the site of a large sawmill complex. Eden House, built by William Henry Wesley in 1897, is restored and furnished with antiques. Mansion tours Monday, Thursday-Sunday, 10 a.m.-3 p.m. Gardens, picnic area. Daily 8 a.m.-sundown.

HOTELS

★★★HILTON SANDESTIN BEACH GOLF RESORT & SPA

4000 S. Sandestin Blvd., Destin, 850-267-9500, 800-367-1271; www.sandestinbeachhilton.com

The 2,400 acres between the Gulf and Choctawatchee Bay are yours at this resort, located 10 miles east of Destin. The resort offers conference facilities and a private beach. 600 rooms. Wireless Internet access. Four restaurants, three bars. Children's activity center. Fitness room, fitness classes available. Beach. Indoor pool, two outdoor pools, children's pool, two whirlpools. Golf. Tennis. Business center. **$$**

★★HOLIDAY INN

1020 Highway 98 E., Destin, 850-837-6181, 877-465-4329; www.hidestin.com

233 rooms. Complimentary full breakfast. Two restaurants, bar. Children's activity center. Fitness room. Beach. Outdoor pool, children's pool, whirlpool. **$$**

★SLEEP INN

10775 Emerald Coast Parkway, Destin, 850-654-7022, 800-638-7949; www.choicehotels.com

77 rooms. Complimentary continental breakfast. Outdoor pool. Pets accepted. High-speed Internet access. **$**

DRY TORTUGAS NATIONAL PARK

With more than 64,000 acres of land and water, this national park not only includes the remains of what was once the largest of the 19th-century American coastal forts, but also the cluster of seven islands known as the Dry Tortugas. The coral keys, upon which the fort sits, were named "las tortugas" (the turtles) in 1513 by Ponce de Leon because so many turtles inhabited these bits of land. The "dry" portion of the islands' name warns mariners of a total lack of fresh water. Tropical ocean birds are the chief inhabitants, and each year between February and September sooty and noddy terns assemble on Bush Key to nest.

Spanish pirates used the Tortugas as a base from which to pillage boats until 1821, when they were driven from the islands. In 1846, the United States, eager to protect its interests in the Gulf of Mexico, began construction of a fort on the 10-acre Garden Key. For more than 30 years, laborers worked on the fort, a rampart that was a half-mile in perimeter with 50-foot-high walls and three tiers designed for 450 guns. Called the "Gibraltar of the Gulf," this massive masonry fort was designed for a garrison of 1,500 men. Only partially completed, Fort Jefferson never saw battle. It was occupied by Union troops during the Civil War.

Resting on an unstable foundation of sand and coral boulders, Fort Jefferson's walls began to crack and shift, making it unsuitable for military defense. In 1863 it became a military prison, confining some 2,400 men. Among them was Dr. Samuel Mudd, who was imprisoned on the island after setting the broken leg of John Wilkes Booth, Abraham Lincoln's assassin. Following two yellow fever epidemics and a hurricane, the fort was abandoned in 1874. In the 1880s it was reconditioned for use as a naval base, coaling station and wireless station; the USS *Maine* sailed from the fort for Havana, where it was blown up, triggering the Spanish-American War. The fort became Fort Jefferson National Monument in 1935 and was renamed Dry Tortugas National Park in 1992.

The fort and islands are accessible by boat or seaplane trips from Key West. There is camping and a picnic area on Garden Key; campers must bring all supplies, including fresh water. Visitor center (daily). Guided tours. Contact the Park Ranger, Key West, 305-242-7700. For transportation information, contact the Greater Key West Chamber of Commerce, 402 Wall St., Old Mallory Square, Key West, 305-294-2587.

★
★ ★
★ ★
★

★★★WATERCOLOR INN

34 Goldenrod Circle, Santa Rosa, 850-534-5000; www.watercolorinn.com

David Rockwell punches up the classic beach house with a modern, edgy look at Florida's WaterColor Inn. Snuggled on the sugary-soft beaches of the serene Gulf Coast, this 499-acre mega resort offers something for everyone. Water rats can kayak, sail, fish or simply splash in the pool (where chilled, mango-scented towels spoil sunbathers), while sybarites can relax at the spa or shop at the many boutiques. Five restaurants showcase everything from pizza to sophisticated coastal cuisine. The sun-dappled guestrooms, complete with uplifting pastel colors and beach views, provide a cozy retreat at the end of a fun-filled day. 60 rooms. Restaurant. Bar. Pool. Tennis. Golf. Spa. Fitness center. Water sport. $$$$

RESTAURANTS

★★DESTIN CHOPS

10343 E. County Highway 30A, Seacrest Beach, 850-231-4050;
www.destinchops30a.com
Seafood, steak menu. Dinner. Bar. Valet parking. Outdoor seating. **$$$**

★★★FISH OUT OF WATER

34 Goldenrod Circle, Santa Rosa, 850-534-5008; www.watercolorinn.com
Located within the Watercolor Inn on Florida's Gulf Coast, Fish Out of Water's understated elegance is the perfect complement to this beachy resort. As its name implies, this restaurant focuses on fish—there's even an ice bar showcasing the day's freshest catch. Sushi is a popular component of the menu, and there are plenty of other tempting dishes including fresh meats and poultry for those who like their fish in the water. The restaurant's exhibition kitchen is an entertaining centerpiece at this lively, but relaxing spot. Seafood menu. Dinner. **$$$**

★★LA PAZ

950 Gulfshore Drive, Destin, 850-837-2247; www.lapaz.com
Mexican menu. Lunch, dinner. Bar. Outdoor seating. **$**

★★MARINA CAFÉ

404 Highway 98 East, Destin, 850-837-7960; www.marinacafe.com
Seafood menu. Dinner. Closed three weeks in January. Bar. Outdoor seating. **$$**

DUNEDIN

One of Florida's oldest coastal towns, Dunedin's name is derived from Edinburgh, Scotland. Several buildings in this community are listed on the National Historical Register.
Information: Greater Dunedin Chamber of Commerce, 301 Main St., Dunedin,
727-733-3198; www.dunedin-fl.com

WHAT TO SEE AND DO

CALADESI ISLAND STATE PARK

1 Causeway Blvd., Dunedin, 727-469-5918;
www.floridastateparks.org/caladesiisland/default.cfm
A 650-acre island accessible only by boat. Swimming, boating (dock); nature trails, picnicking. No vehicles. Ferry service from the mainland, weather permitting. Standard hours. Daily.

HONEYMOON ISLAND STATE RECREATION AREA

1 Causeway Blvd., Dunedin, 727-469-5942;
www.floridastateparks.org/honeymoonisland
Check out one of the few remaining virgin slash pine stands in South Florida along the island's northern loop trail. These large trees serve as important nesting sites for the threatened osprey. The island, with more than 208 species of plants and a wide variety of shore birds, is a prime area for nature study. Swimming; fishing for flounder, snook, redfish, trout, snapper and tarpon; nature trails, picnicking. Ferry service to Caladesi Island State Park. Daily 8 a.m. to sundown.

EVERGLADES NATIONAL PARK

The largest subtropical wilderness in North America, the Everglades National Park is a 2,400-square-mile corner of Florida that is half land and half water, and once covered most of the southern third of the state. From Lake Okeechobee to the northern border of the park, much of the glades have been drained and tamed, leaving an incredibly rich blue-black soil responsible for huge sugar, citrus and winter vegetable crops. In addition to the park, the South Florida Water Management District has developed the remaining area (larger than the state of Delaware) into a huge recreation area with hunting, fishing, boating, camping and sightseeing. The Everglades are easily reached from cities along Florida's east coast—there are 34 access sites located along the canals and the levees that have been constructed to protect 18 counties from flood and drought.

There is no other place in the world like the Everglades, a huge, water-sodden wetland with prairies of saw grass, stands of dwarf cypress, hammocks of cabbage palm, West Indies mahogany, strangler figs and wild orchids. The expanse teems with water birds, alligators, snakes, marsh rabbits, deer, raccoons, bobcats, turtles, largemouth bass, garfish and panfish (wildlife is visible mainly during the winter months). The Everglades are also part of the traditional domain of the Seminole and Miccosukee tribes.

Most of the Everglades are filled with hedges that shoot up 10 feet with barbed blades and needle-sharp edges, appropriately called saw grass. These grassy waters are broken only by clusters of trees and dense vegetation called hammocks. The saw-grass glades give way along the coast to huge, shadowy mangrove swamps interlaced with tranquil winding water lanes.

Much of the national park is impenetrable unless you're accompanied by an experienced guide. The National Park Service has set up marked trails, exhibits and facilities that make a safe excursion into the Everglades possible for any visitor. Fires set accidentally can be a severe danger in the Everglades; ground fires are not permitted. Smoking is also forbidden on nature trails. Pets must be on leashes and are not permitted on the trails or in the backcountry. Information: Park Superintendent, 40001 State Road, Homestead, 305-242-7700; www.nps.gov

FLORIDA

★
★ ★
★ ★
★

SPECIAL EVENTS

HIGHLAND GAMES & SPRING CLAN GATHERING

Michigan and Pinehurst, Dunedin, 727-733-3197; www.dunedinhighlandgames.com
These Games include pipe bands, dance and seven-event athletic competitions. Many people also attend the Gathering of the Clans where they can learn about Scottish traditions or revisit their own heritage. Early March.

TORONTO BLUE JAYS SPRING TRAINING

Dunedin Stadium, 373 Douglas Ave., Dunedin, 800-707-8269;
www.toronto.bluejays.mlb.com
Baseball spring training; exhibition games. Early March-early April.

HOTEL

★★BEST WESTERN YACHT HARBOR INN AND SUITES

150 Marina Plaza, Dunedin, 727-733-4121, 800-447-4728; www.bestwestern.com

55 rooms. Complimentary continental breakfast. Restaurant. Outdoor pool, whirlpool. $

RESTAURANTS

★★★BLACK PEARL

315 Main St., Dunedin, 727-734-3463; www.theblackpearlofdunedin.com

This small restaurant located in the quaint downtown area of Dunedin sources seasonal, fresh ingredients to use in its innovative dishes. Cedar planked salmon comes in a honey glaze with horseradish sauce, while filet mignon is served in a merlot demi-glace. American menu. Dinner. $$$

★★★BON APPETIT

150 Marina Plaza, Dunedin, 727-733-2151; www.bonappetit-restaurant.com

Dine either inside or out at this restaurant just across from the Best Western Yacht Harbor Inn and Suites. The dining room has beautiful views of the Intracoastal. American, French menu. Lunch, dinner, Sunday brunch. Bar. Children's menu. Valet parking. Outdoor seating. $$

★SEA SEA RIDERS

221 Main St., Dunedin, 727-734-1445; www.seaseariders.net

American, seafood menu. Lunch, dinner, Sunday brunch. Bar. Children's menu. Outdoor seating. $$

FLORIDA

★
★★
★★
★

FERNANDINA BEACH

The northern-most city on Florida's east coast, Fernandina Beach is the only incorporated city on Amelia Island. It received its name in 1811 from King Ferdinand VII of Spain. During the course of four centuries, eight flags have flown over this area, starting with the French in 1562, followed by the Spanish and British. In 1812, the Patriots' flag flew, followed in short order by General Sir Gregor MacGregor's personal flag, the Green Cross of Florida, and then, for a brief period, the flag of Mexico. The United States formally took possession of the island in 1821. At the outbreak of the Civil War, the Confederate flag was raised over Fernandina and Fort Clinch, but it was lowered in 1862 in Fort Clinch State Park, when the town was the target of a Union fleet. Today, Fernandina Beach's harbor provides mooring for a large and prosperous shrimping fleet; two local pulp mills produce linerboard for paper containers and chemical cellulose. A 50-block restored Victorian historical district, including redeveloped Centre Street, is located downtown.

Information: Amelia Island Tourist Development Council, 102 Centre St.,
Amelia Island, 904-277-0717, 800-226-3542; www.ameliaisland.org

WHAT TO SEE AND DO

AMELIA ISLAND MUSEUM OF HISTORY

233 S. Third St., Fernandina Beach, 904-261-7378; www.ameliamuseum.org

Recited oral history, using artifacts and exhibits, recounts 400 years of settlement under eight flags; materials from 17th-century Spanish mission archaeological site;

artifacts from 18th-century shipwrecks; 19th-century "Golden Age" decorative arts and photographs. Docent-guided tours. Monday-Saturday 10 a.m.-4 p.m.; closed holidays.

FORT CLINCH STATE PARK

2601 Atlantic Ave., Fernandina Beach, 904-277-7274; www.floridastateparks.org
Found at Florida's most northeastern point, this 1,100-acre park features an old fort with brick ramparts that offer a view of the Georgia shoreline and the Atlantic Ocean. A living history interpretation is provided by park rangers dressed in Union uniforms of the 1864 garrison. Swimming; fishing from a 1,500-foot pier, the shore and jetties; nature trails, picnicking; camping. Visitor center. Daily 8 a.m.-sundown.

HOTELS

★★★GREYFIELD INN

6 N. Second St., Fernandina Beach, 904-261-6408, 866-410-8051; www.greyfieldinn.com
To truly get away from it all, escape to the historic Greyfield Inn, built in 1900. Accessible by private ferry from Fernandina Beach, this inn is a tranquil place to enjoy Cumberland Island's natural beauty and abundant wildlife, including wild horses and many species of birds. Furnished with family heirlooms and antiques, the guest rooms and suites vary widely (not all have private baths). Room rates include breakfast, picnic lunch, gourmet dinner (jacket required) and snacks throughout the day, as well as unlimited use of the inn's sporting, fishing and beach equipment. A two-night minimum stay is required. 17 rooms. Children over 6 years only. Check-in 1 p.m., check-out 11 a.m. Restaurant, bar. Fitness room. $$$$

★HAMPTON INN & SUITES AMELIA ISLAND

19 S. Second St., Fernandina Beach, 904-491-4911, 800-426-7866; www.hamptoninnandsuites.net
122 rooms. Complimentary continental breakfast. Wireless Internet access. Fitness room. Outdoor pool. Business center. $$

SPECIALTY LODGING

HOYT HOUSE BED & BREAKFAST

804 Atlantic Ave., Amelia Island, 904-277-4300, 800-432-2085; www.hoythouse.com
Located in the downtown historic district, this charming yellow-and-blue Victorian was built in the Queen Anne style by a local merchant in 1905. Its guest rooms are decorated in deep, bold colors, and the public rooms feature antiques and oriental rugs. In the yard, a pool and hot tub are surrounded by manicured gardens. 10 rooms. Children over 12 years only. Complimentary full breakfast. Wireless Internet access. Outdoor pool, whirlpool. $$

RESTAURANTS

★★★BEECH STREET GRILL

801 Beech St., Fernandina Beach, 904-277-3662; www.beechstreetgrill.com
Built in 1889, this house has been fully restored and contains many intimate dining areas and fireplaces. It's menu also boasts fresh local seafood and seasonal ingredients. Seafood menu. Dinner. Bar. Children's menu. $$$

★DOWN UNDER

4883 Otis Trail, Fernandina Beach, 904-261-1001
Seafood menu. Dinner. Bar. Children's menu. Closed Monday, Labor Day-March. $$

FORT LAUDERDALE

With more than 300 miles of navigable waterways, 23 miles of Atlantic beaches, and a myriad of rivers, inlets and man-made canals in the Greater Fort Lauderdale area, the city easily lives up to its nickname "the Venice of America." The abundance of water provides ample port for approximately 40,000 boats, not to mention flotillas of visiting vessels. Water taxis ply waterways to hotels, restaurants and sightseeing attractions. Port Everglades, the deepest and perhaps best-known harbor in the state, is also the world's second-largest passenger cruise port. More than 1 million passengers sail from Fort Lauderdale annually.

Fort Lauderdale was named for Major William Lauderdale, who built a fort in 1838 during the Seminole War. The area remained a sleepy strip of oceanfront until the 1950s and 1960s, when college students made it the "spring break capital of the world." The city cracked down on spring breakers in the 1980s in an effort to recapture its reputation, and by the 1990s it was once again a sparkling, family-friendly resort town.

Information: Greater Fort Lauderdale Convention and Visitors Bureau,
1850 E. Broward Blvd., 954-765-4466, 800-227-8669; www.sunny.org

WHAT TO SEE AND DO

BIG CYPRESS SEMINOLE INDIAN RESERVATION SAFARI

Alligator Alley (I-75) to exit 49, then north 19 miles to the park entrance,
800-949-6101, 863-983-6101; www.seminoletribe.com/safari
A 2,200-acre tour site in the Everglades. Billie Swamp Safari eco-tours, airboat rides, day or overnight (reservations required). Ah-Tha-Thi-Ki Museum nearby.

BONNET HOUSE

900 N. Birch Road, Fort Lauderdale, 954-563-5393; www.bonnethouse.org
This 35-acre subtropical, historical estate features uniquely decorated rooms, tropical birds and live monkeys. May-November, Wednesday-Friday 10 a.m.-3 p.m., Saturday to 4 p.m., Sunday noon-4 p.m.; December-April, Tuesday-Saturday 10 a.m.-4 p.m., Sunday from noon.

INTERNATIONAL SWIMMING HALL OF FAME AND AQUATIC COMPLEX

1 Hall of Fame Drive, Fort Lauderdale, 954-462-6536; www.ishof.org
Leading repository for aquatic displays, photos, sculpture, art and memorabilia; computerized exhibits, film and video presentations, aquatic library. Also, two Olympic-size public swimming pools. Museum daily 9 a.m.-5 p.m.

MUSEUM OF ART

1 E. Las Olas Blvd., Fort Lauderdale, 954-525-5500; www.moafl.org
Permanent and changing exhibits feature works by such artists as Dali, Warhol, Picasso and many more. Monday, Wednesday, Friday-Sunday 11 a.m.-7 p.m., Thursday to 9 p.m.; closed holidays.

LAS OLAS BOULEVARD

Las Olas Boulevard is Fort Lauderdale's most fashionable street—it begins at the beach and connects to Riverwalk, a linear park that follows New River to many of the city's best cultural sights. Start out at the famous *Where the Boys Are* beach with the International Swimming Hall of Fame located nearby to the south. In recent years, spring breakers have been replaced by trendsetters. Pass by the shops and cafés and discover the Stranahan House off to your left at 335 S.E. 6th Avenue. Take a tour of Fort Lauderdale's oldest home, built at the turn of the last century, and learn about the days of Indian trading posts and the frontier. Riverwalk, a paved sidewalk for strollers, cyclists and in-line skaters, features educational stations, including one that lets you fiddle around with marine navigational instruments. It passes by charter boats, including the Water Taxi, which will take you anywhere along Fort Lauderdale's extensive system of canals. On Sundays, jazz artists entertain visitors, and there are plenty of park benches where people sit and listen. Toward the end of the walk, you will come to a cluster of cultural attractions. At the **Museum of Art** (*1 E. Las Olas Boulevard*), you'll find impressive exhibits, as well as the museum's own collection. Las Olas Riverfront is a new shopping and entertainment complex and a good place to stop for lunch on the patio overlooking the river. The **Museum of Discovery and Science**, at *401 S.W. 2nd Street* explores physics, space flight, health, fitness and nature. It also has a 3-D IMAX theater that shows science-oriented films. Down the street is Broward Center for the Performing Arts, the destination of evening strollers. The center hosts Florida Grand Opera, Florida Philharmonic, Miami City Ballet and touring Broadway shows. www.lasolasboulevard.com

★
★ ★
★ ★
★

MUSEUM OF DISCOVERY AND SCIENCE AND AUTONATION IMAX 3-D THEATER

401 S.W. Second St., Fort Lauderdale, 954-467-6637; www.mods.org

Hands-on science museum with seven permanent exhibit areas, including KidScience, Space Base, Choose Health, and Florida Ecoscapes. Features Manned Maneuvering Unit space ride and walk-through simulated Florida habitats; traveling exhibitions. IMAX 3D Theater features large-format films shown on five-story screen. Daily; also Saturday-Sunday evenings. Museum Monday-Saturday 10 a.m.-5 p.m., Sunday noon-6 p.m.

RIVERWALK

Las Olas, Fort Lauderdale, 954-468-1541; www.goriverwalk.com

Linear park that connects Las Olas Boulevard to many of the city's other attractions; park runs along New River and hosts Sunday jazz brunches.

STRANAHAN HOUSE

335 S.E. Sixth Ave., Fort Lauderdale, 954-524-4736; www.stranahanhouse.org

Fort Lauderdale's oldest home, once used as a Native American trading post. Tours. Wednesday-Saturday 10 a.m.-3 p.m., Sunday from 1 p.m.

SPECIAL EVENTS

AIR & SEA SHOW

Sunrise Boulevard at A1A, Fort Lauderdale, 954-467-3555; www.airseashow.com
Aerial acrobatics. Includes performances by the U.S. Navy Blue Angels, the U.S. Army Golden Knights and the Canadian Forces Snowbirds. Late April-early May.

BALTIMORE ORIOLES SPRING TRAINING

Fort Lauderdale Stadium, 1301 N.W. 55th St., Fort Lauderdale, www.baltimore.orioles.mlb.com
Baltimore Orioles baseball spring training, exhibition games. Late February-early April.

WINTERFEST

Fort Lauderdale, 954-767-0686; www.winterfestparade.com
Monthlong festival includes a boat parade and downtown New Year's Eve celebration. December.

HOTELS

★★BEST WESTERN OAKLAND PARK INN

3001 N. Federal Highway, Fort Lauderdale, 954-565-4601, 800-633-6279; www.bwoaklandparkinn.com
106 rooms. Complimentary continental breakfast. Wireless Internet access. Restaurant, bar. Fitness room. Indoor pool. Business center. $

★★BEST WESTERN OCEANSIDE INN

1180 Seabreeze Blvd., Fort Lauderdale, 954-525-8115, 800-780-7234; www.bestwestern.com
101 rooms. Complimentary continental breakfast. Wireless Internet access. Restaurant, bar. Outdoor pool. $

★COMFORT SUITES

1800 S. Federal Highway, Fort Lauderdale, 954-767-8700
111 rooms. Complimentary continental breakfast. Outdoor pool. Airport transportation available. $

★★COURTYARD FORT LAUDERDALE EAST

5001 N. Federal Highway, Fort Lauderdale, 954-771-8100, 800-321-2211; www.courtyard.com
104 rooms. Bar. Fitness room. Outdoor pool, whirlpool. $

★★COURTYARD FORT LAUDERDALE WESTON

2000 N. Commerce Parkway, Weston, 954-343-2225, 800-321-2211; www.courtyard.com
174 rooms. Restaurant, bar. Outdoor pool. $

★★EMBASSY SUITES

1100 S.E. 17th St., Fort Lauderdale, 954-527-2700, 800-362-2779; www.embassysuites1.hilton.com
358 rooms, all suites. Complimentary full breakfast. Restaurant, bar. Fitness room. Outdoor pool, whirlpool. Airport transportation available. $$

★★GALLERY ONE, DOUBLETREE GUEST SUITES HOTEL

2670 E. Sunrise Blvd., Fort Lauderdale, 954-565-3800, 800-222-8733;
www.doubletreehilton.com

229 rooms, all suites. Pets accepted, some restrictions; fee. High-speed Internet access. Restaurant, bar. Fitness room. Outdoor pool, whirlpool. Business center. **$$**

★★★HILTON FORT LAUDERDALE AIRPORT

1870 Griffin Road, Fort Lauderdale, 954-920-3300, 800-445-8667; www.hilton.com

Abundant fruit-bearing trees dot the landscape of this secluded hotel located adjacent to the Fort Lauderdale airport. Soundproof guest rooms are decorated in soft, tranquil tones, and the lobby is bright and spacious, with cream-colored marble floors. 388 rooms. Pets accepted; fee. Wireless Internet access. Restaurant, two bars. Fitness room. Outdoor pool, whirlpool. Tennis. Airport transportation available. Business center. **$**

★★★HYATT REGENCY BONAVENTURE

250 Racquet Club Road, Weston, 954-389-3300, 800-238-1234;
www.bonaventurehyatt.com

This recently renovated resort near Fort Lauderdale has rooms with luxury bedding, flatscreen televisions and marble baths. The grounds include three outdoor pools and access to tennis and golf. An onsite Elizabeth Arden Red Door spa offers a full menu of treatments. 496 rooms. Pets accepted, some restrictions; fee. Restaurant, bar. Children's activity center. Fitness room, spa. Indoor pool, outdoor pool, whirlpool. Airport transportation available. Business center. **$$**

★★★HYATT REGENCY PIER SIXTY-SIX

2301 S.E. 17th St., Causeway, Fort Lauderdale, 954-525-6666, 800-233-1234;
www.pier66.hyatt.com

Situated on the Intracoastal Waterway, this hotel offers a 142-slip marina, spa, shops, aquatic club and onsite golf and tennis. Guests won't have to use their car when staying here—in addition to the many onsite activities, a water taxi is available to take guests to the beach, restaurants, and nightclubs. 384 rooms. High-speed Internet access. Five restaurants, four bars. Fitness room, spa. Three outdoor pools, children's pool, whirlpool. Golf, 18 holes. Tennis. Business center. **$$$**

★★★LAGO MAR RESORT AND CLUB

1700 S. Ocean Lane, Fort Lauderdale, 954-523-6511, 800-524-6627;
www.lagomar.com

Five-hundred feet of private beach await guests at this lively resort located between Lake Mayan and the ocean. The beach is dotted with hammocks, cabanas and umbrellas while the pool area, with two beachside pools and a poolside bar, is a tropical oasis. The lobby features a large-scale mosaic built into the floor, lovely architecture and antiques. Guest rooms are decorated in a cool mint, warm coral and pale yellow palette. There's plenty to do here: A putting green, shuffleboard, giant outdoor chess set and table tennis are among the onsite activities; kayak and hammock rentals are also available. 204 rooms. Wireless Internet access. Four restaurants, two bars. Children's activity center. Fitness room. Beach. Two outdoor pools. Tennis. Business center. Spa. **$$**

★★★MARRIOTT HARBOR BEACH RESORT AND SPA

3030 Holiday Drive, Fort Lauderdale, 954-525-4000, Reservations: 800-222-6543;
www.marriottharborbeach.com

This sprawling resort is located on the oceanfront, convenient to cruise ships, shopping and dining. The casual and elegant décor includes fabrics and colors evoking the water and the sun. A gurgling fountain is a fitting soundtrack to the picturesque ocean views. Guest rooms are sunny, and most have balconies. Activities include basketball, bike rentals, beach volleyball, Scuba and Snorkeling, beachside buddies for kids, golf, fishing, yachting and boating and water sports. 637 rooms. High-speed Internet access. Four restaurants, two bars. Children's activity center. Fitness room, fitness classes available, spa. Beach, cabanas. Outdoor pool, whirlpools. Tennis. Business center. Destination weddings, banquet menus. $$$

★★PELICAN GRAND BEACH RESORT

2000 N. Ocean Blvd., Fort Lauderdale, 954-568-9431, 800-525-6232;
www.pelicanbeach.com

159 rooms. Complimentary continental breakfast. Oceanfront dining, poolside cocktail lounge. High-speed Internet access. Restaurant, bar. Oceanfront fitness center. Beach. Outdoor pool. Business center. Concierge service. Underground valet parking. Guest laundry. $$

★★★RENAISSANCE FORT LAUDERDALE HOTEL

1617 S.E. 17th St., Fort Lauderdale, 954-626-1700, 800-627-7468;
www.renaissancehotels.com/fllbr

This Caribbean-inspired hotel has luxurious guest rooms outfitted with pillowtop beds, luxury bedding and down duvets. Decadent spa treatments, a sparkling pool and the eclectic Bin 595 restaurant are just a few of the indulgences the hotel offers. Shopping, beaches and the Florida Everglades are close by. 233 rooms. Wireless Internet access. Restaurant, two bars. Fitness room. Outdoor pool, whirlpool. Business center. $$

★★★★THE RITZ-CARLTON, FORT LAUDERDALE

1 N. Fort Lauderdale Beach Blvd., Fort Lauderdale, 954-465-2300; www.ritzcarlton.com

Elegant, contemporary and utterly luxurious, this oceanfront resort is a stylish escape in busy Fort Lauderdale. Rooms, decorated in neutral tones with mahogany furniture, feature flatscreen TVs with DVD players, beds wrapped in Pratesi linens and balconies with views of the ocean. An 8,500-square-foot spa offers a full menu of treatments, while the sprawling fitness center has spinning classes and a Pilates studio. Cero, the onsite restaurant, serves fresh seafood in a sophisticated setting overlooking the water, and the wine room is a chic place to sample one of the many varietals and chat with the sommelier. 187 rooms. Pool. Spa. Fitness center. Wireless Internet access. Restaurant, bar. $$$$

★★★RIVERSIDE HOTEL

620 E. Las Olas Blvd., Fort Lauderdale, 954-467-0671, 800-325-3280;
www.riversidehotel.com

Experience Old Florida as you walk through the pillared entryway and into the wicker-filled lobby of this Las Olas Boulevard landmark on the New River. Find southeast Asian cuisine at Indigo restaurant or revisit England's colonial period at the Grill Room on Las Olas. 217 rooms. High-speed Internet access. Two restaurants, bar. Outdoor pool. Business center (fax, copy, typing and A/V services available). A seven-story parking garage provides added convenience. Valet parking or self-parking is available. Service animals are accepted. **$$**

★★★SHERATON YANKEE CLIPPER HOTEL
1140 Seabreeze Blvd., Fort Lauderdale, 954-524-5551; www.sheraton.com
The guest rooms here feature dataports, cable television, hair dryers, irons and ironing boards. The hotel's new sports deck allows guests to unwind with a game of bocce ball, basketball, shuffleboard, ping-pong or hopscotch. 500 rooms, seven meeting spaces. Pets accepted, some restrictions; fee. Wireless Internet access. Restaurant, three bars. Fitness room. Beach. Outdoor pool. Business center. **$$**

★TROPIC SEAS RESORT
4616 El Mar Drive, Lauderdale-by-the Sea, 954-772-2555, 800 952-9581;
www.tropicseasresort.com
Pool. **$**

★★★THE WESTIN FORT LAUDERDALE
400 Corporate Drive, Fort Lauderdale, 954-772-1331, 800-937-8461; www.westin.com
This large hotel is located near the Palm Aire golf course and close to the beach. Because it caters to business travelers and conferences, rooms are loaded with technological amenities, from high-speed Internet access to ergonomic desk chairs. 293 rooms. Pets accepted, some restrictions; fee. Restaurant, bar. Children's activity center. Fitness room. Outdoor pool, whirlpool. Business center. **$$**

SPECIALTY LODGINGS

COURTYARD VILLA
4312 El Mar Drive, Lauderdale-by-the-Sea, 954-489-9870, 800-291-3560;
www.courtyardvilla.com
12 rooms. Pets accepted, some restrictions; fee. Complimentary continental breakfast. Wireless Internet access. Whirlpool. Airport transportation available. Business center, spa. **$$**

THE PILLARS AT NEW RIVER SOUND
111 N. Birch Road, Fort Lauderdale, 954-467-9639; www.pillarshotel.com
23 rooms. Outdoor pool. Spa, continental breakfast, business center, high-speed Internet access. **$$**

RESTAURANTS

★★15TH STREET FISHERIES
1900 S.E. 15th St., Fort Lauderdale, 954-763-2777; www.15streetfisheries.com
Seafood menu. Lunch, dinner. Bar. Children's menu. Casual attire. Reservations recommended. Outdoor seating. **$$**

★★ARUBA BEACH CAFÉ
1 E. Commercial Blvd., Lauderdale-by-the-Sea, 954-776-0001
American, seafood menu. Lunch, dinner, Sunday brunch. Three bars. Children's menu. Casual attire. Valet parking. Outdoor seating. **$$**

★★BANGKOK BISTRO

3341 N. Federal Highway, Fort Lauderdale, 954-630-0030
Thai/Sushi menu. Lunch, dinner. Casual attire. Reservations recommended. **$$**

★★BISTRO MEZZALUNA

741 S.E. 17th St., Fort Lauderdale, 954-522-9191; www.bistromezzaluna.com
American, Italian menu. Dinner. Bar. Casual attire. Valet parking. **$$$**

★★★BLUE MOON FISH CO.

4405 W. Tradewinds Ave., Lauderdale-by-the-Sea, 954-267-9888;
www.bluemoonfishco.com
This seafood lover's paradise is set right on the Intracoastal Waterway on the east side
of the bridge. The creative menu has Caribbean accents, and the Art Deco, under-
water-themed interior and waterside patio is usually packed with a seafood-loving
crowd. Seafood menu. Lunch, dinner, Sunday brunch at 11:30. Bar. Children's menu.
Casual attire. Valet parking. Outdoor seating. **$$$**

★★BY WORD OF MOUTH

3200 N.E. 12th Ave., Fort Lauderdale, 954-564-3663; www.bywordofmouthfoods.com
American menu. Lunch (Monday-Friday), dinner (Wednesday-Saturday). Closed Sun-
day. Casual attire. **$$$**

★★CAFE SEVILLE

2768 E. Oakland Park Blvd., Fort Lauderdale, 954-565-1148; www.cafeseville.com
Spanish menu. Lunch, dinner. Bar. Casual attire. Reservations recommended. Closed
Sunday. **$$**

★★★CASA D'ANGELO

1201 N. Federal Highway, Fort Lauderdale, 954-564-1234; www.casa-d-angelo.com
Casa D'Angelo is marked by Corinthian columns and creamy stucco walls. Entrées
include a delicious array of pastas and a selection of fish, chops and steaks. The
500-bottle Italian and Californian wine list includes many gems under $50, and from
late fall to mid-winter, special menus featuring truffles. Italian menu. Dinner. Busi-
ness casual attire. Reservations recommended. Outdoor seating. Closed holidays. **$$$**

★★★CHARLEY'S CRAB

3000 N.E. 32nd Ave., Fort Lauderdale, 954-561-4800, 800-589-6837; www.muer.com
This seafood chain, located on the Intracoastal Waterway, serves volumes of fresh fish
and shellfish. The 600-seat venue attracts a varied crowd of locals and tourists with its
lovely outdoor covered terrace. Seafood menu. Lunch, dinner. Bar. Children's menu.
Casual attire. Valet parking. Outdoor seating. **$$$**

★★★CERO

The Ritz-Carlton, Fort Lauderdale, 1 N. Fort Lauderdale Beach Blvd., Fort Lauderdale,
954-302-6460; www.cerorestaurant.com
Taking advantage of its location, Cero's menu is filled with South Florida-fresh sea-
food fixed with a contemporary French flair. A caviar menu and wine list add to the
decadent dining experience, and the daily breakfast menu features morning favorites
infused with the sunny flavors of the Sunshine State. With fish, steak and osetra and

sevruga at night, and organic eggs and tropical fruits in the morning, Cero has become a must for visitors and a local favorite. Located in The Ritz-Carlton, the dining room is open and features views of the ocean and outdoor seating on the patio. Contemporary French menu. Breakfast, lunch, dinner. **$$$$**

★★EDUARDO DE SAN ANGEL

2822 E. Commercial Blvd., Fort Lauderdale, 954-772-4731; www.eduardodesanangel.com
Mexican menu. Dinner. Bar. Business casual attire. Reservations recommended. Closed Sunday. **$$$**

★★FRENCH QUARTER

215 S.E. Eighth Ave., Fort Lauderdale, 954-463-8000
Cajun/Creole, French menu. Lunch, dinner, late-night. Bar. Casual attire. Reservations recommended. Valet parking. Outdoor seating. Closed Sunday. **$$$**

★★★GRILL ROOM ON LAS OLAS

620 E. Las Olas Blvd., Fort Lauderdale, 954-467-0671, 800-325-3280;
www.riversidehotel.com
Located in the Riverside Hotel, the Grill Room on Las Olas is a stately, elegant restaurant with all the old-world comforts of a classic grill room. The restaurant, a favorite among locals, offers grilled prime steaks, chops and fresh seafood, as well as an extensive 1,500-bottle wine list, a top-grade selection of cigars, a classic cocktail list and a deep, intoxicating selection of single malt scotches and cognacs. Private and alfresco dining are available. Steak menu. Dinner, late-night. Bar. Business casual attire. Reservations recommended. Valet parking. Outdoor seating. Closed Sunday only. **$$$**

★★INDIGO

620 E. Las Olas Blvd., Fort Lauderdale, 954-467-0045; www.riversidehotel.com
Seafood menu. Breakfast, lunch, dinner, late-night, brunch. Bar. Children's menu. Casual attire. Reservations recommended. Valet parking. Outdoor seating. **$$**

★KELLY'S LANDING

1305 S.E. 17th St., Fort Lauderdale, 954-760-7009
Seafood menu. Lunch, dinner. Bar. Children's menu. Casual attire. **$$**

★★LE CAFE DE PARIS

715 E. Las Olas Blvd., Fort Lauderdale, 954-467-2900
Located in the middle of Fort Lauderdale's prime shopping, entertainment and art district, this authentic French restaurant features French posters, antique stoves, tile work and a mural of a French street. Piano entertainment is provided Wednesday-Sunday. French menu. Lunch, dinner. Bar. Casual attire. Reservations recommended. Outdoor seating. **$$**

★★MAI-KAI

3599 N. Federal Highway, Fort Lauderdale, 954-563-3272, 800-262-4524;
www.maikai.com
American, Pacific Rim/Pan-Asian menu. Dinner. Bar. Children's menu. Casual attire. Reservations recommended. Valet parking. Outdoor seating. **$$$**

59

FLORIDA

★
★
★
★

★★★MARK'S LAS OLAS

1032 E. Las Olas Blvd., Fort Lauderdale, 954-463-1000; www.chefmark.com

Mark's Las Olas is a chic, airy restaurant that offers cool, creative seasonal American/Floridian fare and an impressive wine list. Expect plates filled with flashy "Floribbean" flair including seafood like conch, snapper and grouper with interesting accents like coconut, citrus, chiles and rum. International menu. Dinner. Bar. Children's menu. Casual attire. Reservations recommended. Valet parking. Outdoor seating. Fridays and Saturdays open until midnight. **$$$**

★OASIS CAFÉ

600 Seabreeze Blvd., Fort Lauderdale, 954-463-3130;
www.fortlauderdalebeachrestaurants.com

American menu. Lunch, dinner. Bar. Casual attire. Valet parking. Outdoor seating. **$$**

★★★RUTH'S CHRIS STEAK HOUSE

2525 N. Federal Highway, Fort Lauderdale, 954-565-2338; www.ruthschris.com

Founded by the late Ruth Fertel, this branch of the national chain serves melt-in-your-mouth steaks and chops on sizzling plates in a cigar-friendly, masculine atmosphere. Steak menu. Dinner. Bar. Children's menu. Casual attire. Reservations recommended. Valet parking. **$$$**

★★★SAGE FRENCH CAFÉ

2378 N. Federal Highway, Fort Lauderdale, 954-565-2299; www.sagecafe.net

Despite its humble location in a strip mall, this café offers country French cuisine that is worth a special trip. Chef Laurent Tasic's menu is elegantly prepared (and reasonably priced) with dishes like coq au vin, daube de boeuf and a variety of crepes. American, French menu. Lunch, dinner, Sunday brunch. Bar. Children's menu. Casual attire. Outdoor seating. **$$**

★★SEA WATCH

6002 N. Ocean Blvd., Fort Lauderdale, 954-781-2200; www.seawatchfl.com

Seafood menu. Lunch, dinner. Bar. Children's menu. Casual attire. Reservations recommended. Valet parking. Outdoor seating. **$$**

★★★SHULA'S ON THE BEACH

321 N. Fort Lauderdale Beach Blvd., Fort Lauderdale, 954-355-4000; www.donshula.com

Miami Dolphins coach-turned-restaurateur Don Shula and partner Don Gill deliver a high-quality steakhouse with matching service in a memorabilia-packed setting. It is housed in the Sheraton Yankee Trader Hotel and offers views of the ocean. Seafood menu. Breakfast, lunch, dinner. Bar. Children's menu. Business casual attire. Reservations recommended. Valet parking. Outdoor seating. **$$$**

SPA

★★★★THE RITZ-CARLTON SPA, FORT LAUDERDALE

The Ritz-Carlton, Fort Lauderdale, 1 N. Fort Lauderdale Beach Blvd., Fort Lauderdale,
954-465-2300; www.ritzcarlton.com/fortlauderdale

Guests at The Ritz-Carlton can get their bodies bikini-ready with a day at the hotel's spa and fitness center. First, stop in for a yoga class or a run on a treadmill that overlooks the ocean. Now that you've worked oh, so hard, it's time to relax those tired muscles with a De-Stress Muscle Release ($145-215) or a dip in the pool deck Jacuzzi. The 8,500-square-foot Spa at Ritz-Carlton features 11 treatment rooms, including a private couple's suite where you can get his (Balance Men's) and hers (Renew Rose Radiance) facials ($130).

FORT MYERS

Fifteen miles upstream from the Gulf of Mexico on the wide Caloosahatchee River, Fort Myers began as a federal post erected after an Indian raid. Later, settlers came to farm within its protective shadow. Tourism, vegetable and flower growing, and commercial and sport fishing are major activities of the area today.

Information: Lee County Visitor & Convention Bureau, 12800 University Drive,
Fort Myers, 239-338-3500, 800-237-6444; www.fortmyers-sanibel.com

WHAT TO SEE AND DO
CALUSA NATURE CENTER AND PLANETARIUM
3450 Ortiz Ave., Fort Myers, 239-275-3435; www.calusanature.com
More than 100 acres of pine flatwoods and bald cypress swamp. Audubon aviary. Planetarium with star shows and laser light and music shows; exhibits; natural history shop; nature trails (two miles); guided walks. Monday-Saturday 9 a.m.-5 p.m., Sunday 11 a.m-5 p.m.

EDISON WINTER HOUSE & BOTANICAL GARDENS
2350 McGregor Blvd., Fort Myers, 239-334-7419
In 1885 inventor Thomas Edison, ailing at the age of 38, built this 14-acre riverfront estate, where he wintered for the next half century. The house and guesthouse, designed by Edison, were brought by ship from Maine. The complex includes a museum with inventions, mementos and a chemical laboratory; the first modern swimming pool in the state and an extraordinary botanical garden with mature specimens from around the world.

HENRY FORD WINTER HOUSE
2350 McGregor Blvd., Fort Myers, 239-334-7419
"Mangoes," the winter residence of Henry Ford, one of the world's first billionaires, is next door to the house of Ford's good friend, Thomas Edison. The house reflects the home-grown Midwestern values of Ford and his wife, Clara, as well as the effect of extraordinary wealth on their lives.

SOUTH FLORIDA MUSEUM OF HISTORY
2300 Peck St., Fort Myers, 239 321-7430; www.swflmuseumofhistory.com
On display are items of local historical significance. Tuesday-Saturday 10 a.m.-5 p.m.

SPECIAL EVENTS
BOSTON RED SOX SPRING TRAINING
City of Palms Park, 2201 Edison Ave., Fort Myers, 877-733-7699;
www.boston.redsox.mlb.com
Boston Red Sox baseball spring training, exhibition games. Late February-March.

FLORIDA

★
★
★
★
☆

MINNESOTA TWINS SPRING TRAINING

Lee County Sports Complex, 14100 Six Mile Cypress Parkway, Fort Myers,
239-768-427; www.minnesota.twins.mlb.com

Minnesota Twins baseball spring training, exhibition games. Early March-early April.

HOTELS

★★CROWNE PLAZA

13051 Bell Tower Drive, Fort Myers, 239-482-2900, 800-4 96-7621;
www.ichotelsgroup.com

227 rooms. Wireless Internet access. Restaurant, bar. Fitness room. Outdoor pool.
Business center. **$**

★LA QUINTA INN

4850 S. Cleveland Ave., Fort Myers, 239-275-3300, 800-531-5900; www.lq.com

129 rooms. Pets accepted. Complimentary continental breakfast. Outdoor pool. **$**

★★★SANIBEL HARBOUR RESORT & SPA

17260 Harbour Point Drive, Fort Myers, 239-466-4000, 800-767-7777;
www.sanibel-resort.com

Dubbed a fishing paradise in the late 1800s, this 80-acre resort was rebuilt on the original site of the Tarpon House Inn. A Victorian-inspired getaway on the private Punta
Rassa peninsula, the resort offers an extensive spa and fitness center. 240 rooms.
Wireless Internet access, copying and faxing. Five restaurants, three bars. Children's
activity center. Fitness room, fitness classes available, spa. Beach. Indoor pool, three
outdoor pools, whirlpool. Tennis and golf. Business center. **$$$**

RESTAURANTS

★★★HAROLD'S ON BAY

2224 Bay St., Fort Myers, 239-226-1686; www.haroldsonbay.com

Chef and owner Harold Balink serves creative, American recipes in a contemporary din-
ing room in downtown Fort Meyers. Sample several of the small plates such as chilled
duck and arugula salad or truffle seared scallops. Then dig into a main course of grilled
big eye tuna with wasabi mash and stir fried edamame. International menu. Lunch, din-
ner. Bar. Business casual attire. Reservations recommended. Closed Sunday. **$$$**

★LIGHTHOUSE

14301 Port Comfort Road, Fort Myers, 239-489-0770

American menu. Lunch, dinner. Bar. Children's menu. Casual attire. Outdoor seating. **$$**

★★THE PRAWNBROKER

13451-16 McGregor Blvd., Fort Myers, 239-489-2226; www.prawnbroker.com

Seafood, steak menu. Dinner. Bar. Children's menu. Outdoor seating. **$$**

★★★VERANDA

2122 Second St., Fort Myers, 239-334-8634; www.verandarestaurant.com

Two turn-of-the-century homes combine to create a charming Victorian atmosphere
in historic downtown. Try the garden courtyard for a romantic seating option.
American menu. Lunch, dinner. Closed Sunday (except Easter and Mother's Day).

Bar. Business casual attire. Reservations recommended. Valet parking. Outdoor seating. **$$**

FORT MYERS BEACH

Located beside the seven-mile sliver of Estero Island, this town has the Gulf of Mexico on one side and Estero Bay, never more than three blocks away, on the other. The 18th-century pirates are gone, but tourists love to poke in the sand for treasures—most likely they will just find seashells, starfish and sea horses. The beach stretches the entire length of the island and is considered one of the safest in the state.

Information: Greater Fort Myers Beach Chamber of Commerce, 17200 San Carlos Blvd., Fort Myers Beach, 239-454-7500; www.fortmyersbeach.org

SPECIAL EVENT
AMERICAN CHAMPIONSHIP SANDSCULPTING FESTIVAL
Outrigger Beach Resort, 6200 Estero Blvd., Fort Myers Beach, 239-454-7500;
www.fortmyers-sanibel.com
Walk along the beach and check out all the amazing sand creations by sand-sculpting artists from around the world. Early November.

HOTELS
★BEST WESTERN BEACH RESORT
684 Estero Blvd., Fort Myers Beach, 239-463-6000, 800-336-4045;
www.bestwestern.com
75 rooms. Pets accepted, some restrictions; fee. Complimentary continental breakfast. Beach. Outdoor pool. Free parking, free wireless Internet access, free local calls. **$**

★★★PINK SHELL BEACH RESORT & SPA
275 Estero Blvd., Fort Myers Beach, 239-463-6181, 888-222-7465; www.pinkshell.com
With 1,500 feet of beach, this resort is located on 12 acres at the northern end of Estero Island. The whimsical pool, with infinity edges and sculptures of shells and sea horses, is popular with kids. 225 rooms, all suites. Wireless Internet access. Two restaurants. Two bars. Spa. Beach. Three outdoor pools. Tennis. **$$$**

★SANTA MARIA HARBOUR RESORT
7317 Estero Blvd., Fort Myers Beach, 239-765-6700, 888-627-1595;
www.santamariafl.com
50 rooms. Beach. Outdoor pool, whirlpool. **$$$**

RESTAURANTS
★CHARLEY'S BOAT HOUSE GRILL
6241 Estero Blvd., Fort Myers Beach, 239-765-4800; www.boathousegrill.net
American menu. Dinner. Bar. Children's menu. Casual attire. **$$**

★★SNUG HARBOR WATERFRONT
645 Old San Carlos Blvd., Fort Myers Beach, 239-463-8077;
www.snugharborrestaurant.com
American menu. Lunch, dinner, late-night. Bar. Children's menu. Casual attire. Reservations recommended. Outdoor seating. **$$$**

FLORIDA

★
★
★
★

FORT PIERCE

Located on Indian River Drive, the original Fort Pierce was a U.S. Army garrison established in 1837 during the Seminole War. The city formed around the site, with three communities merging into one in 1901. On the west side of the Indian River, the city is linked to the ocean and Hutchinson Island beaches by two bridges and is the marketplace for the cattle ranches, vegetable farms and citrus groves of St. Lucie County. Tourism and commercial fishing round out the economy.

Information: St. Lucie County Chamber of Commerce, 1850 S.W. Fountainview Blvd., 772-595-9999, 888-785-8243; www.stluciechamber.org

WHAT TO SEE AND DO

ST. LUCIE COUNTY HISTORICAL MUSEUM

414 Seaway Drive, Fort Pierce, 772-462-1795

Local and state historical exhibits include 1715 Spanish shipwreck artifacts, military material from Old Fort Pierce, Seminole encampment, items from early industries; restored 1907 house, 1919 American-LaFrance fire engine; changing exhibit gallery. Tuesday-Saturday 10 a.m.-4 p.m., Sunday from noon.

UNDERWATER DEMOLITION TEAM-SEAL MUSEUM.

3300 N. A1A, Fort Pierce, 772-595-5845; www.stlucieco.gov

Diving gear, weapons and apparatus of SEAL (Sea, Air and Land) commandos—successors to US Navy "frogmen" of World War II. Dioramas trace history of the teams; videos of training process. Tuesday-Saturday 10 a.m.-4 p.m.; Sunday noon-4 p.m.

SPECIAL EVENT

NEW YORK METS SPRING TRAINING

Thomas J. White Stadium, 525 N.W. Peacock Blvd., Port St. Lucie, 772-871-2100; www.mets.mlb.com

New York Mets baseball spring training, exhibition games. Mid-February-late March.

HOTEL

★HOLIDAY INN EXPRESS

7151 Okeechobee Road, Fort Pierce, 772-464-5000, 800-465-4329; www.hiturnpike.com

100 rooms. Pets accepted, some restrictions; fee. Complimentary continental breakfast. Outdoor pool, children's pool. Business center. **$**

RESTAURANTS

★★MANGROVE MATTIE'S

1640 Seaway Drive, Fort Pierce, 772-466-1044

American menu. Lunch, dinner. Bar. **$$**

★PEKING CHINESE RESTAURANT

1012 S. Highway 1, Fort Pierce, 772-464-5960

Chinese menu. Lunch, dinner. **$$**

★
★
★
★

FORT WALTON BEACH

A six-mile stretch of sand along Highway 98, Fort Walton Beach is next to the Santa Rosa Sound and the Gulf of Mexico in northwest Florida. Archaeological excavations (begun in 1960) have added historical significance to the city—Temple Mound has yielded artifacts from prehistoric times and between A.D. 1300 and 1700.

Information: Greater Fort Walton Beach Chamber of Commerce,
34 S.E. Miracle Strip Parkway, Fort Walton Beach, 850-244-8191;
www.destin-fwb.com

WHAT TO SEE AND DO

AIR FORCE ARMAMENT MUSEUM

100 Museum Drive, Eglin AFB, 850-651-1808;
www.destin-ation.com/airforcearmamentmuseum

Exhibits include historical aircraft and weapons. Theater. Aircraft from Korean War, Vietnam War and World War II. Daily.

INDIAN TEMPLE MOUND MUSEUM AND PARK

139 Miracle Strip Parkway, Fort Walton Beach, 850-833-9595

Covering an acre of land, this mound served as a major religious and civic center for Native Americans in the area. The ancient temple is re-created in a modern shelter on the original site, which now lies downtown. On the east flank of the mound, a museum houses dioramas and exhibits portraying the Native American settlement over a span of 12,000 years.

HOTELS

★★FOUR POINTS BY SHERATON

1325 Miracle Strip Parkway, Fort Walton Beach, 850-243-8116, 800-874-8104;
www.sheraton4pts.com

216 rooms. Complimentary full breakfast. High-speed Internet access. Two restaurants, two bars. Fitness room. Beach. Two outdoor pools, two whirlpools. $$

★★RAMADA PLAZA BEACH RESORT

1500 Miracle Strip Parkway S.E., Fort Walton Beach,
850-243-9161, 800-874-8962; www.ramadafwb.com

335 rooms. Pets accepted, some restrictions; fee. High-speed Internet access. Restaurant, three bars. Fitness room. Beach. Two outdoor pools, children's pool, whirlpool. Business center. Free parking, free Internet access. $$

GAINESVILLE

This city in the center of the state is home to the University of Florida, a campus of 40,000 students. College sports are the central focus, with football and basketball game-related activities during much of the year.

Information: Alachua County Visitors & Convention Bureau, 30 E. University,
Gainesville, 352-374-5231, 866-778-5002; www.visitgainesville.net

65

FLORIDA

★
★
★
★

WHAT TO SEE AND DO
DEVIL'S MILLHOPPER STATE GEOLOGICAL SITE
4732 Millhopper Road, Gainesville, 352-955-2008; www.floridastateparks.org
This giant sinkhole (500 feet wide, 120 feet deep) was formed when the roof of an underground limestone cavern collapsed. The cool environment allows growth of unique lush vegetation. Access to the bottom is by wooden walkway. Interpretive center; nature walks. Nearby is San Felasco Hammock State Preserve, with rare flora and fauna; nature trails. Wednesday-Sunday 9 a.m.-5 p.m. The park is closed Monday and Tuesday.

FLORIDA MUSEUM OF NATURAL HISTORY
Hull Road and S.W. 34th Street, Gainesville, 352-846-2000; www.flmnh.ufl.edu
The largest museum of natural history in the Southeastern United States, it features a full-scale North Florida Cave exhibit. Monday-Saturday 10 a.m.-5 p.m., Sunday from 1 p.m.

KANAPAHA BOTANICAL GARDENS
4700 S.W. 58th Drive, Gainesville, 352-372-4981; www.kanapaha.org
A 62-acre botanical garden featuring a butterfly garden, large bamboo garden, vinery, hummingbird garden, herb and palm gardens and more. Monday-Wednesday, Friday 9 a.m.-5 p.m., Saturday-Sunday 9 a.m.-dusk.

UNIVERSITY OF FLORIDA
University Avenue and 13th Street Gainesville, 352-392-3261; www.ufl.edu
The 2,000-acre campus has 16 colleges, four schools and 40,000 students. Campus tours available. Monday-Friday 10 a.m. and 2 p.m., Saturday 10 a.m.

UNIVERSITY OF FLORIDA GATORS
352-375-4683; www.gatorzone.com
The University of Florida proudly calls its teams the Gators. They consistently score well in the Southeastern Conference in baseball, football, basketball and golf. The football team won the national championship in 2006, while the basketball captured the national title in 2006 and 2007. They also have an impressive tennis team and are competitive in swimming and soccer. Check the school's Web site, www.ufl.edu, for official standings, team information and tickets.

SPECIAL EVENT
GATORNATIONALS
Gainesville Raceway, 11211 N. County Road, 225, Gainesville, 352-377-0046; www.gainesvilleraceway.com
NHRA drag racing at Gainesville Raceway. Mid-March.

HOTELS
★CABOT LODGE GAINESVILLE
3726 S.W. 40th Blvd., Gainesville, 352-375-2400, 800-843-8735; www.cabotlodge.com
208 rooms. Complimentary continental breakfast. Outdoor pool. Free local phone calls, high-speed Internet access. **$**

★FAIRFIELD INN

6901 N.W. Fourth Blvd., Gainesville, 352-332-8292, 800-228-2800; www.fairfieldinn.com
132 rooms. Complimentary continental breakfast. Outdoor pool. High-speed Internet access, pets not accepted. **$**

★★HOLIDAY INN

1250 W. University Ave., Gainesville, 352-376-1661, 800-465-4329;
www.theuniversityhotel.com
167 rooms. High-speed Internet access. Restaurant, bar. Outdoor pool. Airport transportation available. **$**

SPECIALTY LODGINGS

HERLONG MANSION B&B

402 N.E. Cholokka Blvd., Micanopy, 352-466-3322, 800-437-5664; www.herlong.com
Restored vintage mansion. Veranda. Six rooms. Complimentary continental breakfast. **$$**

MAGNOLIA PLANTATION BED & BREAKFAST INN

309 S.E. Seventh St., Gainesville, 352-375-6653, 800-201-2379; www.magnoliabnb.com
Restored Second Empire house. Five rooms. Pets accepted, some restrictions. Complimentary full breakfast. **$**

RESTAURANT

★★MR. HAN

6944 N.W. 10th Place, Gainesville, 352-331-6400; www.mrhanrestaurant.com
Chinese menu. Lunch, dinner. Bar. **$**

HAINES CITY

Located in the heart of Florida's citrus country, Haines City lies at the foot of a range of rolling hills known as "The Ridge." Originally called Clay Cut, the town eventually took the name of a South Florida Railroad vice president and was subsequently made a regular stop on the line. Nearby sand pits, electronics, the hydraulics industry and tourism help diversify the economy.
Information: Chamber of Commerce, 35610 Highway 27 N., Haines City,
863-422-3751; www.hainescity.com

SPECIAL EVENT

HERITAGE DAYS

Fifth Street and Ledwith Avenue, Haines City, 863-421-3700
Arts and crafts, entertainment. Mid-March.

HOTEL

★QUALITY INN

43824 Highway 27, Davenport, 863-424-2120, 800-424-6423; www.choicehotels.com
104 rooms. Complimentary continental breakfast. Outdoor pool. Business center. Fitness center. Pets not accepted. Wireless Internet access. **$**

FLORIDA

★
★★
★★
★

HALLANDALE BEACH

This oceanfront town is located halfway between Miami and Fort Lauderdale and is part of the sprawl of the Miami Metro area.

Information: www.hallandalebeachfl.gov

WHAT TO SEE AND DO

GULFSTREAM PARK

901 S. Federal Highway, Hallandale Beach, 954-457-6233

Home of the Florida Derby, this famous racetrack has a walking ring decorated with leading stable colors. Bronze plaques in the Garden of Champions honor great Thoroughbreds. January-March, Tuesday-Sunday.

HOTELS

★★★THE DIPLOMAT COUNTRY CLUB AND SPA

501 Diplomat Parkway, Hallandale, 954-883-4000, 888-627-9057;
www.diplomatcountryclub.com

Looking for the ultimate country club–style resort? This sophisticated hotel, situated midway between Fort Lauderdale and Miami, has an 18-hole course that's both challenging and enjoyable. For those in need of a little extra help, the Manny Zerman Golf School provides excellent instruction. Players can even order refreshments to be delivered straight to their location, thanks to the innovative Parview GPS system on each cart. Tennis players will love the well-equipped center and professional staff here, and the garden courtyard spa is a perfect way to end a day on the course or courts. 60 rooms. Restaurant. Spa. Outdoor pool, whirlpool. Golf, 18 holes. Tennis. Fitness center. Business center. Internet access available. $$$

★HAMPTON INN

1000 S. Federal Highway, Hallandale Beach, 954-874-1111, 800-426-7866;
www.hamptoninnhallandale.com

151 rooms. Complimentary continental breakfast. Fitness center. Outdoor pool. Pets not accepted. $

RESTAURANT

★★LYCHEE GARDEN

680 E. Hallandale Beach Blvd., Hallandale, 954-457-5900;
www.lycheegarden.com

Chinese, Japanese menu. Lunch, dinner. Bar. Casual attire. $$

HOLLYWOOD

Born in the real estate boom of the 1920s, Hollywood still rides the crest of tourism. Joseph W. Young, fresh from adventures in California, developed the city and populated it by keeping a fleet of 21 buses on the road to bring in prospective buyers. In addition to the lures of the beach and the busy boulevard, there are several public golf courses in the area.

Information: Greater Hollywood Chamber of Commerce, 330 N. Federal Highway,
954-923-4000, 800-231-5562; www.hollywoodfl.org

WHAT TO SEE AND DO

ANNE KOLB NATURE CENTER AND RECREATION AREA

751 Sheridan St., Hollywood, 954-926-2480

Environmental exhibits and park with nature tours, fishing, canoeing. Early April-late October, daily 8 a.m.-7:30 p.m.; rest of year, to 6 p.m.

HOTELS

★DAYS INN

2601 N. 29th Ave., Hollywood, 954-923-7300, 800-544-8313; www.daysinn.com

114 rooms. Pets accepted; fee. Complimentary continental breakfast. Bar. Fitness room. Outdoor pool, whirlpool. Airport transportation available. $

★★GRAND PALMS HOTEL SPA & GOLF RESORT

110 Grand Palm Drive, Pembroke Pines, 954-431-8800, 800-327-9246;
www.grandpalmsresort.com

137 rooms. Complimentary continental breakfast. Restaurant, bar. Fitness room (fee), fitness classes available, spa. Outdoor pool. Golf, 27 holes. Tennis. $

★★HOLIDAY INN AIRPORT

2905 Sheridan St., Hollywood, 954-925-9100, 800-465-4329; www.ichhotelsgroup.com

150 rooms. Restaurant, bar. Fitness room. Outdoor pool, whirlpool. Spa. Airport transportation available. Business center. Pets not accepted. $$

★★★VILLA SINCLAIR BEACH SUITES & SPA

317 Polk St., Hollywood, 954-450-0000; www.villa-sinclair.com

This beachfront property has individually decorated rooms with flatscreen TVs, DVD players and fully stocked kitchens. Massages are delivered either in-room or alfresco in the massage gazebo. There's also an outdoor hot tub, sauna, bar and barbecue grill for guest use. Six rooms. $$

★★★WESTIN DIPLOMAT RESORT AND SPA

3555 S. Ocean Drive, Hollywood, 954-602-6000, 888-627-9057; www.diplomatresort.com

This elegant yet casual resort offers views of Florida's Gold Coast. Outdoor activities include golf, tennis, boating trips and swimming in the 240-foot lagoon-style pool. 998 rooms. Wireless Internet access. Five restaurants, four bars. Children's activity center. Fitness room, fitness classes available. Beach. Outdoor pool, children's pool, whirlpool. Tennis. Airport transportation available. Business center. $$$

RESTAURANTS

★★BAVARIAN VILLAGE

1401 N. Federal Highway, Hollywood, 954-922-7321;
www.bavarianvillagerestaurant.com

American, German menu. Dinner. Bar. Children's menu. Closed Monday. $$

★★GIORGIO'S GRILL

606 N. Ocean Drive, Hollywood, 954-929-7030; www.giorgiosgrill.com

Mediterranean menu. Dinner, late-night, Sunday brunch. Bars. Casual attire. Reservations recommended. Valet parking. Outdoor seating. $$$

69

FLORIDA

★
★
★
★
★

★★LE PETITE CAFÉ
3308 Griffin Road, Dania, 954-967-9912; www.lepetitcafededania.com
French menu. Lunch, dinner. Bar. Casual attire. Outdoor seating. Closed Monday. **$$**

ISLAMORADA

Islamorada is made up of 18 miles of coral, limestone and sand on four different islands of the Florida Keys. Sport fishing, diving and snorkeling amid coral reefs and shipwrecks are the main tourist attractions. It is the local custom to welcome the spring blossoms of the guaiacum tree, which produces a wood known as lignum vitae that is so dense that it was once used for pulleys and bowling pins. The area got its name, Spanish for "purple isles," when early explorers first saw the island as a distant splash of color, which was, perhaps, the purple bloom of the guaiacum tree.

Information: Chamber of Commerce, 83224 Overseas Highway, Islamorada,
305-664-4503, 800-322-5397; www.islamoradachamber.com

WHAT TO SEE AND DO
HURRICANE MONUMENT
Mile Marker 8, Overseas Highway, Islamorada, 305-664-3661
Memorial to 400 veterans of World War I and others killed in the 1935 hurricane while working on the Overseas Highway. A few veterans are buried in a crypt in the center of the monument.

HOTELS

★★★CHEECA LODGE & SPA
81801 Overseas Highway, Islamorada, 305-664-4651, 866-591-7625;
www.cheeca.com
This property's tropical grounds will remind you of a Caribbean plantation. The resort's guest rooms are decorated with rich, dark woods, plush pillow-top beds, granite vanities and luxurious linens. Recreational options are numerous: snorkeling, scuba diving, parasailing, windsurfing, sailing, fishing (a saltwater lagoon is stocked with a variety of fish) and more. The resort also offers a wonderful children's program and a full-service spa. Nearby attractions include deep-water marinas and dolphin-inhabited lagoons. 199 rooms. Restaurant, bar. Children's activity center. Beach. Two outdoor pools, children's pool. Spa. Fitness center. Golf. Tennis. Airport transportation available. Wireless Internet access. **$$**

★CHESAPEAKE RESORT
83409 Overseas Highway, Islamorada, 305-664-4662, 800-338-3395;
www.chesapeake-resort.com
52 rooms. Fitness room. Outdoor pool, whirlpool. Tennis. Free local calls. **$$$**

★CORAL BAY RESORT
75690 Overseas Highway 1, Islamorada, 305-664-5568; www.thecoralbayresort.com
17 rooms. Beach. Outdoor pool. Airport transportation available. **$$**

★KON TIKI RESORT
81200 Overseas Highway, Islamorada, 305-664-4702; www.kontiki-resort.com
23 rooms. Beach. Outdoor pool. **$$**

★★LIME TREE BAY RESORT

68500 Overseas Highway, Long Key, 305-664-4740, 800-723-4519;
www.limetreebayresort.com

29 rooms. Restaurant, bar. Outdoor pool, whirlpool. **$**

★★PELICAN COVE RESORT AND MARINA

84457 Old Overseas Highway, Islamorada, 305-664-4435, 800-445-4690;
www.pcove.com

63 rooms. Complimentary continental breakfast. Restaurant, bar. Outdoor pool, whirlpool. Tennis. **$**

RESTAURANTS

★★★ATLANTIC'S EDGE

81801 Overseas Highway, Islamorada, 305-664-4651, 866-591-7625;
www.cheeca.com

Located midway between Miami and Key West, Atlantic's Edge at the Cheeca Lodge Resort is a sophisticated spot with waterfront views. Fresh local seafood is the specialty, including Florida lobster and stone crab. American, Caribbean menu. Dinner, Sunday brunch (winter). Children's menu. Casual attire. Valet parking. **$$$**

★★MARKER 88

88000 Overseas Highway, Islamorada, 305-852-9315; www.marker88.info

Continental menu. Lunch, dinner. Bar. Children's menu. **$$$**

★★★PIERRE'S

81600 Overseas Highway, Islamorada, 305-664-3225; www.pierres-restaurant.com

This upper-crust Key West enclave serves a balanced selection of New American dishes. Continental menu. Dinner. Closed Monday June-October. **$$$**

★WHALE HARBOR MARINA

83000 U.S. Highway 1, Islamorada, 305-664-9888; www.whaleharborinn.com

Seafood menu. Lunch, dinner. Bar. Children's menu. **$$**

JACKSONVILLE

Jacksonville, once primarily an industrial and maritime Southern city, now has a new landscape filled with skyscrapers. The Riverwalk near the St. Johns River, Jacksonville's financial focal point, and the Jacksonville Landing, a festive marketplace with events and entertainment, are examples of the city's new modern, prosperous image. Draped around an S curve of the broad St. Johns River, Jacksonville is a major tourist and business center in Florida.

Under the British flag, Jacksonville was known as Cowford, a name that persisted until the purchase of Florida by the United States, when the town was renamed for Andrew Jackson. In the peace following the Seminole War, the city emerged as a prosperous and boisterous harbor town. Jacksonville was occupied by Union troops four times during the Civil War, but emerged during the Reconstruction period as a popular winter resort.

Information: Jacksonville and the Beaches Convention & Visitors Bureau,
550 Water St., 904-798-9111, 800-733-2668; www.jaxcvb.com

WHAT TO SEE AND DO
CUMMER MUSEUM OF ART & GARDENS
829 Riverside Ave., Jacksonville, 904-356-6857; www.cummer.org
Contains 14 galleries and the Tudor Room from the original Cummer Mansion. The mansion's formal gardens were retained as the setting for the gallery. Collection ranges from ancient Egypt to the 20th century and features 700 pieces of early Meissen porcelain and important American paintings. Interactive exhibits. Tuesday, Thursday 10 a.m.-9 p.m., Wednesday, Friday-Saturday to 5 p.m., Sunday noon-5 p.m.

JACKSONVILLE JAGUARS (NFL)
Alltel Stadium, 1 Alltel Stadium Place, Jacksonville, 904-633-6000; www.jaguars.com
Professional football team.

JACKSONVILLE ZOOLOGICAL GARDENS
8605 Zoo Parkway, Jacksonville, 904-757-4462; www.jaxzoo.org
More than 700 mammals, birds and reptiles in natural environments along the Trout River. Train ride; animal shows; restaurant. Daily 9 a.m.-5 p.m.

KINGSLEY PLANTATION
11676 Palmetto Ave., Jacksonville, 904-251-3537;
www.nps.gov/history/NR/travel/geo-flor/21.htm
Plantation house, kitchen house, barn and tabby slave houses reflect 19th-century life on a Sea Island cotton plantation. Ranger programs (seasonal). A National Park Service area. Daily 9 a.m.-5 p.m.

LITTLE TALBOT ISLAND STATE PARK
12157 Heckscher Drive, Jacksonville, 904-251-2320; www.floridastateparks.org
More than 2,500 acres of wide Atlantic beaches and extensive salt marshes teem with life, including migrating birds and sea turtles. Sand dunes, forests. Swimming, surfing, fishing, picnicking, playground, camping. Daily 8 a.m.-sundown

MUSEUM OF SCIENCE AND HISTORY
1025 Museum Circle, Jacksonville, 904-396-6674; www.themosh.org
Interactive exhibits on science, marine mammals and north Florida history, including the natural and physical sciences, wildlife, Native Americans and Civil War artifacts from battleship *Maple Leaf*. Free planetarium, science and reptile shows. Monday-Friday 10 a.m.-5 p.m., Saturday to 6 p.m., Sunday 1-6 p.m.

SPECIAL EVENTS
GATOR BOWL
Alltel Stadium, 1 Alltel Stadium Place, Jacksonville, 904-798-1700; www.gatorbowl.com
One of the major college football bowl games. January 2.

HISTORIC HOME TOUR
2623 Herschel St., Jacksonville, 904-389-2449
Tour representing work of locally prominent architects and builders between 1870 and 1930. Mid-May.

HOTELS

★★COURTYARD BY MARRIOTT

4600 San Pablo Road, Jacksonville, 904-223-1700, 800-321-2211; www.courtyard.com
146 rooms. Restaurant, bar. Fitness room. Outdoor pool, whirlpool. $

★★★CROWNE PLAZA

1201 Riverplace Blvd., Jacksonville, 904-398-8800; www.cpjacksonville.com
Located on the south bank of the St. Johns River on Riverplace Boulevard, this downtown hotel is convenient to the Riverwalk, Prime Osborn Convention Center, Jacksonville International Airport, Alltel Stadium, Jacksonville Landing and historic San Marco. The elegantly furnished rooms feature walk-out balconies. 292 rooms. Wireless Internet access. Two restaurants, two bars. Fitness room. Outdoor pool. Business center. $$

★★EMBASSY SUITES JACKSONVILLE BAYMEADOWS

9300 Baymeadows Road, Jacksonville, 904-731-3555, 800-362-2779;
www.embassysuites.com
277 rooms, all suites. Complimentary full breakfast. Wireless Internet access. Restaurant (children's menu), bar. Fitness room. Indoor pool, whirlpool. Business center. Pets accepted. $$

★HAMPTON INN

1331 Prudential Drive, Jacksonville, 904-396-7770, 800-426-7866; www.hampton-inn.com
118 rooms. Complimentary continental breakfast. Outdoor pool. Pets not accepted. Business center. $

★★HOLIDAY INN

14670 Duval Road, Jacksonville, 904-741-4404, 800-465-4329; www.holiday-inn.com
489 rooms. Pets accepted. Restaurant, bar. Fitness room. Indoor pool, outdoor pool. Tennis. Business center. Wireless Internet access. Valet Parking. Complimentary airport shuttle. $

★★HOLIDAY INN

9150 Baymeadows Road, Jacksonville, 904-737-1700, 800-465-4329;
www.holiday-inn.com
146 rooms. Pets accepted. Restaurant, bar. Fitness room. Outdoor pool. Wireless Internet access. $

★HOMEWOOD SUITES JACKSONVILLE-BAYMEADOWS

8737 Baymeadows Road, Jacksonville, 904-733-9299; www.homewoodsuites.com
116 rooms, all suites. Complimentary continental breakfast. High-speed Internet access. Fitness room. Outdoor pool. Business center. Tennis. Pets not accepted. $

★★★OMNI JACKSONVILLE HOTEL

245 Water St., Jacksonville, 904-355-6664, 800-843-6664; www.omnijacksonville.com
The heated rooftop pool and sundeck overlooking the St. Johns River are not to be missed during a stay at this high-rise hotel in downtown Jacksonville. Luxuriously decorated rooms have pillow-top mattresses, duvets, velvet pillows and plush chairs.

73

FLORIDA

★
★
★
★

354 rooms. Pets accepted, some restrictions; fee. Wireless Internet access. Restaurant, bar. Fitness room. Indoor pool, outdoor pool. Business center. **$$**

★★RADISSON HOTEL

4700 Salisbury Road, Jacksonville, 904-281-9700, 888-201-1788; www.radisson.com
164 rooms. Wireless Internet access. Restaurant, bar. Fitness room. Outdoor pool, whirlpool. Spa. Business center. **$**

★★RADISSON RIVERWALK HOTEL

1515 Prudential Drive, Jacksonville, 904-396-5100; 800-333-3333; www.radisson.com
322 rooms. Wireless Internet access. Restaurant, bar. Fitness room. Outdoor pool. Spa. Tennis. Business center. **$**

★★RAMADA INN MANDARIN

3130 Hartley Road, Jacksonville, 904-268-8080, 800-393-1117; www.ramada.com
152 rooms. Pets accepted; fee. Complimentary full breakfast. Restaurant, bar. Outdoor pool, children's pool. Fitness center. Wireless Internet access. **$**

SPECIALTY LODGING

RIVER SUITES AT CLUB CONTINENTAL

2143 Astor St., Orange Park, 904-264-6070, 800-877-6070; www.clubcontinental.com
Mediterranean-style villa from the 1920s on 30 acres overlooking the St. Johns River. 22 rooms. Pets accepted, some restrictions; fee. Complimentary continental breakfast. Restaurant. Outdoor pool, children's pool. Spa. Tennis. Wireless Internet access. **$**

RESTAURANTS

★AL'S PIZZA

1620 Margaret St., Jacksonville, 904-388-8384; www.alspizza.com
Pizza, Italian menu. Lunch, dinner, late-night. Bar. Children's menu. Casual attire. Outdoor seating. Daily. **$$**

★★★BISTRO AIX

1440 San Marco Blvd., Jacksonville, 904-398-1949; www.bistrox.com
Watch chefs at work in the exhibition kitchen at this restaurant where the menu changes seasonally. Located in the historic downtown district of Jacksonville, it features a brick interior, booths with window views and tables with carved chairs, creating a French bistro-style atmosphere. Continental, French menu. Lunch, dinner. Bar. Casual attire. Outdoor seating. Daily. Credit cards accepted. **$$$**

★★LEMONGRASS

9846 Old Baymeadows Road, Jacksonville, 904-645-9911; www.lemongrassjax.com
Thai menu. Lunch, dinner. Closed Sunday. Bar. Business casual attire. Reservations recommended. Outdoor seating. **$$**

★★★MATTHEW'S

2107 Hendricks Ave., Jacksonville, 904-396-9922; www.matthewsrestaurant.com
Treat yourself to a meal at chef/owner Matthew Medure's namesake restaurant and experience the palate-pleasing European-influenced food that has won this boîte

awards for the past 10 years. The sleek dining room, decorated in soft moss tones with terrazzo floors inlaid with bronze, was originally built as a bank in the 1920s. The chef selects organically grown vegetables and attempts to source most produce and meat from local boutique farms. The food is thoughtful, complex and brilliant. The wine list offers more than 420 selections, and the staff is gifted at helping with pairings. The service is the perfect balance of knowledge, efficiency and charm. Mediterranean menu. Dinner. Closed Sunday. Bar. Business casual attire. Reservations recommended. $$$

★★★MORTON'S, THE STEAKHOUSE

1510 Riverplace Blvd., Jacksonville, 904-399-3933; www.mortons.com

This reputable steakhouse offers dark wood paneling, gold fabric-designed booths and glass signature windows that separate the dining area from the bar. Wine displays and the golf art on the walls add to the steakhouse décor. Steak, Seafood, American menu. Dinner. Bar. Credit cards accepted. Daily. Valet parking. $$$

★★★STERLINGS OF AVONDALE

3551 St. Johns Ave., Jacksonville, 904-387-0700; www.sterlingsofavondale.com

This candlelit dining room has a long-standing reputation for fine dining in the Avondale shopping district. Try the fresh seafood catch of the day, available prepared six different ways from simply grilled to horseradish-crusted with saffron olive oil. American menu. Lunch, dinner, Sunday brunch. Bar. Outdoor seating. $$$

JACKSONVILLE BEACH

Located 15 miles east of Jacksonville, this town has a dual personality; it is a suburban home for many of Jacksonville's commuters, as well as an ocean resort for visitors. With its neighbors—Atlantic Beach, Mayport, Neptune Beach and Ponte Vedra Beach—Jacksonville Beach provides a continuous front of sand and amusement areas. Fishing tournaments, beach events and a variety of other festivities are held year-round.

Information: Jacksonville and the Beaches Convention & Visitors Bureau,
550 Water St., Jacksonville, 904-798-9111, 800-733-2668; www.jaxcvb.com

WHAT TO SEE AND DO

PABLO HISTORICAL PARK

380 Pablo Ave., Jacksonville Beach, 904-241-5657;
www.beachesareahistoricalsociety.com/contact.html

Park includes an original house built for a section foreman of the Florida East Coast Railroad, restored with furnishings from the turn of the century, and the old Mayport Depot, with historic railroad exhibits and memorabilia. Adjacent is a steam locomotive. Monday-Saturday.

HOTELS

★★★THE LODGE AT PONTE VEDRA BEACH

607 Ponte Vedra Blvd., Ponte Vedra Beach, 904-273-9500, 800-243-4304;
www.pvresorts.com

Capitalizing on the historic charm of Ponte Vedra, the Lodge & Club at Ponte Vedra Beach is designed to resemble a European seaside resort. This sister property to the Inn has a Mediterranean flair—all of the rooms and suites overlook the ocean and feature patios or balconies. A sophisticated selection of restaurants and bars awaits diners at the Lodge. 66 rooms. Restaurant, bar. Children's activity center. Fitness room. Three outdoor pools, whirlpool. Golf. Tennis. Spa. Business center. $

★★★PONTE VEDRA INN & CLUB

200 Ponte Vedra Blvd., Ponte Vedra Beach, 904-285-1111, 800-234-7842;
www.pvresorts.com

Open since 1928, this inn, part of the 300-acre Ponte Vedra Resort (which also includes the Lodge), is a traditionalist's haven. The guest rooms and suites are a tribute to classic Floridian décor, with pastel tones, light woods and floral fabrics. The resort offers tennis, golf, horseback riding, water sports, cycling, fishing and sailing. Spend the day sunning by one of the four oceanfront pools or indulging in a treatment at the spa. From nibbles and cocktails to gourmet meals, multiple restaurants cater to many moods. 250 rooms. Restaurant, bar. Children's activity center. Fitness room, spa. Four outdoor pools, children's pool, whirlpool. Golf, 36 holes. Tennis. Airport transportation available. Business center. High-speed Internet access. $$

★★★SAWGRASS MARRIOTT RESORT & BEACH/CLUB

1000 PGA Tour Blvd., Ponte Vedra Beach, 904-285-7777, 800-457-4653;
www.sawgrassmarriott.com

A getaway for the entire family, this resort offers 99 holes of golf and is the official course of the Players Championship. The location is convenient to historic St. Augustine and Jacksonville. 485 rooms. Pets accepted, some restrictions; fee. Restaurant, bar. Children's activity center. Fitness room. Outdoor pool, children's pool, whirlpool. Golf, 99 holes. Spa. Tennis. Business center. $

RESTAURANT

★AQUA GRILL

950 Sawgrass Villa Drive, Ponte Vedra Beach, 904-285-3017; www.aquagrill.net
Seafood menu. Lunch, dinner. Bar. $$

SPA

★★★THE SPA AT PONTE VEDRA INN & CLUB

200 Ponte Vedra Blvd., Ponte Vedra Beach, 904-273-7700; www.pvresorts.com
When your golf or tennis game has worn you down, the Spa at Ponte Vedra is a perfect place to unwind. This spa is a celebration of the classics. An extensive spa menu has 100 different options, from massages and body therapies to facials and salon services. Treat tired muscles to a Swedish, aromatherapy, maternity or reflexology massage. Manicures and pedicures incorporate pressure-point therapy, exfoliating sea salts or paraffin dips.

JENSEN BEACH

Named for Danish sailor John L. Jensen, Jensen Beach celebrates the man who first settled the area that was once a major center of pineapple cultivation. Today, the economy is based on tourism.

Information: Chamber of Commerce, 1900 Ricou Terrace, Jensen Beach,
772-334-3444; www.jensenbeachchamber.biz

SPECIAL EVENT

TURTLE WATCH

2900 N.E. Indian River Drive, Jensen Beach, 772-334-3444

Endangered sea turtles, weighing 200-500 pounds, crawl far up onto the beaches of Hutchinson Island to lay their eggs. Supervised by the Hobe Sound Nature Center. Reservations required. May-early August.

HOTEL

★★COURTYARD BY MARRIOTT

10978 S. Ocean Drive, Jensen Beach, 772-229-1000, 800-321-2211;
www.courtyardhutchinsonisland.com

110 rooms. Restaurant, bar. Fitness room. Beach. Pets not accepted. High-speed Internet access. Outdoor pool. $

RESTAURANTS

★★★11 MAPLE STREET

3224 N.E. Maple St., Jensen Beach, 772-334-7714; www.11maplestreet.net

Housed in an old Florida cottage, this restaurant serves fresh seafood and organic vegetables prepared with contemporary recipes, such as miso-glazed bluefin tuna with sushi rice, bok choy, mushrooms and wasabi. The wine list has more than 200 bottles from around the world. American menu. Dinner. Closed Monday-Tuesday. Outdoor seating. $$

★CONCHY JOE'S SEAFOOD

3945 N.E. Indian River Drive, Jensen Beach, 772-334-1130; www.conchyjoes.com

Riverfront dining. Seafood, steak menu. Lunch, dinner. Bar. Entertainment music. Children's menu. $$

JUPITER

During a storm in 1696, Quaker Jonathan Dickinson and his party were swept ashore near the present-day site of Jupiter. Captured by Native Americans but set free, the survivors marched 225 miles to St. Augustine. Dickinson's tale of his adventures, *God's Protecting Providence*, was widely read in both Europe and America. Jupiter is on the Intracoastal Waterway at the mouth of the scenic Loxahatchee River. A nearly eight-mile stretch of the river, from Riverbend Park in Palm Beach County to the southern boundary of Jonathan Dickinson State Park, forms a component of both the Florida and the National Wild and Scenic Rivers systems.

Information: Jupiter-Tequesta-Juno Beach Chamber of Commerce,
800 N. U.S. Highway 1, 561-746-7111, 800-616-7402; www.jupiterfl.org

WHAT TO SEE AND DO

FLORIDA HISTORY CENTER & MUSEUM

Burt Reynolds Park, 805 N. U.S. Highway 1, Jupiter, 561-747-6639

Exhibits on South Florida culture, Seminole Indians, shipwrecks, railroads; authentic Seminole chickee. Tuesday-Sunday.

JONATHAN DICKINSON STATE PARK

16450 S.E. Federal Highway, Hobe Sound, 772-546-2771; www.floridastateparks.org

Close to where Jonathan Dickinson was first shipwrecked, this park offers more than 10,000 acres between Hobe Sound and the Loxahatchee River and includes the

85-foot-high Hobe Mountain with a 25-foot observation tower, pine flatlands and tropical riverfront. Fishing, boating (ramps), canoeing (rentals); nature trails, bicycling, picnicking (shelters), playground, concession, camping (dump station), cottages. Boat trip (two hours). Guided tours at Trapper Nelson Interpretive Site on river, accessible only by boat. Daily.

JUPITER INLET LIGHTHOUSE AND MUSEUM

500 Captain Armour's Way, Jupiter, 561-747-8380; www.lrhs.org

This redbrick landmark built in 1860 is one of the oldest lighthouses on the Atlantic coast. Houses local historical artifacts and memorabilia. Tours Tuesday-Sunday.

SPECIAL EVENT

BASEBALL SPRING TRAINING

Roger Dean Stadium, 4751 Main St., Jupiter, 561-775-1818

Florida Marlins and St. Louis Cardinals spring baseball training, exhibition games. March-early April.

HOTELS

★BEST WESTERN INTRACOASTAL INN

810 S. Highway 1, Jupiter, 561-575-2936, 800-937-8376; www.bestwestern.com

53 rooms. Complimentary continental breakfast. Outdoor pool. Spa, pets not accepted. High-speed Internet access. **$**

★HOLIDAY INN EXPRESS

13950 Highway 1, Juno Beach, 561-622-4366, 800-272-6380; www.hiejuno.com

108 rooms. Complimentary continental breakfast. Outdoor pool. Golf, tennis. Fitness room. **$**

★★★JUPITER BEACH RESORT & SPA

5 N. A1A, Jupiter, 561-746-2511, 800-228-8810; www.jupiterbeachresort.com

Jupiter has a smaller, more natural appeal than its Palm Beach neighbor, and this casual Caribbean-style resort fits in perfectly. Relax at the private beach or dine and be seen at Sinclair's Ocean Grill. 177 rooms. Two restaurants, two bars. Fitness room. Beach. Outdoor pool. Tennis. Spa. Business center. High-speed Internet access. **$$$**

★JUPITER WATERFRONT INN

18903 S.E. Federal Highway 1, Jupiter, 561-747-9085, 888-747-9085; www.jupiterwaterfrontinn.com

38 rooms. Complimentary continental breakfast. Outdoor pool, Wireless Internet access. whirlpool. **$**

KEY BISCAYNE

This island located just off the downtown Miami coastline is intimate, secluded and tropical. Though damaged by Hurricane Andrew in 1992, the island and its hotels, resorts and condominiums were quickly rebuilt and it is now a top spot for Miamians who want a quick city escape.

Information: Key Biscayne Chamber of Commerce, 88 W. McIntyre St., 305-361-5207, 305-539-3000; www.keybiscaynechamber.org

WHAT TO SEE AND DO

BILL BAGGS CAPE FLORIDA STATE PARK

1200 S. Crandon Blvd., Key Biscayne, 305-361-5811; www.floridastateparks.org

Located at the tip of Key Biscayne, Bill Baggs Cape Florida State Park features the Cape Florida Lighthouse. Built in 1825, the lighthouse is the oldest building in South Florida and has survived numerous battles and hurricanes. The park is a great place for swimming, picnicking, camping and fishing; bicycles, hydrobikes, in-line skates and ocean kayaks are all available to rent. Opened from 8 a.m.-sundown, year-round.

CRANDON PARK

4000 Crandon Blvd., Key Biscayne, 305-361-5421; www.miamidade.gov/parks

More than two miles of beaches attract millions of visitors to Crandon Park each year, where picnic areas, a playground and a colorful carousel provide fun for the whole family. A sand bar just off the shore keeps the water calm and protects wading and swimming areas that range from shallow to nearly 12 feet deep. Lifeguard stations spaced 150 yards apart keep an eye on swimmers and provide updates on water and surf conditions. A variety of concession stands provide everything from umbrella rentals to fast food and souvenirs, but don't expect to have this beach to yourself. The parking areas provide room for more than 3,000 vehicles. The expansive park also features an 18-hole golf course, tennis facilities and a marina.

MANGROVE CYCLES

260 Crandon Blvd., Key Biscayne, 305-361-5555; www.key-biscayne.com/mangrove

If you're headed to Key Biscayne and want to do some biking, Mangrove Cycles has everything you need. From mountain bike rentals to child seats to bikes for kids, there is something for everyone. You'll also find information about biking Key Biscayne, including maps of bike trails and other guides. Mangrove Cycles also sells bikes and accessories and provides maintenance and repair services. Tuesday-Sunday.

HOTEL

★★★★THE RITZ-CARLTON, KEY BISCAYNE

455 Grand Bay Drive, Key Biscayne, 305-365-4500, 800-241-3333;
www.ritzcarlton.com/keybiscayne

Located just outside downtown Miami on the southernmost barrier island in the United States, this resort delivers the intimacy of a private island escape but with the convenient location of a city hotel. Besides 12 acres of oceanfront property, the resort has a 20,000-square-foot spa and 11-court tennis center. The guest rooms feature British colonial furnishings and pastel colors. Cioppino, the resort's signature restaurant, has an Italian-influenced menu with an accent on local seafood. 490 rooms. Wireless Internet access. Two restaurants, two bars. Children's activity center. Fitness room, spa. Beach. Two outdoor pools, children's pool, whirlpool. Tennis. Airport transportation available. Business center. Valet Parking. Golf. $$$$

SPA

★★★★THE RITZ-CARLTON SPA, KEY BISCAYNE

455 Grand Bay Drive, Key Biscayne, 305-365-4500; www.ritzcarlton.com/keybiscane

You don't have to travel far to find a tropical island paradise. Just minutes from Miami's center is a Caribbean-inspired oasis on secluded Key Biscayne. This spa soothes the body and mind with treatments that incorporate healing elements of the land and sea. The extensive spa menu features body therapies, specialized skin care and facials that utilize a holistic approach. The Seawater Therapy restores and balances the skin with a pure, freeze-dried seawater bath. Wellness services include personal training, body sculpting and kickboxing, as well as classes such as tai chi and yoga.

RESTAURANTS

★★★LINDA B STEAKHOUSE

320 Crandon Blvd., Key Biscayne, 305-361-1111; www.Lindabsteakhouse.com
Steak menu. Lunch. Dinner. Bar. Children's menu. Casual attire. Reservations recommended. Outdoor seating. **$$$**

★★THE RUSTY PELICAN

3201 Rickenbacker Causeway, Key Biscayne, 305-361-3818; www.therustypelican.com
American, Italian menu. Lunch, dinner, Sunday brunch. Bar. Children's menu. Casual attire. Reservations recommended. Valet parking. Outdoor seating. **$$$**

KEY LARGO

The longest island in the Keys, Key Largo extends some 30 miles but is seldom more than two miles wide. The Overseas Highway crosses the first bridge at Jewfish Creek to start its southwestward stretch across the keys to Key West. Scattered on the island are marinas catering to the ever-present anglers and skin divers.

Information: Key Largo Chamber of Commerce, Florida Keys Visitor Center, 106000 Overseas Highway, 305-451-4747, 800-822-1088; www.keylargochamber.org

WHAT TO SEE AND DO

DOLPHINS PLUS

31 Corrine Place, Key Largo, 305-451-1993, 866-860-7946; www.dolphinsplus.com
Research and education center that focuses on the interaction between humans and dolphins. Visitors can watch or participate in two- to three-hour programs (reservations required to participate; experienced swimmers only; equipment provided). Minimum age seven years; under age 13 must be accompanied by an adult. Programs for the disabled. Three sessions daily.

JOHN PENNEKAMP CORAL REEF STATE PARK

Key Largo, 305-451-1202, 800-326-3521; www.pennekamppark.com
Just an hour's drive south of Miami, you'll find some of the best snorkeling and scuba diving in the area. John Pennekamp Coral Reef State Park is home to the largest living coral reef in the continental United States. The park has beautiful hiking trails, boardwalks through mangrove swamps and observation decks for bird watching, but the most spectacular part lies offshore. The state park and adjacent national marine sanctuary cover an area of the Atlantic Ocean that is some 25 miles long and three miles out to sea, where fish, coral reefs and marine mammals are carefully protected. Park concessionaires offer all the gear you need to scuba dive and snorkel. You can also sign up for daily boat trips, snorkeling excursions and glass-bottomed boat rides—or better yet, rent a boat to take out on your own. Daily.

JULES' UNDERSEA LODGE

51 Shoreland Drive, Key Largo, 305-451-2353; www.jul.com

The world's only underwater "hotel" is five fathoms deep. Designed to accommodate six divers (introductory diving classes available), the Lodge has an entertainment center, fully stocked galley, dining area, bathrooms and 42-inch windows. Available for three-hour or overnight stays.

HOTELS

★★HOLIDAY INN RESORT AND MARINA

99701 Overseas Highway, Key Largo, 305-451-2121, 800-465-4329;
www.holidayinnkeylargo.com

132 rooms. Wireless Internet access. Two restaurants, two bars. Fitness room. Two outdoor pools, whirlpool. Tennis. Business center. $$

★KEY WEST INN

201 Ocean Drive, Key Largo, 305-451-5081, 800-833-0555; www.keywestinn.com

40 rooms, all suites. Outdoor pool. $

★★★MARRIOTT KEY LARGO BAY BEACH RESORT

103800 Overseas Highway, Key Largo, 305-453-0000, 866-849-3753;
www.marriottkeylargo.com

This resort has comfortable guest rooms decorated with mahogany furniture and tropical prints, granite bathroom countertops and upgraded bed linens. Onsite is a PADI (Professional Association of Diving Instructors) school for scuba diving lessons, specialty certifications, and daily dive and snorkel trips to the coral reef and marine sanctuary is available to guests. For the less adventurous, the property offers volleyball, snorkeling, jet skiing and parasailing. 153 rooms. Restaurant, bar. Fitness room. Outdoor pool, whirlpool. Spa. 18-hole golf. Casual attire. Breakfast, lunch, dinner. $$

★RAMADA KEY LARGO RESORT & MARINA

99751 Overseas Highway, Key Largo, 305-451-3939, 800-843-5397; www.ramadakeylargo.com

92 rooms. Complimentary continental breakfast. Outdoor pool, whirlpool. $

RESTAURANT

★MRS. MAC'S KITCHEN

99336 Overseas Highway, Key Largo, 305-451-3722

American menu. Breakfast, lunch, dinner. Closed Sunday. Children's menu. $$

KEY WEST

Known for its 19th-century gingerbread houses and Cuban foods, Key West is the southernmost city in the continental United States. In 1890, it was also the largest city in Florida. Ponce de Leon may have been the first to spot the island, but Florida Indians often made their way here to trade. The original name was "Cayo Hueso," Spanish for Bone Island. The English, Bahamians, Cubans, New Englanders and Southerners came here to settle and make a living from salvaging wrecked ships, making cigars, sponge gathering, turtling, shrimping and fishing. Following its early burst of prosperity, the city went bankrupt in the 1930s, and an ambitious rehabilitation program was ended by the hurricane that wiped out the Overseas Railroad. However, completion of the Overseas Highway in 1938, along the existing route of the defunct railroad, signaled the start of Key West's present-day affluence. Today, tourism is the main draw. The island is known for its lively gay scene, annual flamboyant Fantasy Fest celebration at Halloween and for being home to writer Ernest Hemingway.

Information: Greater Key West Chamber of Commerce, 402 Wall St., Key West, 305-294-2587; www.keywestchamber.org

WHAT TO SEE AND DO
AUDUBON HOUSE AND TROPICAL GARDENS
205 Whitehead St., Key West, 305-294-2116, 877-294-2470; www.audubonhouse.com
This neoclassical home of sea captain and wrecker John Geiger contains an outstanding collection of 18th- and 19th-century furnishings and re-creates the ambience of the early days of Key West, when Audubon visited the island. Many of the artist's original engravings are on display. Admission includes a CD for a self-guided tour. Daily.

CURRY MANSION
511 Caroline St., Key West, 305-294-5349, 800-253-3466; www.currymansion.com
A 25-room Victorian mansion built in 1899 for the son of Florida's first millionaire; original Audubon prints, period antiques and Tiffany glass; Ernest Hemingway's elephant gun. Self-guided tours. The inn offers 28 elegant, romantic rooms. Daily.

ERNEST HEMINGWAY HOME AND MUSEUM
907 Whitehead St., Key West, 305-294-1136; www.hemingwayhome.com
This Spanish colonial-style house made of native stone was purchased in 1931 by Hemingway, an early visitor to Key West who wrote many of his books here, including *For Whom the Bell Tolls* and *The Snows of Kilimanjaro*. The museum features original furnishings, memorabilia, trees and plants from the Caribbean and other parts of the world, most collected and planted by Hemingway. Daily 9 a.m.-5 p.m.

HARRY S. TRUMAN LITTLE WHITE HOUSE MUSEUM
111 Front St., Key West, 305-294-9911; www.trumanlittlewhitehouse.com
This was the vacation home of the 33rd president, who spent 11 working vacations in Key West between 1946 and 1952. The house has been restored to the period, with original Truman furnishings. Guided tours; video. Daily 9 a.m.-4:30 p.m.

KEY WEST AQUARIUM
1 Whitehead St., Key West, 800-868-7482; www.keywestaquarium.com
Unique and colorful specimens of sea life from the Gulf of Mexico and the Atlantic Ocean; "touch tank" allows visitors to touch and examine live starfish, horseshoe crabs, sea squirts, sea urchins, conchs and more; watch sharks being hand-fed. Guided, narrated tours. Daily 10 a.m.-6 p.m.

SUNSET CELEBRATION—MALLORY PIER
Wall and Duval streets, Key West, 305-292-7700; www.sunsetcelebration.org
A mixture of carnival midway and street theater entertainment by scores of jugglers, magicians, sword swallowers and others that draws crowds of spectators each night, especially in season. Nightly, beginning about 1½ hours before sunset until 1½ hours after.

KEYS ADVENTURE

South of Miami and off Highway 1, the Florida Keys are America's own tropical islands. A laid-back attitude exists here, dress is always casual and life revolves around the water. The Keys are designated marine wildlife refuges, making them one of Florida's most popular destinations for diving.

The Keys stretch for more than 100 miles, beginning with Key Largo. This is the site of John Pennekamp Coral Reef State Park, found at the town's north end, about 40 miles from South Miami. John Pennekamp is known for its snorkeling and glass-bottomed boat tours, but you can also camp and enjoy fishing and other water sports here. Highway 1 continues south, connecting the islands together on a scenic route known as the Overseas Highway. In Islamorada, 20 miles to the south, kids will enjoy a stop at Theater of the Sea where they can watch the sea lion and shark shows and participate in the popular dolphin interaction programs. Manny and Isas is the place to stop for the best home-cooked Cuban food and key lime pie. If you'd rather dine waterside, try Papa Joe's, which is located south of town. Long Key Recreation Area, less than 20 miles south of Islamorada, has camping and picnicking on one of the Keys' few good beaches. North of Marathon (six miles away), the Dolphin Research Center conducts educational and interactive programs. Crane Point Hammock, also in Marathon, is a natural history museum with trails, aquariums and a children's museum. Also, check out the Pigeon Key Historic Site. Here, the welcome center occupies a vintage railroad at the very southern edge of town before the Seven Mile Bridge. From here, you take a tram (you can also walk or bicycle) to a historic site that re-creates an old Bahamian-style railroad-builders settlement from the turn of the last century.

Scenic Seven Mile Bridge is the showpiece of Overseas Highway. It takes you to Bahia Honda State Park, eight miles south of the Pigeon Key visitor center. Here you will find the Keys best beaches, rated among the top in the country. You can snorkel, kayak, swim and fish in the marina here. Campgrounds, cabins and beautiful beaches provide a great opportunity to relax.

Down the road four miles lies the largest Florida Key, Big Pine Key. It is also one of the most natural of the Keys, home to the National Key Deer Refuge, which protects the diminishing diminutive white-tailed deer. Fishing and lobstering are popular pastimes in this community. A couple of miles south, at Torch Key, find some of the Keys' best snorkeling and diving in an area known as Looe Key National Marine Sanctuary. Continue south (about 15 miles) to Key West, best known for its sunset celebrations, all-night carousing and festival scene. Its historic Old Town area is full of great dining, shopping, historic sites and museums. Among the most well-known attractions are the Hemingway Home, the Key West Aquarium and the Little White House. Take the Conch Train around town to learn about the island's fascinating history. Check out Fort Zachary Taylor State Historic Site for more history and a beach picnic. (approximately 154 miles): www.floridakeysadventures.com

WRECKER'S MUSEUM—THE OLDEST HOUSE

322 Duval St., Key West, 305-294-9501; www.oirf.org

The oldest house in Key West, built in 1830 with a unique "conch" construction. Once the house of sea captain and wrecker Francis B. Watlington, the museum now houses displays of Key West's wrecking industry, historic documents, ship models, toys and antiques. Garden for rent. Daily 10 a.m.-4 p.m.

SPECIAL EVENTS

FANTASY FEST

1111 12th St., Key West, 305-296-1817; www.fantasyfest.net

Parade, costume contest, masquerade ball. Late October.

HEMINGWAY DAYS FESTIVAL

908 Whitehead St., Key West, 305-294-2587; www.hemingwaydays.net

Readings from Hemingway's works, talks, book signings. Mid-late July.

OLD ISLAND DAY

10 Old Mallory Square, Key West, 305-294-9501

A series of 10 different events that includes house and garden tours, orchid and art shows and a conch shell-blowing contest. December-March.

HOTELS

★BEST WESTERN KEY AMBASSADOR RESORT INN

3755 S. Roosevelt Blvd., Key West, 305-296-3500, 800-432-4315; www.keyambassador.com

100 rooms. Complimentary continental breakfast. Bar. Outdoor pool. High-speed Internet access. Pets not accepted. Airport courtesy shuttle. $

★★★CASA MARINA RESORT

1500 Reynolds St., Key West, 305-296-3535, 866-397-6342; www.casamarinaresort.com

This sprawling resort is located on Kokomo Beach, the largest beach in Key West. Scuba dive, relax by the oceanfront pools and visit the Sunday veranda brunch at Flagler's restaurant. 311 rooms. Wireless Internet access. Two restaurants, two bars. Children's activity center. Fitness room. Beach. Two outdoor pools, children's pool, whirlpool. Tennis. Business center. Pets accepted. $$

★★★CROWNE PLAZA HOTEL KEY WEST-LA CONCHA

430 Duval St., Key West, 305-296-2991, 800-745-2191; www.laconchakeywest.com

On the southernmost part of the island sits the highest building in Key West. Built in 1926, it is listed on the National Register of Historic Places. The lobby features tropical décor with wicker furniture, palm leaf fans, marble flooring and lots of cozy seating. Guest rooms are decorated with mahogany antiques and plush bedding, and some rooms have refrigerators. The seventh-floor observatory offers panoramic views of the Gulf, ocean and Duval Street. 16 rooms. Restaurant, three bars. Fitness room. Outdoor pool. Wireless Internet access. $$

★★★DOUBLETREE GRAND KEY RESORT

3990 S. Roosevelt Blvd., Key West, 305-293-1818, 888-310-1540;
www.grandkeyresort.doubletree.com

This tropical resort is situated just one mile from the Key West airport. Guests can enjoy hotel-sponsored water sports at the private beach or try their hand at a game of badminton. A free shuttle is provided to the airport, beach, golf course and historic Old Town. Guest rooms and suites feature blue and yellow cottage-style décor. 216 rooms. Bar. Fitness room. Outdoor pool, whirlpool. $$

★★HOLIDAY INN KEY WEST

3850 N. Roosevelt Blvd., Key West, 305-294-6681, 800-465-4329;
www.holidayinnkeywest.com

141 rooms. Complimentary continental breakfast. Wireless Internet access. Restaurant, bar. Outdoor pool, whirlpool. $$

★★★HYATT KEY WEST RESORT & SPA

601 Front St., Key West, 305-809-1234, 800-233-1234; www.hyatt.com

A tropical setting with lush gardens and ponds inhabited by a large variety of turtles can be found at this hotel in downtown Key West. Brightly colored guest rooms offer balconies and great views of the Gulf. Area attractions and shops are nearby. 118 rooms. Pets accepted; fee. Restaurant, bar. Fitness room. Beach. Outdoor pool, whirlpool. Wireless Internet access. Spa. $$$

★★★LA MER AND DEWEY HOUSE

504-506 South St., Key West, 305-296-6577, 800-354-4455;
www.southernmostresorts.com

Located on the south end of the island, this inn is only a few steps from the beach. Fresh flowers are placed in each of the guest rooms, which are decorated in a tropical, contemporary style and feature microwaves and minirefrigerators. A continental breakfast and afternoon tea are served in the cozy parlor. 11 rooms. Complimentary continental breakfast. Restaurant, bar. Beach. Outdoor pool. Wireless Internet access. $$$

★★★LITTLE PALM ISLAND RESORT & SPA

28500 Overseas Highway, Little Torch Key, 305-515-4004, 800-343-8567;
www.littlepalmisland.com

Accessible by boat or seaplane, this private island has white-sand beaches and towering palm trees. Intimate and seductive, the thatched-roof bungalows have rattan furnishings, gauzy canopied beds and are blissfully technology free, without TVs or phones. The resort entices with simple pleasures, like snoozing in the sun, visiting the spa (which features indoor and outdoor massage services) and floating in the freshwater pool. Dinner is served at the onsite restaurant under a tiki-torch-lit, star-filled sky. 30 suites. Children over 16 years only. Complimentary continental breakfast. Restaurant, two bars. Fitness room, fitness classes available. Spa. Outdoor pool, whirlpool. Airport transportation available. $$$$

★★★MARQUESA HOTEL

600 Fleming St., Key West, 305-292-1919, 800-869-4631; www.marquesa.com

Listed on the National Register of Historic Places, this hotel is private and peaceful and is located in the heart of the historic district. Rooms and suites are decorated with

FLORIDA

★
★
★
★

antiques and soft floral prints. Cafe Marquesa serves fine contemporary American cuisine. 27 rooms. Children over 13 years only. Wireless Internet access. Restaurant, bar. Two outdoor pools. Business center. Pets not accepted. Reservations recommended. $$$

★★★OCEAN KEY RESORT & SPA

0 Duval St., Key West, 305-296-7701, 800-328-9815; www.oceankey.com
Located in Old Town, this is the home of the famous Sunset Pier nightly sunset celebrations. Rooms are colorful and eclectic and decorated with sleigh beds and wicker furniture. Fishing, scuba and sightseeing trips are available for at the onsite marina. 100 rooms. Wireless Internet access. Two restaurants, two bars. Fitness room, fitness classes, spa. Outdoor pool. $$$

★★★PIER HOUSE RESORT AND CARIBBEAN SPA

1 Duval St., Key West, 305-296-4600, 800-723-2791; www.pierhouse.com
This Gulf-front resort offers white sand, the Caribbean Spa (with a waterfall Jacuzzi) and several restaurants and bars. Have a drink at the infamous Chart Room Bar, where Jimmy Buffett is said to have begun his career. The décor here is classic Key West, and the grounds are landscaped with lush garden walkways and tropical trees and plants. 142 rooms. Pets accepted, some restrictions; fee. Children over 21 years only. Wireless Internet access. Two restaurants, four bars. Fitness room, fitness classes available, spa. Beach. Outdoor pool, whirlpool. $$$

★★RADISSON HOTEL KEY WEST

3820 N. Roosevelt Blvd., Key West, 305-294-5511, 888-201-1718; www.radisson.com
145 rooms. Wireless Internet access. Restaurant, two bars. Fitness room. Outdoor pool. Business center. $$

★★★THE REACH RESORT

1435 Simonton St., Key West, 305-296-3535, 866-397-6427; www.reachresort.com
Private balconies, pastel décor and a natural sand beach make this oceanfront Old Town resort a relaxing hideaway. Still, there's plenty to do, from shopping Duval Street to sunset cruises to dining at the Mediterranean-style Sands Restaurant and Lounge. 150 rooms. Wireless Internet access. Restaurant, two bars. Fitness room. Beach. Outdoor pool, whirlpool. Airport transportation available. Business center. $$

★★★SHERATON SUITES KEY WEST

2001 S. Roosevelt Road, Key West, 305-292-9800, 800-452-3224;
www.sheratonkeywest.com
This all-suite, nonsmoking hotel is across the street from Smather's Beach. All rooms have refrigerators, microwaves and coffee makers, and some feature balconies. A complimentary shuttle service transports guests to and from the airport and historic Old Key West. Adding to the tropical setting is the outdoor pool, complete with a cascading waterfall. 182 rooms. Pets accepted, some restrictions. Restaurant, bar. Fitness room. Outdoor pool. Business center. Tennis. Golf. Fitness Center. $$$

★★SOUTHERNMOST HOTEL

1319 Duval St., Key West, 305-296-6577, 800-354-4455; www.southernmostresorts.com
127 rooms. Wireless Internet access. Restaurant, bar. Beach. Two outdoor pools, whirlpool. Multilingual staff. $$

★★SOUTHERNMOST ON THE BEACH

508 South St., Key West, 305-296-6577, 800-354-4455; www.southernmostresorts.com

48 rooms. Wireless Internet access. Restaurant, bar. Beach. Three outdoor pools, whirlpool. **$$**

★★★SUNSET KEY GUEST COTTAGES

245 Front St., Key West, 305-292-5300, 800-937-8461; www.westin.com

The Sunset Key Guest Cottages resort is located on a secluded 27-acre island called Sunset Key, just 10 minutes by boat from the Hilton Key West Resort and Marina. The cottages feature traditional Key West architecture and have kitchens, living and dining areas, CD and DVD/VHS players and a beverage and pantry bar. Try the free-form garden pool with whirlpools or sip a tropical drink at Flippers Pool Bar. There is 24-hour boat transportation to the Hilton Key West Resort, located in Old Town Key West. 37 rooms. Complimentary continental breakfast. High-speed Internet access. Restaurant, bar. Children's activity center. Fitness room. Beach. Outdoor pool, two whirlpools. Tennis. **$$$$**

★★★WESTIN KEY WEST RESORT AND MARINA

245 Front St., Key West, 305-294-4000, 800-937-8461;
www.westinkeywestresort.com

Overlooking the Gulf of Mexico and next to Mallory Square, this Victorian-inspired resort sits at the northwest edge of Key West's Old Town. Rooms are decorated with upscale tropical décor, and most have private balconies and water views. The resort marina offers a variety of water sports and a nightly sunset festival on the pier. 178 rooms. Wireless Internet access. Three restaurants, two bars. Children's activity center. Fitness room. Beach. Outdoor pool, whirlpool. Business center. Valet parking. **$$$**

SPECIALTY LODGINGS

ARTIST HOUSE GUEST HOUSE

534 Eaton St., Key West, 305-296-3977, 800-582-7882; www.artisthousekeywest.com

This Queen Anne/Victorian mansion was the former residence of Key West artist Gene Otto. Rooms are furnished with antiques and oriental rugs. Seven rooms. Children over 12 years only. Complimentary continental breakfast. Spa. **$$**

BLUE PARROT INN

916 Elizabeth St., Key West, 305-296-0033, 800-231-2473; www.blueparrotinn.com

Guest rooms are decorated with wicker, mahogany and rattan furniture. The exterior features lush, tropical gardens, an upstairs balcony and a front porch, where the resident blue parrot is usually perched in his cage. 11 rooms. Children over 16 years only. Complimentary continental breakfast. Outdoor pool. **$**

CURRY MANSION INN

511 Caroline St., Key West, 305-294-5349, 800-253-3466; www.currymansion.com

This well-recognized Victorian-style bed and breakfast is located next to the original Curry Mansion, which was built in 1899 by Florida's first millionaire. The lobby's Tiffany glass sliding doors are a prelude to the beautiful wicker and antique-filled rooms. 28 rooms. Pets accepted, some restrictions. Complimentary full breakfast. Outdoor pool, whirlpool. Business center. Wireless Internet access. **$$$**

★
★
★
★
★

DUVAL HOUSE

815 Duval St., Key West, 305-292-9491, 800-223-8825;
www.duvalhousekeywest.com

Situated between the Gulf and the ocean in a residential neighborhood, this bed and breakfast has seven historic buildings, all more than 100 years old and decorated with lots of wicker, colorful bedspreads and local art. Cozy front porches with whitewood balconies and stair railings add to the inviting exterior. 28 rooms. No children allowed. Complimentary continental breakfast. Outdoor pool. **$$**

HERON HOUSE

512 Simonton St., Key West, 305-294-9227, 800-294-1644; www.heronhouse.com

Another charming location in the historic district of Old Town is steps from Duval Street. Private decks and patios border the well-manicured, orchid-strewn pathways of this quiet, relaxed house. 23 rooms. No children allowed. Complimentary continental breakfast. Outdoor pool. **$$$**

ISLAND CITY HOUSE HOTEL

411 William St., Key West, 305-294-5702, 800-634-8230; www.islandcityhouse.com

A combination of antiques and contemporary décor add to the warm atmosphere of this downtown inn. Historic buildings that date to the 1880s feature guest rooms with full kitchens. 24 rooms, all suites. Complimentary continental breakfast. Outdoor pool. Spa. **$$**

OLD TOWN MANOR

511 Eaton St., Key West, 305-292-2170, 800-294-2170; www.oldtownmanor.com

Built in 1886, the main house is a restored Victorian mansion decorated with lots of historic memorabilia. The grounds feature tropical gardens and brick walkways. Guests have free access to the Eaton Lodge Villas' outdoor pool, located one block away. 13 rooms. Pets accepted, some restrictions; fee. Children over 12 years only. Complimentary continental breakfast. **$$**

RESTAURANTS

★★ANTONIA'S

615 Duval St., Key West, 305-294-6565; www.antoniaskeywest.com

Italian menu. Dinner. Daily. Bar. **$$**

★★BAGATELLE

115 Duval St., Key West, 305-296-6609; www.bagatelle-keywest.com

American seafood menu. Breakfast, lunch, dinner. Bars. Outdoor seating. **$$$**

★★★CAFE MARQUESA

600 Fleming St., Key West, 305-292-1244; www.marquesa.com

This contemporary American restaurant is located in the Marquesa Hotel in the historic district. Breads and desserts are baked fresh daily and accompany specialties like lobster and diver scallops with Thai basil sauce. The show kitchen brings life to the intimate 50-seat dining room. American menu. Dinner. Bar. **$$$**

★★★FLAGLER'S STEAKHOUSE

1500 Reynolds St., Key West, 305-296-3535, 866-397-6342; www.casamarinakeywest.com

Located in the historic Casa Marina Resort, this traditional steakhouse, named for railroad magnate Henry Flagler, is popular both for dinner and its Sunday brunch buffet. Seafood, steak menu. Breakfast, lunch, dinner, Sunday brunch. Bar. Children's menu. Valet parking. Outdoor seating. **$$$**

★HALF SHELL RAW BAR

231 Margaret St., Key West, 305-294-7496

Seafood menu. Lunch, dinner. Bar. Outdoor seating. **$$**

★★★HARBOUR VIEW CAFE

1 Duval St., Key West, 305-296-4600; www.pierhouse.com

This restaurant at the south end of Duval Street is right on the Gulf and offers sunset views and a great menu. The décor is contemporary and clean, with a blue-and-white color scheme and unusual light and dark wood floors. Nightly entertainment includes a piano bar and local jazz groups. Seafood menu. Breakfast, lunch, dinner. Bar. Children's menu. Casual attire. Reservations recommended. Outdoor seating. **$$$**

★★KELLY'S CARIBBEAN BAR, GRILL & BREWERY

301 Whitehead St., Key West, 305-293-8484; www.kellyskeywest.com

Pan American airlines first tickets were sold in this building in 1927. American, Caribbean menu. Lunch, dinner. Bar. Children's menu. Outdoor seating. **$$**

★★★LOUIE'S BACKYARD

700 Waddell Ave., Key West, 305-294-1061; www.louiesbackyard.com

This waterfront restaurant serves a seafood heavy menu and has a spacious outdoor patio with ocean views. Dishes include sautéed Key West shrimp with bacon and stoneground grits and sea scallops in orange chile broth. Caribbean menu. Lunch, dinner. Bar. Reservations recommended. Indoor, Outdoor seating. **$$$**

SPA

★★★★SPA TERRE AT LITTLE PALM ISLAND

28500 Overseas Highway, Little Torch Key, 305-515-3028, 800-343-8567;
www.littlepalmisland.com

Reconnecting with body and soul is the philosophy behind Little Palm Island's Spa Terre. The menu is filled with massages and body treatments, many inspired by Indonesian and Thai techniques and traditions. Spend an hour unwinding with a Swedish, sports or aromatherapy massage, or let heated volcanic river rocks do the work in a hot stone massage. Tired feet and lower legs are soothed with reflexology, while skin is revived with the detoxifying Caribbean seaweed body mask or the rehydrating cucumber and aloe wrap.

KISSIMMEE

Known as cattle country for more than 75 years, Kissimmee is also famous for being the gateway to Walt Disney World and several other central Florida attractions.

Information: Kissimmee-St. Cloud Convention and Visitors Bureau, 1925 E. Irlo Bronson Memorial Highway, 407-944-2400, 800-327-9159; www.floridakiss.com

WHAT TO SEE AND DO

GATORLAND

14501 S. Orange Blossom Trail, 407-855-5496, 800-393-5297; www.gatorland.com

For the quintessential Florida experience, visit this 110-acre park and wildlife pre-serve with thousands of alligators and crocodiles. Shows include Jungle Crocs, the Up Close Encounters snake show, Gator Wrestlin' and the Gator Jumparoo where large alligators jump out of the water to grab food from a trainer's hand. Daily 9 a.m.-6 p.m.

GREEN MEADOWS PETTING FARM

1368 S. Poinciana Blvd., Kissimmee, 407-846-0770; www.greenmeadowsfarm.com

Two-hour guided tours encourage hands-on experience with more than 200 farm animals, cows for milking, hay rides, pony rides and free pumpkins (October). Daily 9:30 a.m.-4 p.m.

OLD TOWN

5770 W. U.S. Highway 192, Kissimmee, 407-396-4888; www.old-town.com

Replica turn-of-the-century Florida village with brick-lined streets; specialty shops and restaurants, general store, Ferris wheel, Windstorm roller coaster and Kids Town with 10 rides, daily noon-11 p.m. Stores daily 10 a.m.-11 p.m.

SPECIAL EVENTS

HOUSTON ASTROS SPRING TRAINING

Osceola County Stadium, 630 Heritage Park Way, Kissimmee, 407-839-3900; www.houston.astros.mlb.com

Houston Astros baseball spring training, exhibition games. Early March-early April.

SILVER SPURS RODEO

Silver Spurs Arena, 1875 Silver Spurs Lane, Kissimmee, 407-677-6336, 800-783-7205; www.silverspursrodeo.com

The largest rodeo east of the Mississippi River, the Silver Spurs Rodeo is held in a new 8,300-seat, enclosed, state-of-the-art arena. The 12 luxury boxes come complete with food and beverage service. February and October.

HOTELS

★★★GAYLORD PALMS RESORT AND CONVENTION CENTER

6000 W. Osceola Parkway, Kissimmee, 407-586-0000; www.gaylordpalms.com

Located in Kissimmee, Gaylord Palms is also only five minutes from Walt Disney World. The contemporary guest rooms reflect regions of Florida. Bold colors define the Key West wing; a breezy, natural style pervades the Everglades; European ele-gance dominates the St. Augustine rooms; and Emerald Bay is the perfect choice for modern sophisticates. Each room includes a flatscreen computer equipped with the "I-connect" program, allowing guests to send room-to-room emails, make dining reservations, request valet service and more. 1,406 rooms. Wireless Internet access. Four restaurants, five bars. Children's activity center. Fitness room, fitness classes available, spa. Two outdoor pools, whirlpool. Airport transportation available. Busi-ness center. $$

★
★ ★
★ ★
★

★★SARATOGA RESORT VILLA

4787 W. Irlo Bronson Memorial Highway 192, Kissimmee,
407-397-0555, 800-936-9417; www.saratogaresortvillas.com

150 villas. Restaurant, bar. Fitness room. Outdoor pool, children's pool, whirlpool.
Tennis. Business center. Spa. Wireless Internet access. **$**

★★★RADISSON RESORT ORLANDO

2900 Parkway Blvd., Kissimmee, 407-396-7000, 800-333-3333;
www.radisson.com/orlando-celebration

This beautifully designed resort is set on 20 acres. Meeting spaces are available, and
families traveling here will enjoy the supersized pool complete with a waterfall, and
water slide. 718 rooms. Restaurant, bar. Fitness room. Two outdoor pools, children's
pool, two whirlpools. Tennis. Business center. **$**

★★RADISSON WORLDGATE RESORT

3011 Maingate Lane, Kissimmee, 407-396-1400, 800-333-3333;
www.radissonworldgate.com

566 rooms. Pets accepted, some restrictions; fee. Wireless Internet access. Three restaurants, two bars. Fitness room. Two outdoor pools, whirlpool. Tennis. Airport transportation available. Business center. **$**

RESTAURANTS

★★ARABIAN NIGHTS

3081 Arabian Nights Blvd., Kissimmee, 407-239-9223, 800-553-6116;
www.arabian-nights.com

American menu. Dinner. Bar. Children's menu. Business casual attire. Reservations
recommended. **$$$**

★AZTECA'S MEXICAN RESTAURANT

809 N. Main St., Kissimmee, 407-933-8155 www.mexrestaurant.com

Mexican menu. Lunch, dinner. Children's menu. Casual attire. Reservations recom-
mended. Outdoor seating. **$$**

★★CHARLEY'S STEAK HOUSE

2901 Parkway Blvd., Kissimmee, 407-396-1646; www.talkofthetownrestaurants.com

Steak menu. Dinner. Bar. Children's menu. Business casual attire. Reservations rec-
ommended. Outdoor seating. **$$$**

★★KOBE JAPANESE STEAK HOUSE

2901 Parkway Blvd., Kissimmee, 407-396-8088; www.kobesteakhouse.com

Japanese menu. Dinner. Bar. Children's menu. Casual attire. Reservations recom-
mended. **$$**

★★KOOLS OAK FIRE GRILL

7725 W. Irlo Bronson Memorial Highway, Kissimmee, 407-239-7166;
www.koolsorlando.com

Steak menu. Dinner. Bar. Children's menu. Casual attire. Reservations recommended. **$$**

FLORIDA

★
★
★
★
★

★★PACINO'S ITALIAN RISTORANTE
5795 W. Irlo Bronson Memorial, Kissimmee, 407-239-4141; www.pacinos.com
Italian, steak menu. Dinner. Bar. Children's menu. Casual attire. Reservations recommended. Outdoor seating. $$

SPA
★★★★CANYON RANCH SPACLUB AT GAYLORD PALMS RESORT
6000 W. Osceola Parkway, Kissimmee, 407-586-2051, 800-742-9000;
www.canyonranch.com
An outpost of the award-winning Arizona-based spa chain, the Canyon Ranch Spa-Club at Gaylord Palms reflects its sister properties' dedication to excellence. The Euphoria treatment begins with a scalp massage followed by a botanical body mask, a gentle buffing and a warm water soak, and ends with a relaxing oil massage. Marine products from the coast of Brittany serve as the inspiration behind the Aqua Lift Replenishing Facial while the Canyon Stone Massage uses oils and warm basalt stones to release tension. From deep-cleansing and antioxidant facials to shiatsu and head, neck or shoulder massages, this spa has something to satisfy every need.

LAKE WORTH
Adjacent to Palm Beach, Lake Worth offers all the advantages of the Gold Coast without straining the budget. A free local transportation system is available here. On the west shore of saltwater Lake Worth, which is part of the Intracoastal Waterway and separated from the ocean by Palm Beach, the city maintains beach and recreation facilities. Tourism is the principal activity of this town, which is named for General William J. Worth, a hero of the Seminole and Mexican wars.
Information: Greater Lake Worth Chamber of Commerce, 501 Lake Ave.,
Lake Worth, 561-582-4401; www.lwchamber.com

SPECIAL EVENTS
GULFSTREAM POLO FIELD
4550 Polo Club Road, Lake Worth, 561-965-2057
Matches Friday and Sunday.

PALM BEACH POLO
Palm Beach Polo and Country Club, 11199 Polo Club Road, Wellington,
561-798-7000, 800-257-1038; www.palmbeachpolo.com
Whether you're a polo aficionado or you've never seen a match before, attending one of these fast-paced games under the lights is an experience. The setting is very informal, so you may even get to meet and talk to some of the players after the game. Saturday evenings in late January-early April.

HOTEL
★★HOLIDAY INN
7859 Lake Worth Road, Lake Worth, 561-968-5000, 800-325-8193;
www.holiday-inn.com/westpalmbeach
114 rooms. Restaurant, bar. Fitness room. Outdoor pool. Tennis. Two meeting rooms. Wireless Internet access. $

RESTAURANT
★★JOHN G'S
10 S. Ocean Blvd., Lake Worth, 561-585-9860; www.johngs.com
American, Seafood menu. Breakfast, lunch. Daily. Casual attire. Outdoor seating.
Credit cards not accepted. $

LAKELAND
Located in central Florida, this city's name comes from the 13 lakes found within the
city limits. Thousands of acres of citrus groves and several citrus packing and pro-
cessing plants are in the area. Tourism, agriculture and phosphate mining are integral
parts of Lakeland's economy.
Information: Lakeland Area Chamber of Commerce, 35 Lake Morton Drive,
863-688-8551; www.lakelandchamber.com

WHAT TO SEE AND DO
POLK MUSEUM OF ART
800 E. Palmetto St., Lakeland, 863-688-7743; www.polkmuseumofart.org
Collection of Pre-Columbian art, Asian and decorative art; contemporary and historical photography, sculpture; changing exhibits. Student Gallery. Lectures, films,
performances. Tuesday-Saturday 10 a.m.-4 p.m., Sunday from 1 p.m.

SPECIAL EVENT
DETROIT TIGERS SPRING TRAINING
Marchant Stadium, 2301 Lakeland Hills Blvd., Lakeland, 863-686-8075;
www.springtrainingonline.com
Detroit Tigers baseball spring training, exhibition games. Early March-early April.

HOTELS
★★HOLIDAY INN
3405 S. Florida Ave., Lakeland, 863-646-5731, 800-465-4329; www.holidayinn.com
Located in Lakeland, the official winter home of the Detroit Tigers, this hotel caters to
baseball fans from both Florida and Michigan. 171 rooms. Complimentary continental
breakfast. Restaurant, bar. Fitness room. Outdoor pool, whirlpool. Wireless Internet
access. $

★HOWARD JOHNSON EXECUTIVE CENTER
3311 Highway 98 N., Lakeland, 863-688-7972, 800-446-4656;
www.lakelandfloridahotels.com
118 rooms. Complimentary full breakfast. Wireless Internet access. Restaurant, bar.
Outdoor pool, children's pool. Pets accepted; fee. Business center. $

LONGBOAT KEY
Nearly 11 miles long, Longboat Key is located between Sarasota Bay and the Gulf of
Mexico and is surrounded by beaches. Discovered in 1593 when Hernando de Soto
made his historic landing nearby, Longboat Key did not receive recognition until the
early 1900s, when circus magnate John Ringling took an interest in surrounding Sarasota. The area's beaches provide good surf fishing and swimming.
Information: Chamber of Commerce, 6960 Gulf of Mexico Drive, Longboat Key,
941-383-2466

FLORIDA

★
★
★
★

HOTELS

★★★THE COLONY BEACH & TENNIS RESORT

1620 Gulf of Mexico Drive, Longboat Key, 941-383-6464, 800-282-1138;
www.colonybeachresort.com

The Colony Beach Resort is located on an island just off the coast of Sarasota. This all-suite property has rooms that reflect a tropical feel with wicker furnishings and brightly colored accessories. The Colony wins rave reviews for its 21-court tennis facility, considered the top center in the country. Players cool off with a dip in the freshwater, beachside pool while the spa and salon are on hand to pamper postmatch. 232 rooms, all suites. Restaurant, bar. Children's activity center. Fitness room. Outdoor pool, whirlpool. Tennis. Airport transportation available. Business center. Spa. $$$

★★★HILTON LONGBOAT KEY BEACH RESORT

4711 Gulf of Mexico Drive, Longboat Key, 941-383-2451, 800-445-8667;
www.longboatkey.hilton.com

This resort has a 400-foot private beach on the Gulf of Mexico and is convenient to exclusive shopping and restaurants. 102 rooms. Two restaurants, two bars. Fitness room. Beach. Outdoor pool. Pets not accepted. High speed Internet access. $$

★★★LONGBOAT KEY CLUB AND RESORT

301 Gulf of Mexico Drive, Longboat Key, 941-383-8821, 888-237-5545;
www.longboatkeyclub.com

The Longboat Key Club and Resort is found on the barrier island of Longboat Key off the Sarasota coast. Located here are 45 holes of golf, 38 Har-Tru tennis courts, a comprehensive fitness center with spa treatments and a private beach with water sports. Dining options include five restaurants ranging from poolside to elegant tables with a view. 218 rooms. Five restaurants, bar. Children's activity center. Fitness room. Beach. Outdoor pool, whirlpool. Golf, 45 holes. Tennis. $$

RESTAURANTS

★★★THE COLONY DINING ROOM

1620 Gulf of Mexico Drive, Longboat Key, 941-383-6464, 800-282-1138;
www.colonybeachresort.com

Views of the ocean provide the backdrop for dinner at this restaurant inside the Colony Beach resort. Try the madras curry lobster risotto or skillet-seared snapper. Caribbean, Continental menu. Breakfast, lunch, dinner, late-night, Sunday brunch. Bar. Children's menu. Business casual attire. Reservations recommended. Valet parking. Outdoor seating. Spa. $$$

★★★EUPHEMIA HAYE

5540 Gulf of Mexico Drive, Longboat Key, 941-383-3633; www.euphemiahaye.com
Located in a lush, tropical garden, this restaurant serves dishes such as roast duckling with bread stuffing and flambéed prime pepper steak. The Haye Loft is a dessert and gourmet coffee room, and a great spot for sampling one of the many ports on the dessert wine menu. International menu. Dinner. Closed three weeks in September. Bar. Business casual attire. Reservations recommended. $$$

★MOORE'S STONE CRAB
800 Broadway St., Longboat Key, 941-383-1748, 888-968-2722; www.stonecrab.cc
Seafood menu. Lunch, dinner. Bar. Children's menu. Casual attire. $$

MAITLAND

This Orlando suburb is famous for hosting the annual Florida Film Festival. A quaint downtown is the hub of activity for the area.
Information: Maitland Area Chamber of Commerce, 110 N. Maitland Ave., 407-644-0741; www.maitlandchamber.com

SPECIAL EVENT
FLORIDA FILM FESTIVAL
1300 S. Orlando Ave., Maitland, 407-644-6579; www.floridafilmfestival.com
Rated one of the top 10 film festivals in the United States, the Florida Film Festival is held annually in mid-March and features more than 50 feature, documentary and short films over a 10-day period. The festival utilizes multiple venues for screenings, from the artsy-eclectic Enzian Theater in Maitland to the 20-screen Loews Universal Cineplex located at Universal CityWalk in Orlando. Intimate chats with stars and filmmakers are great for stargazers and wannabe moviemakers alike. Mid-March.

SPECIALTY LODGING
THURSTON HOUSE
851 Lake Ave., Maitland, 407-539-1911, 800-843-2721; www.thurstonhouse.com
This restored 1885 Queen Anne Victorian house overlooks the lake on a secluded wooded property. Three rooms. Children over 12 years only. Complimentary full breakfast. $$

RESTAURANT
★★★ANTONIO'S LA FIAMMA
611 S. Orlando Ave., Maitland, 407-645-1035; www.antoniosonline.com
Italian menu. Lunch, dinner. Bar. Casual attire. Closed Sunday. $$$

MARATHON

Transformed from a little fishing village by developers who invested $15 million in the area, Marathon has become the hub of the Middle Keys. Its name originated when an East Coast Railroad engineer groaned, "It's getting to be a marathon," after hearing that the construction of the tracks was to continue southward. Today, tourism and sport fishing are the mainstays of the economy.
Information: Chamber of Commerce, 12222 Overseas Highway,
305-743-5417, 800-262-7284; www.floridakeysmarathon.com

WHAT TO SEE AND DO
MUSEUMS AND NATURE CENTER OF CRANE POINT HAMMOCK
5550 Overseas Highway, Marathon, 305-743-3900; www.cranepoint.net
Exhibits on coral reefs, shipwrecks, Native Americans, wildlife, pirates; nature trails. Also located here is the Florida Keys Children's Museum. Daily.

FLORIDA

★
★★
★★
★

HOTELS

★★★HAWKS CAY RESORT

61 Hawk's Cay Blvd., Duck Key, 305-743-7000, 888-443-6393; www.hawkscay.com

The tropical setting at this resort features a saltwater lagoon and multiple-heated freshwater pools, a children's pool and whirlpools. There's plenty to do with eight tennis courts, a fitness room, a kids' club, golf privileges and water sports. There are also several dolphins at the resort, and guests can get close to them through the dolphin program. 180 rooms. Restaurant, bar. Children's activity center. Fitness room. Two outdoor pools, whirlpool. Tennis. Airport transportation available. Spa. Business center. $$$

★★HOLIDAY INN MARATHON-MARINA

13201 Overseas Highway, Marathon, 305-289-0222, 800-465-4329;
www.ichotelsgroup.com

This family-friendly hotel is located on the water and has its own marina with slip, boat and water sport rentals. Book scuba or snorkeling time at the property's dive center. The hotel has an outdoor pool with tiki bar, children's pool, fitness center, restaurant, bar and complimentary continental breakfast. 72 rooms. Complimentary continental breakfast. Restaurant, bar. Outdoor pool. Fitness center. Wireless Internet access. $

MARCO ISLAND

Marco Island, the largest and northernmost of the Ten Thousand Islands, was once occupied by a cannibalistic tribe that prevented settlement on the island until the late 1800s. Later, the Doxsee Clam Factory established itself on the island, but it wasn't until the 1960s when dredges were constructed that Marco became a flourishing resort community. Today, the island is noted for its luxurious hotels, restaurants and golf courses.

Information: Marco Island Area Chamber of Commerce, 1102 N. Collier Blvd., 239-394-7549; www.marco-island-florida.com, www.ichotelsgroup.com

WHAT TO SEE AND DO

COLLIER-SEMINOLE STATE PARK

20200 Tamiami Trail E., Naples, 239-394-3397; www.floridastateparks.org

Approximately 6,400 acres with historic displays and native plant communities. Fishing, boating (ramp, canoe rentals), nature trails, picnicking, concession, camping. Boat tour. Seminole villages nearby. Daily.

HOTELS

★★★HILTON MARCO ISLAND BEACH RESORT

560 S. Collier Blvd., Marco Island, 239-394-5000, 800-445-8667;
www.marcoisland.hilton.com

Guests at this resort can enjoy a large variety of water sports including sailing, parasailing and jet skiing, or stay dry and play tennis or volleyball. The 11,000 square feet of meeting space makes this place a popular choice for meeting planners. 300 rooms. Complimentary continental breakfast. Restaurant. Bar. Children's activity center. Fitness room, spa. Beach. Outdoor pool, whirlpool. Tennis. Business center. $$

★★★MARCO BEACH OCEAN RESORT
480 S. Collier Blvd., Marco Island, 239-393-1400, 800-715-8517;
www.marcoresort.com
This hotel is located on Marco Island's white-sand Crescent Beach. Each suite is exquisitely furnished and includes a multitude of luxurious amenities, including marble showers and vanity tops, fully equipped kitchens and floor-to-ceiling sliding glass doors. 98 suites. Restaurant, bar. Fitness room, spa. Beach. Outdoor pool, whirlpool. Golf. Tennis. Business center. **$$$**

★★★MARRIOTT MARCO ISLAND RESORT GOLF CLUB AND SPA
400 S. Collier Blvd., Marco Island, 239-394-2511, 800-438-4373;
www.marcoislandmarriott.com
This Gulf-front hotel's rooms and suites sit along a long stretch of white sand. Golfers can visit the onsite golf club. Relax at the pool or try one of the five restaurants. 727 rooms. High-speed Internet access. Five restaurants, bar. Children's activity center. Fitness room. Beach. Two outdoor pools, whirlpool. Golf. Tennis. Business center. Spa. **$$**

RESTAURANTS
★★CAFE DE MARCO
244 Palm St., Marco Island, 239-394-6262;
www.marcoislandrestaurants.com/demarco.htm
Seafood menu. Dinner. Closed Sunday (off-season); holidays. Children's menu. Casual attire. Outdoor seating. **$$**

★★KONRAD'S
599 S. Collier Blvd., Marco Island, 239-642-3332; www.konradsrestaurant.com
German, seafood, steak menu. Dinner. Closed Sunday (summer). Bar. Children's menu. Casual attire. Valet parking. Outdoor seating. **$$**

★★MAREK'S COLLIER HOUSE
1121 Bald Eagle Drive, Marco Island, 239-642-9948; www.mareksrestaurant.com
International menu. Dinner. Closed Sunday-Monday (May-October). Casual attire. **$$$**

★SNOOK INN
1215 Bald Eagle Drive, Marco Island, 239-394-3313; www.snookinn.com
Seafood, steak menu. Lunch, dinner. Bar. Children's menu. Casual attire. Outdoor seating. Daily. Reservations recommended. **$$**

★SU'S GARDEN
537 Bald Eagle Drive, Marco Island, 239-394-4666
Chinese menu. Lunch, dinner. Casual attire. **$$**

MARIANNA
The Chipola River bisects Marianna, the center of Jackson County. East is Merritts Mill Pond and its source, an underwater cave at Blue Springs.
Information: Jackson County Chamber of Commerce, 4318 Lafayette St.,
Marianna, 850-482-8061; www.jacksoncounty.com

FALLING WATERS STATE PARK

1130 State Park Road, Chipley, 850-638-6130; www.floridastateparks.org

It covers more than 150 acres and features a waterfall that flows into a 100-foot sink-hole, which has moss- and fern-covered walls. Swimming; nature trails, picnicking, camping. Daily.

FLORIDA CAVERNS STATE PARK

3345 Caverns Road, Marianna, 850-482-1228; www.floridastateparks.org

This 1,300-acre park includes a limestone cavern and a network of caves with unusual stalactites and stalagmites. Cavern tours (daily). The Chipola River, which helped form the cavern, flows through the park, going underground for a short distance. Swimming, fishing, canoeing, nature trails, picnicking, camping. Visitor center.

HOTEL

★QUALITY INN

2175 Highway 71 S., Marianna, 850-526-5600, 800-638-7949; www.qualityinn.com

80 rooms. Pets accepted; fee. Complimentary continental breakfast. Outdoor pool. Wireless Internet access. **$**

RESTAURANT

★TONY'S

4133 Lafayette St., Marianna, 850-482-2232, 850-482-7606

American, Italian menu. Lunch, dinner. Closed Saturday-Sunday. Children's menu. **$$**

MELBOURNE

With its location next to both Cape Canaveral and the Kennedy Space Center, Melbourne's present and future is deeply rooted in the space age. Many large electronic firms have been established here in the last decade, making the town a leader in technology. Fishing is available from the causeways, the rivers, Lake Washington and the Atlantic Ocean. Boating, sailing, waterskiing, sailboarding and jet skiing are also popular.

Information: Melbourne-Palm Bay Area Chamber of Commerce,

1005 E. Strawbridge Ave., 321-724-5400, 800-771-9922; www.melpb-chamber.org

WHAT TO SEE AND DO

FLORIDA INSTITUTE OF TECHNOLOGY

150 W. University Blvd., Melbourne, 321-674-8000; www.fit.edu

On the main campus is the Florida Tech Botanical Garden, which features rare and exotic palms. Daily.

LIBERTY BELL MEMORIAL MUSEUM

Wels Park, 1601 Hickory St., Melbourne, 321-727-1776; www.honoramerica.org

This museum houses a full-size replica of the Liberty Bell cast by the same foundry that cast the original Liberty Bell. Also on display are historic documents; patriotic memorabilia including flags, weapons, paintings, ships, aircraft, military uniforms and artifacts dating back to the Revolutionary War. Monday-Friday 10 a.m.-4 p.m.

HOTELS

★★CROWNE PLAZA MELBOURNE OCEANFRONT

2605 N. Highway A1A, Indialantic, 321-777-4100, 800-465-4329;
www.cpmelbourne.com
270 rooms. Pets accepted; fee. Restaurant, bar. Fitness room. Beach. Outdoor pool,
whirlpool. Tennis. Spa. Business center. Wireless Internet access. **$**

★★DOUBLETREE GUEST SUITES MELBOURNE BEACH OCEANFRONT

1665 N. Highway A1A, Indialantic, 321-723-4222, 800-810-1528; www.doubletree.com
207 rooms, all suites. Pets accepted; fee. Complimentary continental breakfast. Restaurant, bar. Beach. Outdoor pool, whirlpool. Fitness center. High-speed Internet access. **$**

MIAMI

The glamour, the excitement, the international flair—Miami is a new-world city,
located in southeast Florida between the Everglades and the Atlantic Ocean. Known
for its diverse culture and ethnicities, Miami is a gateway to Latin America and has
more than 600 hotels, 7,000 restaurants, 650 churches and synagogues, 40 foreign
consuls and 35 hospitals. More than 9.5 million visitors come here each year. The
recent real estate boom is most notable in Miami, where dozens of high-rise condo-
minium buildings are under construction.

To most visitors, Miami includes both the city of Miami and its across-the-bay
twin, Miami Beach. Each is a separate community, and each is vigorously different in
personality. Miami is older, more settled and sophisticated. Miami Beach is youth on
a fling. The city of Miami has the bustle of business, rush hour traffic and skyscrapers. This is a city of luxury houses, palm-bordered boulevards, Art Deco architecture
and souvenir shops in the midst of a downtown with new, ultramodern office towers,
hotels, condominiums and shopping malls.

Biscayne Bay serves as the buffer between the two communities. Along this shore,
on the Miami side, runs Biscayne Boulevard (Highway 1), lined with hundreds of
stately royal palms—a street where anything from a free glass of orange juice to a
$2 million yacht can be casually acquired. The Miami River winds through the heart
of the city, and seven causeways form lifelines to the sandy shores of Miami Beach.
Another causeway links the mainland with Key Biscayne to the south.

Miami was a remote tropical village of frame houses until Henry Morrison Flagler
brought his East Coast Railway here in 1896 and spurred community development.
Miami's growth was steady but unspectacular, until the 1920s when the great Florida
land boom brought 25,000 real estate salesmen to town. In 1925, downtown property
was selling at $20,000 a front foot and $100 million was spent in construction. The
bubble burst when a mighty hurricane hit in 1926, but Miami had the natural assets
to come back strong. The city's growth continues at an unflinching pace today, solidly
based on year-round tourism, international commerce and trade, industry and agriculture. The Port of Miami is the largest embarkation point for cruise ships in the world.
Suburbs include Coral Gables, Hialeah, Hollywood, Key Biscayne and Miami Beach.
See individual alphabetical listings.

Information: Greater Miami Convention and Visitors Bureau, 701 Brickell Ave.,
305-539-3000, 800-933-8448; www.miamiandbeaches.com

99

FLORIDA

★
★
★
★

WHAT TO SEE AND DO

BARNACLE HISTORIC STATE PARK

3485 Main Highway, Miami, 305-442-6866; www.floridastateparks.org/TheBarnacle

Dade County's oldest house, Barnacle was built by yacht designer Ralph Middleton Munroe with beams fashioned from shipwreck salvage he collected. Considered an engineering feat, ropes and pulleys opened skylights, allowing air to circulate and cool the house in the era before air-conditioning. The tropical hardwood forest surrounding it is a rare example of Miami's native landscape. One-hour tours take in both the heirloom-filled home and bayside boathouse. Friday-Monday 9 a.m.-4 p.m.

BAYFRONT PARK

301 N. Biscayne Blvd., Miami, 305-358-7550; www.bayfrontparkmiami.com

A 32-acre green space with history, downtown Miami's Bayfront Park was created from the 1926 dredging of Biscayne Bay, which it faces, and became politically infamous in 1933 as the site of an assassination attempt on President Franklin Delano Roosevelt. In 1987, famed Japanese sculptor Isamu Noguchi oversaw the park's redesign, installing a double helix-shaped sculpture to memorialize the astronauts killed in the 1986 *Challenger* space shuttle explosion. On a daily basis the park draws strollers and dog walkers to its fountain, while its amphitheater frequently stages music festivals. Daily.

THE DEERING ESTATE AT CUTLER

16701 S.W. 72nd Ave., Miami, 305-235-1668; www.deeringestate.com

Built in the early 1900s, the estate provides a glimpse of life for wealthy Florida pioneers. Tour the homes and natural preserves or explore the waterfront by kayak. Daily 10 a.m.-5 p.m.

FLORIDA GRAND OPERA

8390 N.W. 25th St., Miami, 305-854-1643, 800-741-1010; www.fgo.org

Enjoy opera classics like *Don Giovanni* and *Turandot* during the Florida Grand Opera's November-May season. A traveling show, the FGO also stages performances at both the Miami-Dade County Auditorium in Miami and the Broward Center for the Performing Arts in Fort Lauderdale.

FLORIDA MARLINS (MLB)

Pro Player Stadium, 2267 N.W. Dan Marino Blvd., Miami, 305-626-7400;
www.floridamarlins.com

This multi-championship team plays at Pro Player Stadium (formerly called Joe Robbie Stadium), which is also the home of the NFL's Dolphins. Tickets are usually easy to obtain, as the stadium seats more than 50,000 people in its signature teal-and-orange chairs.

FLORIDA PANTHERS (NHL)

Bank Atlantic Center, 1 Panthers Parkway, Sunrise, 954-835-7000; www.panthers.nhl.com

Many were skeptical when professional hockey came to Florida in the 1990s, but they were silenced when the Panthers advanced to the Stanley Cup Finals in 1996, losing to the Colorado Avalanche. Still, the team and the game have caught on with local fans, and the Panthers are usually competitive in the challenging Eastern Conference.

LITTLE HAVANA

S.W. Eighth Street, between S.W. 11th and S.W. 17th avenues

Just south of downtown, Southwest Eighth Street, also known as "Calle Ocho," is the epicenter of Cuban exile culture in Miami. A flood of islanders seeking refuge from ruler Fidel Castro in the 1960s settled in this modest neighborhood, painting it in tropical colors and opening cafés and nightclubs. Although many of the original inhabitants have moved out of the neighborhood to be replaced by later waves of Latin immigrants, Little Havana is a lively nightlife destination for authentic Cuban food, music, hand-rolled cigars and intense games of dominoes.

MIAMI ART MUSEUM

101 W. Flagler St., Miami, 305-375-3000; www.miamiartmuseum.org

The Miami Art Museum (MAM) showcases art created throughout the western hemisphere from 1940 to the present. Although the museum does feature a permanent collection, it is better known for its special exhibits and events, which can vary dramatically throughout the year. The MAM is located in the same plaza as the Philip Johnson-designed Cultural Center, the Miami-Dade Public Library and the Historical Museum. Guided tours are available. Tuesday-Friday 10 a.m.-5 p.m., Saturday-Sunday from noon.

MIAMI DOLPHINS (NFL)

Dolphin Stadium, 2269 Dan Marino Blvd., Miami, 305-623-6100;
www.miamidolphins.com

The Dolphins are one of the NFL's most celebrated franchises, and were coached for many years by Don Shula, who owns the NFL mark for most coaching victories in a career. The 1973 Dolphins team is still the only one in NFL history to go through an entire NFL season and playoffs undefeated, behind players like Larry Czonka and Bob Griese. The team shares Pro Player Stadium with the Florida Marlins and regularly draws sizeable crowds to all home games.

MIAMI HEAT (NBA)

American Airlines Arena, 601 Biscayne Blvd., Miami, 786-777-4328; www.miamiheat.com

Since entering the NBA as an expansion team with the Charlotte Hornets in 1988, the Heat has become one of the most popular teams and the winner of the 2007 national championship. Their home, American Airlines Arena, is located near Bayside Marketplace, a great place to spend some time before or after the game.

MIAMI METROZOO

12400 S.W. 152nd St., Miami, 305-251-0400; www.miamimetrozoo.com

After a long-overdue expansion, most of the exhibits at Metrozoo are now surrounded by moats instead of high fences, so you have a clear view of the animals. The grounds are expansive and visitors can stroll through nearly 300 acres of park, much of it paved with sidewalks that make it easy to push a stroller (you can rent special animal strollers at the gate). Nearly 800 animals live in the park, including rare white Bengal tigers in an exhibit that features a replica of an ancient Cambodian temple. Other exotic animals include orangutans, elephants, gorillas, chimps, rhinos and bears. There's also a children's petting zoo and an observation deck that overlooks the African Lobe. Daily 9:30 a.m.-5:30 p.m.

FLORIDA

★
★
★
★

MIAMI MUSEUM OF SCIENCE

3280 S. Miami Ave., Miami, 305-646-4200; www.miamisci.org

From interactive exhibits to displays on south Florida's earliest human residents, the Miami Museum of Science brings history, ecology and scientific research to life. The museum's newest feature, created in cooperation with the Smithsonian, offers an adventurous approach to history and includes never-before-seen artifacts. As visitors move through the 3,200-square-foot exhibit, they join an expedition, retracing archae-ologists' steps as they journeyed through jungles and unearthed Mayan ruins through-out the Americas. The exhibit features 150 artifacts from the Smithsonian's National Museum of Natural History, including four large stone carvings from Nicaragua that were sent to the Smithsonian in 1849 and have not been displayed in more than 100 years. While you're in the neighborhood, consider visiting the Vizcaya Museum and Gardens, located across the street. Daily 10 a.m.-6 p.m.

MIAMI SEAQUARIUM

4400 Rickenbacker Causeway, Key Biscayne, 305-361-5705;
www.miamiseaquarium.com

Ever since the 1960s, when the television show *Flipper* was filmed here, the Miami Seaquarium has been one of the city's top tourist draws. Located on 38 acres of Bis-cayne Bay shore, the marine mammal aquarium presents crowd-pleasing dolphin and killer whale shows throughout the day, while sea lions perform under a geodesic dome built by architectural whiz Buckminster Fuller. Additional exhibits feature sharks, tropical fish, crocodiles and manatees, an endangered species the park actively rescues and rehabilitates. For further immersion, sign up for the two-hour dolphin swim program under the instruction of a trainer (for an additional $140). Daily 9:30 a.m.-6 p.m.

MUSEUM OF CONTEMPORARY ART

Joan Lehman Building, 770 N.E. 125th St., North Miami, 305-893-6211; www.mocanomi.org

If you appreciate modern art, the Museum of Contemporary Art is worth the trip to North Miami. Opened in 1996, this state-of-the-art building was designed by acclaimed architect Charles Gwathmey and features 23,000 square feet of exhibit space. The museum is known for its daring, provocative exhibits. Shows change eight to 10 times per year. Call for information about the current exhibits. Tuesday-Saturday 11 a.m.-5 p.m., Sunday from noon.

PARROT JUNGLE & GARDENS

1111 Parrot Jungle Trail, Miami, 305-258-6453; www.parrotjungle.com

Newly relocated to Watson Island in Biscayne Bay, Parrot Jungle populates its 18.6-acre spread with 3,000 exotic animals, including orangutans, reptiles and birds. The park's highlight, a 20-minute winged wonders show, presents scores of parrots, cockatoos and macaws trained to astonish by roller skating, among other antics. Make sure to check out the rare albino alligator. Daily 10 a.m.-6 p.m.

TROPICAL PARK

7900 S.W. 40th St., Miami, 305-226-8316; www.miamidade.gov

One of the largest sports-oriented parks in Dade County, Tropical Park features every-thing from bike trails to basketball to trout fishing. Four lakes offer a variety of water sports, from freshwater swimming to a lake stocked with bass, catfish and bluegill. A third lake is set aside for paddle boating, and the fourth lake provides a cool place to nap. The park offers separate playing areas for soccer, softball, football, volleyball and basketball. You'll also find racquetball and tennis facilities (including 12 lighted wheelchair-accessible tennis courts). The park provides a bike path, and the trails that wind their way around the lakes are considered one of the best places for jogging in the Miami area. Paddle boat and bike rentals are available. Daily sunrise-sunset.

VIZCAYA MUSEUM AND GARDENS
3251 S. Miami Ave., Miami, 305-250-9133; www.vizcayamuseum.com
In 1914, retired International Harvester magnate James Deering employed 1,000 workers (10 percent of Miami's population at the time) to construct his winter home, modeled on Italian Renaissance architecture of the 16th century. Deering died in 1925, and in 1952 the county acquired and began restoring his deteriorating dream home and its surrounding gardens, now a National Historic Landmark. Inside the villa, 34 rooms showcase furniture and decorative art from the 15th through the 19th centuries. The multiterraced gardens are similarly lavish, with decorative urns, cascades, reflecting pools and a maze. Daily 9:30 a.m.-5 p.m.

SPECIAL EVENTS
CALLE OCHO FESTIVAL
1400 S.W. First St., Miami, 305-644-8888; www.carnavalmiami.com/calle8
The Calle Ocho Festival is a celebration of Cuban life in Miami that attracts crowds from around the world. (Eighth Street, along which the festival is held, is better known by the Spanish translation "Calle Ocho," even on most official street signs). The event holds many records, including the world's second-largest street fair (after Carnival in Brazil); the world's longest conga line, with 119,000 dancers shaking their hips to live music by Gloria Estefan in 1998; and the world's largest pinata (27 feet long and 10,000 pounds). Past festivals have attracted nearly 1.5-million people, even though the festival only lasts one day. Mid-March.

COCONUT GROVE ARTS FESTIVAL
3390 Mary St., Coconut Grove, 305-447-0401; www.coconutgroveartsfest.com
This annual festival is one of the country's best attended arts festivals. Set in Coconut Grove, the festival spans several city blocks and features more than 300 artists and crafts-people, as well as fine cuisine, live music and other entertainment. Special events are also available for kids. Late February.

FED EX ORANGE BOWL
Dolphin Stadium, 2269 Dan Marino Blvd., Miami, 305-341-4700; www.orangebowl.org
Orange Bowl Football Game (January). Two weeks of activities also include a tennis tournament, 10K footrace and regatta series. December-early January.

HOTELS
★★COURTYARD MIAMI AIRPORT SOUTH
1201 N.W. LeJeune Road, Miami, 305-642-8200, 800-321-2211; www.courtyard.com
125 rooms. Restaurant, bar. Fitness room. Outdoor pool, whirlpool. Tennis. Airport transportation available. Business center. Wireless Internet access. $

★★DOUBLETREE GRAND HOTEL BISCAYNE BAY

1717 N. Bayshore Drive, Miami, 305-372-0313, 800-222-8733;
www.biscaynebay.doubletree.com

212 rooms. Three restaurants, bar. Fitness room. Outdoor pool, whirlpool. Pets not accepted. $

★★DOUBLETREE HOTEL

2649 S. Bayshore Drive, Coconut Grove, 305-858-2500, 800-222-8733;
www.coconutgrove.doubletree.com

196 rooms. Restaurant, bar. Fitness room. Outdoor pool. Business center. Pets not accepted. $$

★★★★FOUR SEASONS HOTEL MIAMI

1435 Brickell Ave., Miami, 305-819-5053, 800-332-3442; www.fourseasons.com

This contemporary hotel is located in downtown Miami's newly buzzing Brickell neighborhood. Guest rooms and suites are decorated with cool earth tones and distinctive artwork. The 50,000-square-foot splash spa at the onsite Sports Club/LA has 10 treatment rooms and a unique menu of offerings. The hotel features a fine-dining restaurant, Acqua, which serves up Latin-inspired fare, and two lounges, including the skytop, poolside Bahia, where locals and travelers alike gather for cocktails. 305 rooms. Pets accepted, some restrictions. High-speed Internet access. Restaurant, two bars. Children's activity center. Fitness room, fitness classes available, spa. Outdoor pool, children's pool, whirlpool. Airport transportation available. Business center. $$$

★★★GRAND BAY COCONUT GROVE

2669 S. Bayshore Drive, Miami, 305-858-9600, 866-725-3647; www.grandbaymiami.com

This tropical getaway located in the Miami neighborhood of Coconut Grove. Pastel colors and a breezy elegance define the interior of this resort. Java addicts line up at the resort's Starbucks, while food lovers go to Bice, one of the top restaurants in town. 177 rooms. Pets accepted; fee. High-speed Internet access. Restaurant, bar. Fitness room. Outdoor pool, whirlpool. Business center. $$$

★★★GROVE ISLE HOTEL & SPA

4 Grove Isle Drive, Coconut Grove, 305-858-8300, 800-884-7683; www.groveisle.com

Set on a secluded private island on Biscayne Bay, this resort's tropical rooms and suites have glossy, terra-cotta-tiled floors and floor-to-ceiling windows that open onto private terraces. 49 rooms. Pets accepted, some restrictions; fee. Wireless Internet access. Restaurant, bar. Fitness room, fitness classes available, spa. Outdoor pool, whirlpool. Tennis. Airport transportation available. Business center. $$$

★★★HILTON MIAMI AIRPORT AND TOWERS

5101 Blue Lagoon Drive, Miami, 305-262-1000, 800-445-8667; www.hilton.com

Located just south of the airport, this Hilton is accessible off 57th Avenue south of Highway 836. Exotic birds in cages and saltwater tanks with exotic fish live inside. Tennis, basketball and a jogging trail are among the onsite activities offered here. 500 rooms. Wireless Internet access. Two restaurants, two bars. Fitness room, fitness classes available. Outdoor pool, whirlpool. Tennis. Airport transportation available. Business center. $$

★★★INN AT FISHER ISLAND

1 Fisher Island Drive, Fisher Island, 305-535-6000, 800-537-3708;
www.fisherisland.com

Near Miami in Biscayne Bay, this 216-acre island was once the Vanderbilt family's private winter hideaway. Recalling the grandeur of the 1920s, the Inn at Fisher Island maintains exclusivity with its small number of rooms and suites. Whether you're sunning poolside or dining in the refined Vanderbilt Mansion, the inn resembles an idyllic country club. Amenities include the Pete Dye-designed nine-hole course; 18 grass, hard and clay courts; and the spa Internazionale. A favorite of boaters, Fisher Island has two deep-water marinas with 131 slips. 61 rooms. Pets accepted, some restrictions; fee. High-speed Internet access. Eight restaurants, five bars. Children's activity center. Fitness room, fitness classes available, spa. Beach. Five outdoor pools. Golf, nine holes. Tennis. Business center. $$$$

★★★INTERCONTINENTAL HOTEL MIAMI AT MIAMI CENTER

100 Chopin Plaza, Miami, 305-577-1000, 800-327-3005; www.ichotelsgroup.com

This Biscayne Bay hotel is located in the financial district at the corner of Chopin Plaza and Biscayne Boulevard. Bayside Marketplace and Bayfront Park are both within walking distance, and many shops and restaurants are nearby. Guest rooms are spacious and overlook the bay, city or port. 34 floors, 641 rooms, 34 suites. Wireless Internet access. Three restaurants, two bars. Fitness room, fitness classes available. Outdoor pool. Airport transportation available. Business center. $$

★★★JW MARRIOTT HOTEL MIAMI

1109 Brickell Ave., Miami, 305-329-3500, 800-228-9290; www.marriott.com

This sleek hotel in the city center is 18,000 square feet and has contemporary architecture and stylish interior design. The spacious rooms and suites have large work spaces and state-of-the-art technology. The fitness center and an outdoor stainless steel pool keep fitness routines in check. Three restaurants and 24-hour room service ensure that no craving goes unmet. 296 rooms. High-speed Internet access. Two restaurants, two bars. Fitness room, spa. Onsite parking, fee, valet parking, fee. Outdoor pool, whirlpool. Airport transportation available. Business center. $$$

★★★★MANDARIN ORIENTAL, MIAMI

500 Brickell Key Drive, Miami, 305-913-8288, 866-526-6567;
www.mandarinoriental.com

With its waterfront location and contemporary interior design, this hotel is an island of calm in the middle of downtown Miami. Located on tiny Brickell Key, opposite the city center, this outpost of the Asian hotel group is favored for its skyline views, Azul restaurant and man-made white-sand beach. Sign up for the hotel's South Beach Experience, which includes transportation to South Beach, a private beach cabana and access to the pool and restaurant at the famed Casa Casuarina. After the beach, retreat to one of the luxurious guest rooms decorated in a contemporary Asian-influenced style with bamboo hardwood floors, simple furnishings and white fabrics. 327 rooms. Pets accepted, some restrictions; fee. High-speed Internet access. Two restaurants, two bars. Fitness room, fitness classes available, spa. Beach. Outdoor pool, whirlpool. Airport transportation available. Business center.

★★★MARRIOTT DORAL GOLF RESORT AND SPA

4400 N.W. 87th Ave., Miami, 305-592-2000, 800-713-6725; www.doralresort.com

You'll find five 18-hole championship courses at this 650-acre oasis in northwest Miami. Play the famous Dick Wilson and Robert von Hagge Blue Monster course, shop, dine, play tennis, or have a treatment in the 168,000-square-foot spa. 793 rooms. Restaurant, bar. Children's activity center. Fitness room, spa. Indoor pool, five outdoor pools, children's pool, whirlpool. Golf, 90 holes. Tennis. Business center. $$$

★★★MARRIOTT MIAMI BISCAYNE BAY

1633 N. Bayshore Drive, Miami, 305-374-3900, 800-228-9290; www.marriott.com

Perfect for the frequent business traveler, this hotel is minutes from Miami International Airport and overlooks Biscayne Bay in downtown Miami. 580 rooms. High-speed Internet access. Fridge and cable TV. Restaurant, three bars. Fitness room. Outdoor pool, whirlpool. Airport transportation available, onsite parking, fee. Valet parking, fee. Business center. $$

★★★MAYFAIR HOTEL & SPA

3000 Florida Ave., Miami, 305-441-0000, 800-433-4555; www.mayfairhotelandspa.com

Mayfair House is housed in an avant-garde building featuring a lush, central courtyard. Each suite features its own unique name, character and design, as well as hand-carved mahogany furniture and a Japanese-style hot tub or Roman tub. Stained-glass windows and antique artwork decorate this 12,000-square-foot space. 179 rooms, all suites. Pets accepted, some restrictions. Restaurant, bar. Fitness room, spa. Outdoor pool, whirlpool. Business center. $$

★★★THE MUTINY HOTEL

2951 S. Bayshore Drive, Miami, 305-441-2100, 888-868-8469; www.mutinyhotel.com

Near Coconut Grove's shopping and restaurant district, the Mutiny Hotel features suites designed in a tropical British colonial motif, each with a full kitchen and two televisions. Most have private balconies with views of the bay or city. From here, plan day trips for sailing, fishing, diving or sea kayaking. 120 rooms, all suites. Wireless Internet access. Restaurant, bar. Fitness room. Outdoor pool, whirlpool. Airport transportation available. Business center. $$$

★★★★THE RITZ-CARLTON, COCONUT GROVE

3300 S.W. 27th Ave., Miami, 305-644-4680, 800-241-3333; www.ritzcarlton.com

This palatial hotel is recognized for its impeccable service—technology, travel, bath and even pet butlers cater to your every need. The spacious spa offers dozens of treatments, and a shimmering pool with views over Coconut Grove is a prime spot for sunbathers and people-watchers. The lobby lounge serves cocktails and afternoon tea, while Bizcaya Grill serves steaks prepared to perfection. 115 rooms. High-speed Internet access. Restaurant, three bars. Fitness room, spa. Outdoor pool. Pets not accepted. Airport transportation available. $$

★★★SHULA'S HOTEL & GOLF CLUB

6842 Main St., Miami Lakes, 305-821-1150, 800-247-4852; www.donshulahotel.com

Namesake of the venerable Miami Dolphin's coach, Shula's Hotel is a lush South Florida compound where Dolphins photographs and bronze sculptures dedicated to the Florida Marlins share 500 acres with fish ponds and tropical gardens. The resort has two 18-hole golf courses, nine tennis courts, a well-equipped gym and several swimming pools. 205 rooms. Restaurant, bar. Fitness room, spa. Two outdoor pools, whirlpool. Golf, 36 holes. Tennis. Business center. **$$**

★★★SOFITEL MIAMI
5800 Blue Lagoon Drive, Miami, 305-264-4888, 800-763-4835; www.sofitel.com
Close to the airport, this hotel is located off 57th Avenue and south of the Dolphin Freeway. Rooms are contemporary and elegant and feature high-speed Internet access. 281 rooms. Pets accepted. Restaurant, bar. Fitness room. Outdoor pool. Tennis. Airport transportation available. Business center. **$$**

★★TRAVEL INN HOTEL
1050 N.W. 14th St., Miami, 305-324-0200; www.travelinncivic.com
200 rooms. Wireless Internet access. Restaurant. Fitness room. Outdoor pool. Airport transportation available. **$**

SPA

★★★★★THE SPA MANDARIN ORIENTAL, MIAMI
500 Brickell Key Drive, Miami, 305-913-8332; www.mandarinoriental.com
This three-story, 15,000-square-foot spa is a destination in itself. Miamians book massage appointments here months in advance to take full advantage of the views and the work of the expert technicians. The décor makes the most of earthy materials, from natural stone to bamboo floors. The six VIP suites occupy the top floor of the spa and include private relaxation rooms, some with personal multi-jet tubs. Those who can't pry themselves from the beach can opt for a massage in one of the beachfront cabanas. The spa also features a full fitness facility, salon services, and pilates, yoga and tai chi classes.

RESTAURANTS

★★★★AZUL
500 Brickell Key Drive, Miami, 305-913-8358; www.mandarinoriental.com
Mediterranean and Asian flavors marry at Azul at the Mandarin Oriental Miami, where chef Clay Conley crafts a menu made from the day's fresh catch and seasonally fresh ingredients. Miso-marinated hamachi is accompanied by edamame rice, shrimp dumplings and sake butter sauce, while a grilled lamb chop might rest alongside a harissa-marinated lamb loin with smoked eggplant. Wash down these delicacies with an exclusive wine from a selection that boasts more than 700 bottles. Lunch, dinner. Bar. Children's menu. Business casual attire. Reservations recommended. Valet parking. Outdoor seating.

★★★BALEEN
4 Grove Island Drive, Miami, 305-858-8300; www.groveisle.com
An eclectic, contemporary, seafood-centered menu is served at Baleen, an intimate restaurant. This serene oasis is set in a vista of plush outdoor greenery, complete with waterfront views. Inventive fish dishes include fried Chinese-style snapper with coconut rice and sweet-tart black bean sauce and wood-roasted day-boat scallops. International menu. Breakfast, lunch, dinner, Sunday brunch. Bar. Business casual attire. Reservations recommended. Valet parking. Outdoor seating. **$$$**

★CAFÉ MED

3015 Grand Ave., Miami, 305-443-1770; www.cafemedmiami.com

Italian menu. Lunch, dinner. Bar. Children's menu. Casual attire. Outdoor seating. **$$**

★★CAFE TU TU TANGO

3015 Grand Ave., Miami, 305-529-2222; www.cafetututango.com

International/Fusion menu. Lunch, dinner, late-night. Bar. Children's menu. Casual attire. Outdoor seating. **$$**

★★★THE CAPITAL GRILLE

444 Brickell Ave., Miami, 305-374-4500; www.thecapitalgrille.com

This steakhouse chain is located in the financial district of Miami. Known for its in-house aged meats, the Capital Grille also boasts a broad selection of fresh seafood and rich desserts, as well as a well-trained waitstaff. The interior features traditional steakhouse décor—dark wood, a prominent bar area, wine display racks and private dining areas. Steak menu. Lunch, dinner. Bar. Business casual attire. Reservations recommended. Valet parking. **$$$**

★★CASA JUANCHO

2436 S.W. Eighth St., Miami, 305-642-2452; www.casajuancho.com

Spanish menu. Lunch, dinner, late-night. Bar. Casual attire. Reservations recommended. Valet parking. **$$**

★★FLEMING

8511 S.W. 136th St., Miami, 305-232-6444; www.flemingatasteofdenmark.com

Continental menu. Dinner. Bar. Business casual attire. Reservations recommended. **$$**

★FLORIDITA CAFE & GRILL

44 N.E. First St., Miami, 305-373-3060

Latin menu. Breakfast, lunch. Closed Saturday-Sunday. Casual attire. **$**

★★★LA PALOMA

10999 Biscayne Blvd., North Miami, 305-891-0505

Ornate décor with real and faux antiques, a value-packed early menu and old-fashioned continental cuisine attract an adoring crowd of seniors to this North Miami restaurant. Swiss menu. Lunch, dinner. Bar. Children's menu. Valet parking. **$$**

★★MAMA JENNIE'S

11720 N.E. Second Ave., Miami, 305-757-3627; www.mamajennies.com

Italian menu. Lunch, dinner. Children's menu. Casual attire. Outdoor seating. **$**

★★MOJITOS CUBAN RESTAURANT

11401 N.W. 12th St., Miami, 305-406-1002; www.mojitos.com

Cuban menu. Lunch, dinner, late-night. Bar. Casual attire. Outdoor seating. **$$**

★★★NEOMI

18001 Collins Ave., Sunny Isles, 305-692-5600; www.trumpsonesta.com

As the Trump International Sonesta Beach Resort's signature restaurant, Neomi satisfies the eyes as well as the taste buds. The resort is located on some of the most exclusive real estate in South Beach. The menu is contemporary with tropical influences and features such favorites as lobster bisque, B.L.T. soup, heirloom tomato salad, Key West shrimp, lamb chops with buttered stone-ground grits and key lime pie. American menu. Breakfast, lunch, dinner. Bar. Children's menu. Business casual attire. Reservations recommended. Valet parking. Outdoor seating. **$$$**

★★OLD LISBON

1698 S.W. 22nd St., Miami, 305-854-0039; www.oldlisbon.com

Spanish menu. Lunch, dinner. Children's menu. Casual attire. Reservations recommended. Valet parking. **$$**

★★PERRICONE'S MARKETPLACE

15 S.E. 10th St., Miami, 305-374-9449; www.perricones.com

Italian menu. Breakfast, lunch, dinner, late-night, Sunday brunch. Bar. Casual attire. Valet parking. Outdoor seating. **$$**

★TOBACCO ROAD

626 S. Miami Ave., Miami, 305-374-1198; www.tobacco-road.com

Established in 1912, Tobacco Road is Miami's oldest bar. American menu. Lunch, dinner, late-night. Bar. Casual attire. Valet parking. Outdoor seating. **$$**

★★TONY CHAN'S WATER CLUB

1717 N. Bayshore Drive, Miami, 305-374-8888; www.tonychans.com

Chinese menu. Lunch, dinner. Bar. Casual attire. Reservations recommended. Valet parking. **$$$**

★VERSAILLES

3555 S.W. Eighth St., Miami, 305-444-0240

Cuban menu. Breakfast, lunch, dinner. Casual attire. Reservations recommended. **$$**

MIAMI BEACH

The hotels, the celebrities, the scene—Miami Beach is one of the most glamorous destinations in the world for sunseekers. Located on an island that is only 10 miles long and between one and three miles wide, the area was created from a wilderness of palmettos and a sandbar infested with snakes and mosquitoes. When John S. Collins failed in an attempt to develop avocado groves here he turned to real estate. To join his proposed residential colony with Miami, he built what was then the longest wooden bridge in the United States. Collins auctioned off land (much of it under swamp water at the time), and dredged sand from the bay to transform it into solid ground. This created a yacht basin and several small islands. A pair of elephants, giveaways, super-salesmanship and a talented press agent helped finish the transformation from jungle to resort.

The area is renowned for its Art Deco architecture, evident in the beachfront hotels and buildings revitalized in the early 1990s. Though some say Miami Beach's day in the sun as a hot spot is long over (thanks to flocks of tourists and an influx of chain hotels and restaurants), it's still an exciting, unique place to visit, the closest thing the United States has to European sybaritic favorites like St. Tropez or Ibiza.

Information: Chamber of Commerce, 1920 Meridian Ave., Miami Beach, 305-674-1300; www.miamibeachchamber.com

ART DECO DISTRICT

From Sixth to 23rd streets, Lenox Court to Ocean Drive, 305-672-2014

A designated national historic district, this square-mile concentration of Art Deco, streamline *moderne* and Spanish Mediterranean Revival architecture is the most unique in the nation. Former Art Deco apartment buildings, ballrooms and warehouses have been restored to pastel-and-neon luminosity and sometimes serve as canvases for murals, trompe l'oeil images and elaborate graffiti created by local artists. Special events include classic films, exhibits, music, lectures and fashions. Guided walking tours Thursday evening and Friday, Saturday and Sunday mornings.

BASS MUSEUM OF ART

2121 Park Ave., Miami Beach, 305-673-7530; www.bassmuseum.org

Located in South Beach's Art Deco district, the Bass Museum features more than 3,000 works and claims title as the most comprehensive collection of art in the region. Highlights include Renaissance canvases by Botticelli and Rubens, Rembrandt sketches, Japanese woodblock prints and architectural photos charting the history of Miami Beach. Design fans will also appreciate the streamlined addition by Arata Isozaki, which includes outdoor sculpture terraces. Tuesday-Wednesday, Friday-Saturday 10 a.m.-5 p.m.; Thursday to 9 p.m.; Sunday 11 a.m.-5 p.m.

CASA CASUARINA

1116 Ocean Drive, Miami Beach, 305-672-6604; www.casacasuarina.com

This Ocean Drive mansion, built in the 1930s, is infamous for being the former home of famed Italian fashion designer Gianni Versace. Versace was gunned down on the front steps in 1997 by serial killer Andrew Cunanan. The house was later bought by a telecommunications billionaire who turned it into a private club and event space. The lavish house, with its outdoor, fountained courtyard, can be rented for private parties, and luxe guestrooms are available for overnight stays.

THE JEWISH MUSEUM

301 Washington Ave., Miami Beach, 305-672-5044; www.jewishmuseum.com

The Jewish Museum is dedicated to telling the story of the Florida Jewish Experience since 1763. Exhibits include a portrait series by well-known Jewish artists. The museum is housed in a former synagogue that had been built in 1936. The building has been fully renovated and in keeping with much of the rest of South Beach, has an Art Deco design with a copper dome, a marble bimah and 80 stained-glass windows. Admission is free on Saturdays. Tuesday-Sunday 10 a.m.-5 p.m.; closed on Monday, Jewish and civil holidays.

LINCOLN ROAD

Miami Beach

Second only to Ocean Drive in popularity, Lincoln Road has a wider range of restaurants and shops than on the more touristy Ocean Drive. Blocked off to traffic from Alton Road to Washington Avenue, this pedestrian mall is an ideal place to spend a few hours wandering through shops and art galleries and enjoying a meal at an outdoor café.

SOUTH BEACH

Extends south from Dade Boulevard, concentrated mainly along Ocean Drive

This area was spared from demolition through the efforts of citizens and local designers who began repainting and restoring Art Deco buildings from the 1920s, 1930s and 1940s using bright pastel colors. Subsequent redevelopment of the area transformed the structures into eclectic boutiques, galleries, hotels, nightclubs and restaurants specializing in alfresco dining overlooking the ocean.

THE WOLFSONIAN

1001 Washington Ave., Miami Beach, 305-531-1001; www.wolfsonian.fiu.edu

This Mediterranean Revival-style building has a collection of more than 80,000 European and American *objets d'art,* including furnishings, architectural elements, murals and poster art. Designs from the Industrialist through the Postmodern eras are the focus here. Academic year, Monday-Tuesday, Friday-Saturday 11 a.m.-6 p.m., Thursday to 9 p.m., Sunday noon-5 p.m.; summer, Thursday-Friday noon-9 p.m., Saturday-Sunday noon-6 p.m.

SPECIAL EVENTS
ART BASEL MIAMI

300 W. 41st St., Miami Beach, 305-674-1292; www.artbaselmiamibeach.com

This annual art festival has become the country's most important for established and emerging contemporary artists. Sister to the famed Art Basel show in Switzerland, the event takes place at 220 leading art galleries and various spots around Miami. First weekend in December.

ART DECO WEEKEND

Art Deco district, 305-672-2014; www.artdecoweekend.com

A celebration of Art Deco and popular culture from the 1930s. Vintage cars, music, tours and entertainment throughout the district. Mid-January.

INTERNATIONAL BOAT SHOW

Miami Beach Convention Center, 1901 Convention Center Drive,
Miami Beach, 305-673-7311; www.miamiboatshow.com

The annual Miami boat-fest takes over three venues showcasing ship varieties ranging from one-man wave runners to 75-foot executive yachts.

HOTELS
★★★ALBION HOTEL

1650 James Ave., Miami Beach, 305-913-1000, 800-782-3557; www.rubellhotels.com

The Albion Hotel's Art Deco building resembles an ocean liner, complete with port-holes for viewing swimmers. Guest rooms feature Art Deco décor and CD players, spa bathrobes and custom-made cucumber-scented bath amenities. 100 rooms. Pets accepted, some restrictions; fee. Two restaurants, bar. Fitness room. Outdoor pool. Airport transportation available. **$$**

★★★ALEXANDER ALL-SUITE OCEANFRONT RESORT

5225 Collins Ave., Miami Beach, 305-865-6500, 800-327-6121; www.alexanderhotel.com

Take in the West Indies-inspired décor at this all-suite resort on Millionaire's Row. Climb the spiral staircase to Shula's Steak House, take a dip in the lagoon pools or

FLORIDA

★
★
★
★
★

enjoy the view from your terrace. 133 rooms, all suites. Pets accepted, some restrictions; fee. Two restaurants, two bars. Fitness room, fitness classes available, spa. Beach. Two outdoor pools, two whirlpools. Airport transportation available. Business center. $$$

★★★BLUE MOON HOTEL

944 Collins Ave., Miami Beach, 305-673-2262, 800-553-7739;
www.bluemoonhotel.com
South Beach is home to the Blue Moon Hotel, a charming Mediterranean-style boutique hotel listed on the National Register of Historic Places. The surroundings are inviting, and well-appointed guest rooms are bright and stylish, featuring separate sitting areas, minibars and bathrobes. 75 rooms. Restaurant, bar. Outdoor pool, whirlpool. Business center. $$

★★CARDOZO HOTEL

1300 Ocean Drive, Miami Beach, 305-535-6500, 800-782-6500;
www.cardozohotel.com
43 rooms. Restaurant, bar. $$

★★CASA GRANDE SUITE HOTEL

834 Ocean Drive, Miami Beach, 305-672-7003, 866-420-2272;
www.casagrandesuitehotel.com
34 rooms, all suites. Pets accepted; fee. Restaurant, bar. Beach. $$$$

★★COURTYARD MIAMI BEACH OCEANFRONT

3925 Collins Ave., Miami Beach, 305-538-3373, 800-503-1432; www.courtyard.com
263 rooms. Restaurant, bar. Fitness room. Outdoor pool, whirlpool. $

★★★DELANO

1685 Collins Beach, Miami Beach, 305-672-2000, 800-697-1791; www.delanohotelmiami.com
The Delano almost single-handedly brought life back to Miami's South Beach. This Art Deco-turned-contemporary hotel opened in the mid-90s to much fanfare. Rooms and suites are the last word in minimalism, with clean lines and simple furnishings all in white. The poolside cabanas remain the place to see and be seen. 194 rooms. Wireless Internet access. Three restaurants, two bars. Children's activity center. Fitness room, fitness classes available, spa. Beach. Outdoor pool. Airport transportation available. Business center. $$$$

★★★FONTAINEBLEAU MIAMI BEACH RESORT

4441 Collins Ave., Miami Beach, 305-538-2000, 800-548-8886; www.fbresorts.com
This Miami Beach landmark is a three-building resort sitting on 20 tropical acres. With 190,000 square feet of meeting space it is a major business destination, but not without significant draws for leisure travelers such as the half-acre multi-pool with waterfalls. Though the pool will be closed this year for renovation, the seventh floor pool remains open, as does access to the beach. 1,328 rooms. Pets accepted. High-speed Internet access. Two restaurants, two bars. Children's activity center. Fitness room. Beach. Outdoor pool, children's pool, whirlpool. Business center. $$

112

FLORIDA

★
★ ★
★ ★
★

mobiltravelguide.com

★★FOUR POINTS BY SHERATON

4343 Collins Ave., Miami Beach, 305-531-7494, 800-525-6994; www.fourpoints.com
216 rooms. High-speed Internet access. Restaurant, bar. Fitness room. Beach. Outdoor pool, whirlpool. Business center. **$$**

★★★HOTEL NASH

1120 Collins Ave., Miami Beach, 305-674-7800, 800-403-6274; www.hotelnash.com
Housed in a building originally constructed in 1935, the Hotel Nash prides itself on elegant style and attentive service. A variety of rooms and suites are available, each appointed with modern blond wood furnishings and cool ivory tones. There are three small spa pools here—one freshwater, one saltwater and one mineral water—as well as the popular Mark's South Beach restaurant. The beach is just a block away, and great shopping and dining are nearby. 55 rooms. Complimentary continental breakfast. High-speed Internet access. Restaurant, bar. Fitness room, spa. Three outdoor pools, whirlpool. Airport transportation available. **$$**

★★★HOTEL OCEAN

1230 Ocean Drive, Miami Beach, 305-672-2579, 800-783-1725; www.hotelocean.com
Rooms at this oceanfront boutique hotel are decorated with crisp linens in fresh colors of the sea, contemporary furniture and flatscreen TVs. The concierge can secure VIP passes to South Beach's hottest clubs. A new location of Hosteria Romana, an authentic Italian restaurant, recently opened at the hotel. 27 rooms. Pets accepted; fee. Complimentary continental breakfast. High-speed Internet access. Restaurant, bar. Beach. Whirlpool. Airport transportation available. **$$$**

★★★★LOEWS MIAMI BEACH HOTEL

1601 Collins Ave., Miami Beach, 305-604-1601, 800-235-6397; www.loewshotels.com
This hotel's architecture blends Art Deco landmark the St. Moritz hotel with new construction to form a thoroughly modern hotel. Guest rooms are decorated in the soothing hues of sun, sand and sea. Celebrity chef Emeril Lagasse gives the seafood-heavy menu at his onsite restaurant, Emeril's South Beach, a Creole accent. 790 rooms. Pets accepted. High-speed Internet access. Direct access to beach. Three restaurants, three bars. Children's activity center. Fitness room, fitness classes available, spa. Beach. Outdoor pool, whirlpool. Airport transportation available. Business center. **$$$**

★MARLIN HOTEL-AN ISLAND OUTPOST HOTEL

1200 Collins Ave., Miami Beach, 305-604-3595; www.marlinhotel.com
13 rooms. Pets accepted, some restrictions; fee. Wireless Internet access. Restaurant, bar. **$$**

★★★MARRIOTT SOUTH BEACH

161 Ocean Drive, Miami Beach, 305-536-7700, 800-228-9290; www.marriott.com
A full-service oceanfront resort on the southern edge of South Beach, the stylish Marriott, though newly constructed, keeps pace with its Art Deco neighbors via a vintage-inspired exterior and Art Deco accents. Guest rooms are comfortable and business-ready with dual-line phones and high-speed Internet access. A spacious pool is connected to the beach. 236 rooms. High-speed Internet access. Restaurant, bar.

FLORIDA

★
★
★
★
☆

Fitness room, spa. Beach. Outdoor pool, whirlpool. Airport transportation available. Business center. $$$

★★★MERCURY RESORT & SPA

100 Collins Ave., Miami Beach, 305-398-3000; www.mercuryresort.com

This all-suite boutique hotel is just a block from the beach. Sleek and modern, the guest rooms feature Italian furniture in creamy neutral tones. Amenities include two TVs, a music system with CD library, imported linens and marble baths with whirlpool spa. The resort's three restaurants offer everything from sushi to comfort food, while the onsite day spa offers hot stone massage and four-handed Thai massage. 39 rooms. Pets accepted, some restrictions. High-speed Internet access. Three restaurants, bar. Fitness room, spa. Outdoor pool, whirlpool. Airport transportation available. $$$

★★★MIAMI BEACH RESORT & SPA

4833 Collins Ave., Miami Beach, 305-532-3600, 866-767-6060;
www.miamibeachresortandspa.com

This boutique-style resort with Old World charm is located on Millionaires Row. 424 rooms. Wireless Internet access. Three restaurants, two bars. Fitness room, spa. Beach. Outdoor pool, children's pool. Business center. $$$

★★★NATIONAL HOTEL

1677 Collins Ave., Miami Beach, 305-532-2311, 800-327-8370; www.nationalhotel.com

This restored historic hotel functions as the heart of the South Beach Art Deco district. The famous long, narrow pool and its snack bar is a popular place to see and be seen. 151 rooms. High-speed Internet access. Two restaurants, two bars. Fitness room, fitness classes available. Beach. Two outdoor pools. Business center. $$$$

★★RALEIGH MIAMI BEACH

1775 Collins Ave., Miami Beach, 305-534-6300, 800-848-1775; www.raleighhotel.com

104 rooms. Pets accepted. Wireless Internet access. Three restaurants, three bars. Beach. Outdoor pool. Airport transportation available. $$$

★★★RENAISSANCE EDEN ROC MIAMI BEACH RESORT AND SPA

4525 Collins Ave., Miami Beach, 786-276-0526, 800-319-5354; www.edenrocresort.com

Closed until February 2008 for renovations, this mid-century Miami Beach classic will have updated amenities. The oceanfront bar is a boardwalk hotspot, but don't miss drinks in the lobby lounge, faithfully outfitted with mid-century modern sofas and chairs. 632 rooms. Pets accepted, some restrictions; fee. High-speed Internet access. Two restaurants, two bars. Children's activity center. Fitness room, fitness classes available, spa. Beach. Two outdoor pools, two whirlpools. Airport transportation available. Business center. $$$

★★★★THE RITZ-CARLTON, SOUTH BEACH

1 Lincoln Road, Miami Beach, 786-276-4000, 800-241-3333; www.ritzcarlton.com

This landmark property, originally designed by legendary Miami architect Morris Lapidus, boasts an ideal location—the foot of South Beach's Lincoln Road Mall on the Atlantic Ocean. Rooms feature nautical hues, views of the ocean and luxury touches like marble baths and feather-topped beds. The 16,000-square-foot La Maison de Beaute Carita spa is the centerpiece of the resort. Dining choices abound here, including restaurants that feature Caribbean, New American and Floridian cuisine served in a variety of elegant and informal settings. 375 rooms. Pets accepted, some restrictions; fee. High-speed Internet access. Four restaurants, four bars. Children's activity center. Fitness room, spa. Beach. Outdoor pool, whirlpool. Airport transportation available. Business center.

★★★ROYAL PALM

1545 Collins Ave., Miami Beach, 786-276-0100; www.royalpalmmiamibeach.com
Where Ocean Drive ends, the high-rise Royal Palm Resort begins, splitting the distance between the party scene south and luxury hotels north—both walking distance from this hotel. The resort sees plenty of business traffic bound for the massive convention center nearby. Beach concierge service includes chaise lounges and umbrellas. Color-mad artist Romero Britto decorated the lobby restaurant, ensuring that every breakfast is an eye-opener. 414 rooms. Pets accepted; fee. Wireless Internet access. Restaurant, three bars. Fitness room, fitness classes available. Beach. Outdoor pool, whirlpool. Airport transportation available. Business center. $$$

★★★★THE SETAI

2001 Collins Ave., Miami Beach, 305-520-6000; www.setai.com
Set on the oceanfront, rooms at the Setai are sleek and simple with hardwood floors, neutral tones, crisp white linens and black granite bathrooms. Luxurious amenities include in-room tubs, Aqua di Parma bath products, waterfall showers and plasma televisions. The Spa at the Setai features private spa suites with ocean views and a fully-equipped gym with personal trainers. At the end of the day, satiate your appetite with a meal at the Restaurant, where a menu of French- and Asian-inspired fare awaits. 75 rooms. High-speed Internet access. Restaurant, bar. Fitness room, fitness classes available, spa. Outdoor pool. $$$$

★★★THE TIDES HOTEL

1220 Ocean Drive, Miami Beach, 305-604-5070, 800-439-4095;
www.thetideshotel.com
This Art Deco landmark has been completely reimagined by star designer Kelly Wearstler. Her signature Hollywood regency style is lightened to reflect the beachfront location, with crisp white linens, natural materials of bleached wood and shell and glamorous touches from zebra rugs to guilt mirrors. The new onsite restaurant, La Marea, is an exercise in style and restraint, from the beach chic décor to the Mediterranean menu. 45 rooms, all suites. Pets accepted, some restrictions; fee. Wireless Internet access. Restaurant, two bars. Fitness room. Outdoor pool. Business center. $$$$

RESTAURANTS
★★BALANS

1022 Lincoln Road, Miami Beach, 305-534-9191; www.balans.co.uk
International menu. Breakfast, lunch, dinner, brunch. Bar. Casual attire. Reservations recommended. Outdoor seating. $$

★
★
★
★
★

★BIG PINK

157 Collins Ave., Miami Beach, 305-532-4700; www.bigpinkrestaurant.com

American menu. Breakfast, lunch, dinner, late-night. Bar. Children's menu. Casual attire. Outdoor seating, free delivery. **$$**

★★★★BLUE DOOR

1685 Collins Ave., Miami Beach, 305-674-6400; www.delano-hotel.com

You don't have to take a test to eat at Blue Door, but a certain level of cultural literacy is necessary to fully appreciate the experience. For example, you must appreciate that the chef giving Blue Door's French cuisine a Pan-Asian and tropical twist (think duck breast with nine-spice ginger sauce) is the acclaimed Claude Troisgras. You must appreciate that architect Philippe Starck designed the all-white, tropical-cool décor of the restaurant and Delano hotel. Dinner is also theater here, and it always earns a rave review. French, Brazilian menu. Breakfast, lunch, dinner, Sunday brunch. Bar. Children's menu. Business casual attire. Reservations recommended. Valet parking. Outdoor seating. **$$$**

★★★BONDST LOUNGE

150 20th St., Miami Beach, 305-398-1806; www.townhousehotel.com

Located in the swank Town House Hotel, Bond Street is a Zen tribute to Japanese cuisine tweaked for the chic American palate. Everyone from the waitstaff to the diners—delicately snacking on shimmering slices of sushi and sashimi while sipping cool saketinis—looks as though they just stepped out of the pages of a fashion magazine. Japanese, sushi menu. Dinner, late-night. Bar. Casual attire. **$$**

★★CAFFE MILANO

850 Ocean Drive, Miami Beach, 305-532-0707; www.cafemilano.com

Italian menu. Lunch, dinner, late-night. Bar. Children's menu. Casual attire. Reservations recommended. Valet parking. Outdoor seating. **$$$**

★★★CHINA GRILL

404 Washington Ave., Miami Beach, 305-534-2211; www.chinagrillmgt.com

The sibling of the original New York hotspot does just as well at serving loud, happy crowds its splashy signature family-style Chinese fare. Make sure to try the Peking duck and endive salad and the ahi sashimi tempura with wasabi dipping sauce. Pan-Asian menu. Lunch, dinner, late-night. Bar. Children's menu. Casual attire. Reservations recommended. Valet parking. Outdoor seating. **$$**

★★ESCOPAZZO

1311 Washington Ave., Miami Beach, 305-674-9450; www.escopazzo.com

Italian menu. Dinner, late-night. Bar. Business casual attire. Reservations recommended. **$$$**

★FLÛTE CHAMPAGNE LOUNGE

500 S. Pointe Drive, Miami Beach, 305-674-8680; www.flutebar.com

American menu, desserts and appetizers. Late-night. Closed Thanksgiving, Christmas. Bar. Casual attire. Outdoor seating. **$**

★★FRONT PORCH CAFÉ
1418 Ocean Drive, Miami Beach, 305-531-8300
American menu. Breakfast, lunch, dinner. Outdoor seating. **$$**

★★★JOE ALLEN
1787 Purdy Ave., Miami Beach, 305-531-7007; www.joeallenrestaurant.com
Located on the west side of South Beach overlooking Biscayne Bay, Joe Allen offers a great selection of simple and hearty dishes in a lively and comfortable room. The restaurant's appeal is its ability to turn out well-prepared, moderately priced and stylish comfort food like burgers, meatloaf and wood-fired pizzas. American menu. Lunch, dinner, late-night, Sunday brunch. Bar. Casual attire. Reservations recommended. **$$**

★★LARIOS ON THE BEACH
820 Ocean Drive, Miami Beach, 305-532-9577
Cuban menu. Lunch, dinner, late-night. Bar. Children's menu. Casual attire. Reservations recommended. Valet parking. Outdoor seating. **$$**

★★★MARK'S SOUTH BEACH
1120 Collins Ave., Miami Beach, 305-604-9050; www.chefmark.com
At Mark's South Beach, chef Mark Militello offers savvy Floridian cuisine, with Caribbean, Asian and local ingredients in signature dishes such as the potato-crusted Pacific oysters with horseradish, crème fraîche and caviar; peppercorn/lavender-spiced Moulard duck breast with wild rice pecan flan and foie gras huckleberry sauce; and a tasting of exotic homemade sorbets with watermelon carpaccio and Mojito nage. But the food isn't the only attraction here—the restaurant offers indoor and outdoor Art Deco dining. American menu. Lunch, dinner, Sunday brunch. Bar. Casual attire. Valet parking. Outdoor seating. **$$$**

★★NEMO
100 Collins Ave., Miami Beach, 305-532-4550; www.nemorestaurant.com
International menu. Lunch, dinner, Sunday brunch. Bar. Business casual attire. Reservations recommended. Valet parking. Outdoor seating. **$$$**

★★NEWS CAFÉ
800 Ocean Drive, Miami Beach, 305-538-6397; www.newscafe.com
International menu. Breakfast, lunch, dinner, late-night. Bar. Casual attire. Valet parking. Outdoor seating. **$$**

★★OSTERIA DEL TEATRO
1443 Washington Ave., Miami Beach, 305-538-7850
Italian menu. Dinner. Closed Sunday. Bar. Business casual attire. Reservations recommended. Valet parking. **$$**

★★★PACIFIC TIME
915 Lincoln Road, Miami Beach, 305-534-5979; www.pacifictime.biz
The Asian-influenced, perfectly prepared food is just as enticing as the people-watching at this Lincoln Road eatery. East-West cuisine often seems jumbled, but the kitchen here delivers clean, bright flavors and exciting combinations like filet of

sole in lemongrass and tomato broth, and savory lamb and wild mushroom dumplings. Pacific-Rim/Pan-Asian menu. Dinner. Bar. Casual attire. Reservations recommended. Valet parking. Outdoor seating. $$$

★★SHOJI SUSHI

100 Collins Ave., Miami Beach, 305-532-4245; www.shojisushi.com

Japanese, sushi menu. Lunch, dinner, late-night. Bar. Casual attire. Reservations recommended. Outdoor seating. $$$

★★★SMITH AND WOLLENSKY

1 Washington Ave., Miami Beach, 305-673-2800, 888-517-8325;
www.smithandwollensky.com

This branch of the national steakhouse chain features an elegant space with a waterfront location where you can enjoy its fabulous prime-grade beef, dry aged in-house for 28 days. Whether you feast on the double sirloin, filet mignon or sliced steak Wollensky, you'll put the signature, oversized steak knife to good use. At lunch service during spring's Wine Week, $10 will buy you a sample from up to 10 selections from the extensive wine list. Steak menu. Lunch, dinner, late-night. Bar. Casual attire. Reservations recommended. Valet parking. Outdoor seating. $$$

★★SUSHI ROCK CAFÉ

1351 Collins Ave., Miami Beach, 305-532-2133; www.sushirockcafe.com

Sushi menu. Lunch, dinner, late-night. Bar. Casual attire. Outdoor seating. $$

★★★TUSCAN STEAK

433 Washington Ave., Miami Beach, 305-534-2233; www.chinagrillmanagement.com

You would expect an exemplary "biftecca alla fiorentina" at a restaurant called Tuscan Steak and that's what you get. The excellent Tuscan food, served family style, and the beautifully renovated Art Deco space attract a fashionable, noisy crowd. Italian, steak menu. Dinner. Bar. Business casual attire. Reservations recommended. Valet parking. $$$

★★★★WISH

801 Collins Ave., Miami Beach, 305-674-9474; www.wishrestaurant.com

Dining at Wish, located in the Hotel, is paradise. Avocado, watermelon, plantains, cilantro and ginger are used to perfectly accent everything on the menu, from ceviche and salad to fish, poultry and beef. The kitchen is careful to balance the familiar with the exotic so that the menu remains exciting. Because this is the land of the lean, you won't find a cream sauce in sight. But the sauces are divine. Clean and light, brightened with citrus juices or vegetable purées, olive oil and herbs, they practically sparkle on the plate. There's a house cocktail list in addition to an extensive international wine list. American, pan-Asian menu. Breakfast, lunch, Tuesday-Sunday. Bar. Children's menu. Business casual attire. Reservations recommended. Valet parking. Outdoor seating. $$$

★★★YUCA

501 Lincoln Road, Miami Beach, 305-532-9822; www.yuca.com

Opened in 1989, Yuca—an acronym for Young Urban Cuban-Americans—is the original icon of Nuevo Latino cuisine in South Beach. It continues to serve Cuban fare in a splashy dining room filled with a who's who of local notables. While there has been a succession of chefs in the kitchen, the cuisine has not suffered. Plantains, lime, cilantro and other spices punctuate the menu. Cuban, Latin American menu. Lunch, dinner. Bar. Business casual attire. Reservations recommended. Outdoor seating. $$

SPAS

★★★★THE RITZ-CARLTON, SOUTH BEACH SPA

1 Lincoln Road, Miami Beach, 786-276-4000, 800-241-3333; www.ritzcarlton.com

Sybarites book appointments at this Carita spa to experience therapies that beautify and detoxify. Carita is well-known for its anti-aging treatments, which can be experienced in many of the facial and body treatments. Relaxation is paramount here, where massage therapies cover everything from Swedish, Shiatsu and deep tissue varieties to more unique sand stone therapy. Services include pre- and post-party therapies, while those who overindulge at the beach can seek solace in the spa's nourishing after-sun treatments.

★★★★THE SPA AT THE SETAI

2001 Collins Ave., Miami Beach, 305-520-6000; www.setai.com

Asian simplicity and elegance are the inspiration for this tranquil oceanfront retreat. Surrounded by lush gardens and with views of the Atlantic Ocean, the Spa at the Setai feels like a remote haven tucked away in a corner of Southeast Asia. Four treatment suites feature private steam rooms and showers for quiet relaxation before or after treatments. The Balinese massage is a deep-pressure technique that relieves muscular tension and stimulates the lymphatic system. Or try the Langkawi Bamboo Body Polish, during which tiny rejuvenating pearls of bamboo and ginseng are used to invigorate the body and mind and improve circulation.

MOUNT DORA

This central Florida town north of Orlando has a quaint, historic downtown that's as American as apple pie. The area is antique-shopping heaven and beautiful Lake Dora provides a scenic backdrop. Shaded by lovely oak trees and nestled in rolling hills—an oddity in Florida—Mount Dora has a large collection of specialty shops as well as unusual restaurants and an inn.

Information: Mount Dora Area Chamber of Commerce, 341 Alexander St.,
Mount Dora, 352-383-2165; www.mountdora.com

WHAT TO SEE AND DO

RENNINGER'S TWIN MARKETS

20651 Highway 441, Mount Dora, 352-383-3141; www.renningersflorida.com

Renninger's, a massive complex located on 117 acres just east of town, boasts not only an Antique Center but also a Farmer's & Flea Market on weekends. Antique Mart, Saturday-Sunday 9 a.m.-5 p.m., Farmer's & Flea Market 8 a.m.-4 p.m.

TOURING MOUNT DORA AND OCALA

Travel north out of Orlando on Highway 441 to reach the charming Victorian town of Mount Dora on Route 46. Known for its antique shops, bed and breakfasts and biking trails, downtown Mount Dora offers shopping, great dining spots and a chance to check out the remarkable architecture of the area. Stop in at Royellou Museum, which is housed in the old city firehouse and jail. Take your pick of sightseeing adventures: The *Miss Dora* tour boat takes you through a canal between two lakes to see wildlife and Old Florida scenery, and the *Mount Dora Cannonball* and the *Dora Doodlebug* offer tours via rail.

Out of Mount Dora, follow Route 19A to Route 19 and travel straight into the spring lands of Ocala National Forest. You can also continue on Highway 441 (via Highway 27) into historic Ocala itself. Ocala National Forest, about 20 miles from Mount Dora, provides vast pineland acreage famous for its mineral springs that is divided into several different recreational areas where you can camp, canoe, swim, hike and dive. Juniper Springs (located on Route 40, west of Route 19) offers the most to see and do, including a scenic waterwheel-powered mill at the rock-edged spring swimming hole.

On the way to Jupiter Springs, you will pass Silver Springs, Florida's original theme park. The setting for many Tarzan movies, Silver Springs became famous when it introduced glass-bottom boat rides, which are still conducted over crystal-clear waters into woods filled with free-roaming monkeys. Inside the park, shows, safaris and other attractions feature all kinds of creatures. The park also contains an antique car and racecar museum and a petting zoo. Next door, Wild Waters Water Park is open for cooling off during the warm months.

Downtown Ocala and surrounding residential streets feature vintage architecture. In the old movie theater you will find Discovery Science Center, fun for the kids with hands-on science experiments and games. Be sure to ride around the Ocala countryside to look at the pure green mineral springs-fed grass and the thoroughbred horse ranches that take advantage of the natural setting. Some of the horse farms welcome visitors; check with the local chamber of commerce. *Approximately 75 miles.*

HOTELS

★★LAKESIDE INN

100 N. Alexander St., Mount Dora, 352-383-4101, 800-556-5016; www.lakeside-inn.com

88 rooms. Complimentary continental breakfast. Restaurant. Outdoor pool. Tennis. **$**

★★★MISSION INN GOLF RESORT

10400 County Road 48, Howey-in-the-Hills, 352-324-3101, 800-874-9053;
www.missioninnresort.com

Built in 1924 by the city's namesake, William Howey, this resort was restored by the Beucher family in 1969. Its Spanish colonial buildings and manicured courtyard gardens remain in its ownership today. Golf is the highlight with 36 championship holes. 176 rooms. Restaurant, bar. Fitness room. Outdoor pool, whirlpool. Golf, 36 holes. Tennis. Airport transportation available. Business center. **$$**

RESTAURANT

★★★EL CONQUISTADOR

10400 Country Road 48, Howey-in-the-Hills, 352-324-2024;
www.missioninnresort.com

This fine dining restaurant housed in the Mission Inn resort overlooks the central plaza and offers a menu of classically prepared seafood and steak options. Monthly wine dinners are a popular local event. Continental menu. Dinner. Bar. Reservations recommended. $$$

NAPLES

Named after the Italian city and complete with a "Bay of Naples," this Gulf of Mexico resort community has grown steadily since 1950. Ten miles of beach and a 1,000-foot fishing pier are tourist favorites. Naples is also home to more than 60 golf courses and a stop on the Senior PGA Tour.

Information: Naples Area Chamber of Commerce, 2390 Tamiami Trail North,
239-262-6376; www.napleschamber.org

WHAT TO SEE AND DO

CARIBBEAN GARDENS: THE ZOO IN NAPLES

1590 Goodlette-Frank Road, Naples, 239-262-5409; www.caribbeangardens.com

A 52-acre botanical garden with animals, birds and plants from around the world; boat tours, wild animal shows, tropical bird circus, lectures. Picnic area, snack bar, petting zoo, gift shop. Daily 9:30 a.m.-5:30 p.m.

CORKSCREW SWAMP SANCTUARY

375 Sanctuary Road, Naples, 239-348-9151; www.corkscrew.audubon.org

This National Audubon Society preserve contains one of the largest stands of mature bald cypress trees; two-mile boardwalk loops through the swamp; self-guided tour. Picnic area. Visitor center. Mid-April-late September, daily 7 a.m.-7:30 p.m.; October-mid-April, daily 7 a.m.-5:30 p.m.

DELNOR-WIGGINS PASS STATE RECREATION AREA

11100 Gulfshore Drive, Naples, 239-597-6196; www.floridastateparks.org

This beachfront island park is known for fishing, shelling and swimming; picnicking, observation tower, loggerhead turtle talks in summer. Daily 8 a.m.-sundown.

ROOKERY BAY NATIONAL ESTUARINE RESEARCH RESERVE

300 Tower Road, Naples, 239-417-6310; www.rookerybay.org

This 9,400-acre reserve encompasses a variety of habitats, including extensive mangrove forests, sea grasses, salt marshes and upland pine flatwoods; various wildlife and bird species can be observed; slide shows, interpretive displays, nature center with boat and canoe trips (winter) and guided boardwalk tours. Fishing; hiking. Daily.

HOTELS

★★★BAYFRONT INN FIFTH AVENUE

1221 Fifth Ave. S., Naples, 239-649-5800, 800-382-7941; www.bayfrontinnnaples.com

One mile from the beach, this hotel is located on the bay and within walking distance to Tin City, Bayfront Marketplace and other shops. Guest rooms feature a contemporary décor with rich, dark wood. The restaurant and bar offer a relaxing place to sit

★
★
★
★
★

and enjoy the view of the bay. A 12-slip marina is located here, and boat rentals are offered. 98 rooms. Complimentary continental breakfast. Wireless Internet access. Restaurant, bar. Outdoor pool, whirlpool. Business center. $$

★BEST WESTERN NAPLES INN & SUITES

2329 N. Ninth St., Naples, 239-261-1148, 800-243-1148; www.bestwesternnaples.com
110 rooms. Complimentary continental breakfast. High-speed Internet access. Children under 18 free in same room. Pets not accepted. Two outdoor pools, whirlpools. Business center. $

★★★EDGEWATER BEACH HOTEL & CLUB

1901 Gulf Shore Blvd. N., Naples, 888-325-7711; www.edgewaternaples.com
This contemporary beachfront hotel offers suites with a crisp, clean design and plenty of luxury amenities. Beds are topped with fluffy duvets, rooms have plasma TVs, the bathrooms have modern granite surfaces and rainshowers, and kitchens come fully stocked. The resort offers a long stretch of sandy beach, heated outdoor pool and fully renovated fitness facility. 126 rooms. Restaurant, bar. Children's activity center. Fitness room. Outdoor pool. $$$

★★★HILTON NAPLES AND TOWERS

5111 Tamiami Trail N,. Naples, 239-430-4900, 800-445-8667; www.hiltonnaples.com
This richly decorated hotel is located in Naples' business and shopping districts and near the beach. Contemporary guest rooms and the lobby area are tastefully decorated, and lush grounds surround the pool area. Onsite activities include basketball, ping-pong and bicycling. The ever popular Shula's Steakhouse serves lunch and dinner. 199 rooms. Wireless Internet access. Restaurant, bar. Fitness room. Outdoor pool, whirlpool. Airport transportation available. Business center. $$

★★★HYATT REGENCY COCONUT POINT

5001 Coconut Road, Bonita Springs, 239-444-1234, 800-233-1234;
www.coconutpoint.hyatt.com
From the secluded beach to the 140-foot water slide, this resort revolves around water. Even the onsite Stillwater Spa echoes the aquatic theme. Comfortable guest rooms feature Floridian décor in tropical shades of peach and sage, marble-topped vanities and balconies with views. The hotel is located between Fort Myers and Naples and close to the Southwest International Airport. 456 rooms. Restaurant, bar. Fitness room. Two outdoor pools, children's pool, whirlpool. Airport transportation available. Business center. $$$

★INN AT NAPLES

4055 Tamiami Trail N., Naples, 239-649-5500, 800-895-8858; www.innofnaples.com
99 rooms. Pets accepted, some restrictions; fee. Complimentary continental breakfast. Wireless Internet access. Fitness room. Outdoor pool. Business center. $$

★INN AT PELICAN BAY

800 Vanderbilt Beach Road, Naples, 239-597-8777, 800-597-8770;
www.innatpelicanbay.com
100 rooms. Complimentary continental breakfast. Wireless Internet access. Bar. Fitness room. Outdoor pool, whirlpool. Business center. $$

★★★INN ON FIFTH

699 Fifth Ave. S., Naples, 239-403-8777, 888-403-8778; www.naplesinn.com

Formerly a bank built in the 1950s, this elegant inn is richly decorated in Mediterranean décor and features marble flooring, elaborate chandeliers and wrought-iron balconies. Situated in the heart of downtown Naples, this hotel is surrounded by boutiques and restaurants. 87 rooms. Complimentary continental breakfast. Restaurant, bar. Fitness room. Outdoor pool, whirlpool. $$$

★★★LAPLAYA BEACH & GOLF RESORT

9891 Gulf Shore Drive, Naples, 239-597-3123, 800-237-6883; www.laplayaresort.com

With the Gulf on one side and the bay on the other, this resort has beautiful views from every direction. Waterfalls and lush plants surround the pool area, and a large covered porch awaits guests who want to relax in one of the rocking chairs. Shuffleboard, bike rentals, wave runners and parasailing are among the activities offered onsite. 189 rooms. Pets accepted, some restrictions. Restaurant, bar. Children's activity center. Fitness room, spa. Beach. Outdoor pool, whirlpool. Golf. $$$

★★★NAPLES BEACH HOTEL & GOLF CLUB

851 Gulf Shore Blvd. N., Naples, 239-261-2222, 800-455-1546;
www.naplesbeachhotel.com

Orchids are the theme here, with various colors and sizes displayed throughout the hotel. Rooms feature plantation shutters and balconies. One- and two-bedroom suites are also available. Volleyball, kayaks, paddleboats and bike rentals are all onsite, as are boutiques and a golf shop. 318 rooms. Restaurant, bar. Children's activity center. Outdoor pool. Golf. $$$

123

★★★NAPLES GRANDE BEACH RESORT

475 Seagate Drive, Naples, 239-597-3232, 888-422-6177;
www.naplesgranderesort.com

The Naples Grande Resort & Club captures the elegance of this western Florida resort town. Spacious guest rooms are richly decorated and well equipped, with lots of attention to detail. Contemporary one- and two-bedroom villas are also available. Three miles of beach fronting the Gulf of Mexico are accessed by a tram that winds its way through some of the resort's 300 acres of mangrove forest. 474 rooms. Complimentary continental breakfast. Three restaurants, two bars. Children's activity center. Fitness room, fitness classes available, spa. Beach. Five outdoor pools, children's pool, three whirlpools. Golf, 18 holes. Tennis. Business center. $$$

★★PARK SHORE RESORT

600 Neapolitan Way, Naples, 239-263-2222, 888-627-1595; www.parkshorefl.com

156 rooms, all suites. Restaurant, bar. Children's activity center. Outdoor pool, whirlpool. Tennis. $$$

★★QUALITY INN & SUITES GOLF RESORT

4100 Golden Gate Parkway, Naples, 239-455-1010, 800-277-0017;
www.naplesgolfresort.com

170 rooms. Restaurant, bar. Outdoor pool, whirlpool. Golf. $

FLORIDA

★
★
★
★
★

★★★★THE RITZ-CARLTON GOLF RESORT, NAPLES

2600 Tiburon Drive, Naples, 239-593-2000, 800-241-3333; www.ritzcarlton.com

Greg Norman's award-winning Tiburon golf course is the focal point at the Ritz-Carlton Golf Resort, Naples. Just three miles down the road from its beachfront sister property, the course is legendary for its beauty and challenge. The onsite Rick Smith Golf Academy offers its innovative instructional techniques. The resort's architecture presents a fresh take on the Mediterranean villa, with vibrant colors, red-tiled roof and striped awnings. Guests may take advantage of the sister property's spa and other amenities, though many choose to remain here, with fantastic dining options and splendid views. 295 rooms. Pets accepted, some restrictions; fee. High-speed Internet access. Restaurant, two bars. Children's activity center. Fitness room. Outdoor pool, whirlpool. Golf, 36 holes. Tennis. Airport transportation available. Business center. $$$

★★★★★THE RITZ-CARLTON, NAPLES

280 Vanderbilt Beach Road, Naples, 239-598-3300, 800-241-3333;
www.ritzcarlton.com

Three miles of white-sand beaches attract visitors to this Mediterranean-inspired resort. Take part in water sports, sample the menu at the full-service spa or take the shuttle to the Ritz Carlton Golf Resort just down the road. Guest rooms are beautifully appointed with European-style décor. The hotel's multimillion dollar art collection of 18th- and 19th-century British and American pieces is on prominent display throughout the property. Seven restaurants run the gamut from casual poolside cafés and beach pavilions to formal establishments that encourage guests to dress for dinner. 463 rooms. High-speed Internet access. Seven restaurants, six bars. Children's activity center. Fitness room, fitness classes available, spa. Beach. Two outdoor pools, children's pool, whirlpool. Golf, 36 holes. Tennis. Airport transportation available. Business center. $$$$

★★VANDERBILT BEACH RESORT

9225 Gulfshore Drive North, Naples, 239-597-3144, 800-243-9076;
www.vanderbiltbeachresort.com

50 rooms. High-speed Internet access. Restaurant, bar. Beach. Outdoor pool. Tennis. $

RESTAURANTS

★★★★ARTISANS IN THE DINING ROOM

280 Vanderbilt Beach Road, Ritz-Carlton, Naples, 239-598-3300, 800-241-3333;
www.ritzcarlton.com

Artisans is an intimate space that gives the feeling of dining in a private home, even if it's a home that is more like a castle. The space is elaborately decorated with dark-wood china cabinets, tropical floral arrangements and 19th-century paintings. The capable kitchen staff prepares a menu degustation and a blind tasting menu, a selection of dishes prepared at the chef's whim. The gifted wine stewards will confidently assist in pairing wines with the meal. The champagne brunch on Sundays comes with live jazz and enough food to keep you satiated for the rest of the week. Seafood menu. Dinner, Sunday brunch. Closed Monday; also August-early September. Bar. Children's menu. Business casual attire. Reservations recommended. Valet parking. Outdoor seating. $$$$

★★BAYSIDE SEAFOOD GRILL

4270 N. Gulf Shore Blvd., Naples, 239-649-5552; www.baysideseafoodgrillandbar.com

Seafood menu. Lunch, dinner, Sunday brunch. Two bars. Children's menu. Casual attire. Valet parking. Outdoor seating. **$$**

★★BHA! BHA! PERSIAN BISTRO

847 Vanderbilt Beach Road, Naples, 239-594-5557; www.bhabhapersianbistro.com

Persian menu. Lunch, dinner, Sunday brunch. Casual attire. Reservations recommended. Outdoor seating. **$$**

★★★BLEU PROVENCE

1234 Eighth St. S., Naples, 239-261-8239; www.bleuprovencenaples.com

Perfect for special occasions, this downtown Old Naples restaurant features whitewashed floors and tables topped with candles and fresh flowers. Located in an upscale neighborhood, the outdoor garden is enhanced with Italian lights for a warm ambience. A wine selection of 12,000 bottles and 1,000 varieties is available. French, Mediterranean menu. Dinner. Bar. Business casual attire. Reservations recommended. Outdoor seating. **$$$**

★★BOATHOUSE

990 Broad Ave. S., Naples, 239-643-2235; www.boathousenaples.com

Seafood menu. Lunch, dinner. Bar. Children's menu. Casual attire. Outdoor seating. **$$$**

★★CAMPIELLO

1177 Third St. S., Naples, 239-435-1166; www.campiello.damico.com

Italian menu. Lunch, dinner. Bar. Casual attire. Reservations recommended. Outdoor seating. **$$$**

★GASTRONOMIA CIAO

835 Fourth Ave. S., Naples, 239-263-3889; www.ristoranteciao.com

Italian menu. Lunch. Casual attire. Closed Saturday-Sunday. **$$**

★★★THE GRILL

280 Vanderbilt Beach Road, Naples, 239-598-3300, 800-241-3333;
www.ritzcarlton.com

Situated right off the lobby of the Ritz-Carlton, Naples, The Grill feels like an exclusive club with its warm, wood paneling, exclusive artwork and fireplace and live music nightly. The menu, created by chef de Cuisine Trevor Hill, focuses on All-American cuisine. The emphasis is on grilled meats, including filet mignon, ribeye, New York strip, Colorado rack of lamb, veal and pork chops. Seafood and fowl are also available with choices such as fennel-glazed chilean sea bass. The chef even offers a heart-healthy menu with items such as wild salmon seared in olive oil. Steak menu. Dinner. Closed August-early September. Bar. Children's menu. Business casual attire. Reservations recommended. Valet parking. **$$$$**

★★LE BISTRO

842 Neopolitan Way, Naples, 239-434-7061

French menu. Dinner. Casual attire. Outdoor seating. Closed Sunday; holidays; also early June-early October. **$$**

FLORIDA

★
★
★
★

★★★LEMONIA

2600 Tiburon Drive, Naples, 239-593-2000, 800-241-3333; www.ritzcarlton.com

Chef Massimo Veronesi studied all over Verona, Tuscany and Milan before honing his skills at the Ritz-Carlton Golf Resort, Naples. Under his charge, Lemonia offers both indoor and alfresco dining and a contemporary Tuscan menu. Dishes include marinated salmon tartare with basil, tarragon and citrus fruit dressing, or crispy Mediterranean sea bass with tomato compote and saffron sauce. For a different kind of indulgence, visit the restaurant on Sunday morning for its spectacular brunch buffet. Italian menu. Breakfast, lunch, dinner, Sunday brunch. Bar. Children's menu. Business casual attire. Reservations recommended. Valet parking. Outdoor seating. $$$

★★MAXWELL'S ON THE BAY

4300 N. Gulf Shore Blvd., Naples, 239-263-4421; www.maxwellsonthebay.com

Seafood menu. Lunch, dinner, Sunday brunch. Bar. Children's menu. Casual attire. Valet parking (dinner). Outdoor seating. $$$

★★PEWTER MUG

12300 N. Tamiami Trail, Naples, 239-597-3017; www.pewtermug.net

Seafood, steak menu. Dinner. Bar. Children's menu. Casual attire. $$

★★ST. GEORGE & THE DRAGON

936 Fifth Ave. S., Naples, 239-262-6546; www.stgeorgeandthedragon.com

American menu. Lunch, dinner. Bar. Children's menu. Jacket required (main dining room). Valet parking. Closed Sunday; December 25. $$$

★TONY'S OFF THIRD

1300 Third St. S., Naples, 239-262-7999; www.tonysoffthird.com

American, bakery, pastry menu. Breakfast, lunch, dinner. Casual attire. Outdoor seating. $

SPA

★★★★THE RITZ-CARLTON SPA, NAPLES

280 Vanderbilt Beach Road, Naples, 239-598-3300, 800-241-3333;
www.ritzcarlton.com

This spa features 33 treatment rooms, hot and cold plunge pools, saunas and steam rooms. Therapies draw from the healing effects of land and sea, like the Sea Holistic, an exfoliating relaxation experience utilizing marine salt crystals. The Golden Shimmer is a full body treatment that exfoliates with extracts of pure gold and Artemisia. The onsite fitness center offers personal training, group exercise classes and nutrition consultation, as well as a one-on-one equipment orientation session designed to acclimate guests to the fitness center.

OCALA

In the central highlands of the state, Ocala has become a focal point for excursions in what's called "ridge" country. There are approximately 500 thoroughbred breeding and training farms here in addition to farms raising other breeds. The Ocala Breeders Sales Pavilion is host to eight horse sales a year.

Information: Ocala/Marion County Chamber of Commerce, 110 E. Silver Springs Blvd.,
352-629-8051; www.ocalacc.com

WHAT TO SEE AND DO

OCALA NATIONAL FOREST

3199 N.E. Highway 315, Ocala

The largest developed area of this approximately 383,000-acre forest is Salt Springs. With a constant temperature of 72 degrees and a flow of 52 million gallons per day, Salt Springs provides swimming, a bathhouse, boating (rentals), hiking, picnicking and camping (some hook-ups). Juniper Springs and Fern Hammock have a combined daily flow of more than 15 million gallons at a constant 72 degrees (private canoes allowed, some rentals). Swimming, a bathhouse, picnicking, camping, trailer facilities and a visitor center. Fees may be charged at recreation sites.

HOTELS

★HAMPTON INN

3434 S.W. College Road, Ocala, 352-854-3200, 800-426-7866; www.hamptoninn.com

152 rooms. Complimentary full breakfast. Fitness room. Outdoor pool. **$**

★★★HILTON OCALA/SILVER SPRINGS

3600 S.W. 36th Ave., Ocala, 352-854-1400, 877-602-4023; www.hiltonocala.com

This six-acre property is near the famous horse farms of Marion County. The 6,500 square feet of meeting space appeals to business travelers, but there are other pursuits here, including a pool, two beach volleyball courts and a putting green. 196 rooms. Pets accepted. High-speed Internet access. Restaurant, bar. Fitness room. Outdoor pool, whirlpool. Tennis. Business center. **$**

★★QUALITY INN

3621 W. Silver Springs Blvd., Ocala, 352-629-0381, 800-424-6423; www.choicehotels.com

269 rooms. Pets accepted; fee. Restaurant, bar. Fitness room. Outdoor pool, whirlpool. **$**

SPECIALTY LODGING

SEVEN SISTERS INN

820 S.E. Fort King St., Ocala, 352-867-1170, 800-250-3496; www.sevensistersinn.com

Enjoy a quiet evening on the porch of this restored Victorian inn. A library and sitting room offer a comfortable place for socializing. 13 rooms. Children over 12 years only. Complimentary full breakfast. Business center. **$**

ORLANDO

Most people hear the word Orlando and immediately think theme parks. Orlando may be famous for being the theme park capital of the world, but the irony is that only one of the major parks is even *in* the city. Orlando is actually as close to an urban oasis as it gets. Live oaks edge picturesque brick-lined streets surrounding the central focal point of Lake Eola. While you can still find some orange trees dotting the yards of surrounding homes—and breathe in the citrus aroma during orange blossom time— Orlando is now home to more commerce than agriculture, housing the headquarters of many of the world's leading businesses.

It's hard to believe that this metropolis began as an offshoot of a military outpost in 1838 in the midst of the Seminole Wars. It served as a trading post known as Jernigan (named after the area's first permanent settlers) until 1857, when the U.S. Post Office officially adopted the new name of Orlando. Legends abound surrounding the origins of its name—one version has the town named after the lead in Shakespeare's *As You Like It;* another claims that it honors a man named Orlando who died on a journey to Tampa. Probably the most popular tale is that the city was named for Sentinel Orlando Reeves, who was killed during the Seminole War as he attempted to fire a warning shot to his fellow soldiers.

Orlando is a favorite for a devoted colony of year-round visitors. The metro area has 300 lakes within its limits and retains an open, parklike atmosphere. More than 100 attractions can be found in Orlando. To accommodate all the tourists, there are 110,000 hotel rooms, 52 million square feet of retail space and 4,500 restaurants.
Information: Orlando/Orange County Convention and Visitors Bureau,
9800 International Drive, 407-685-9800; www.orlandoinfo.com

WHAT TO SEE AND DO

AMWAY ARENA
600 W. Amelia, Orlando, 407-849-2001; www.orlandocentroplex.com
The 17,740-seat Amway Arena in downtown Orlando is home to the Orlando Magic basketball team, the Orlando Seals hockey team and the Orlando Predators arena football team. Plenty of other events take place here, including top-name concerts, rodeos, the circus, ice shows and much more. The center opened in 1989 and is still affectionately called the Orena (Orlando Arena) by old-timers.

BOB CARR PERFORMING ARTS CENTRE
401 W. Livingston St., Orlando, 407-849-2577; www.orlandovenues.net
Home to the Orlando Opera, the Florida Theatrical Association and the Orlando Celebrity Concert Association, the Bob Carr Performing Arts Centre hosts a multitude of performances, ranging from opera and ballet to rock concerts to the symphony and the annual Broadway Series, in the 2,518-seat hall. Ticket prices vary by event.

GRAND CYPRESS GOLF CLUB
1 N. Jacaranda, Orlando, 800-835-7377; www.grandcypress.com
The Grand Cypress has 45 holes designed by Jack Nicklaus. The North, South and East courses have nine holes each and can be played in different combinations, while the New course sports 18 holes all by itself. The New course is designed to look like St. Andrews in Scotland, with stone walls along the 15th and 17th holes and deep pot bunkers lining some of the fairways. There's little water and only a few trees, so golfers can enjoy hitting a driver off of many tees without dire consequences.

HARRY P. LEU GARDENS
1920 N. Forest Ave., Orlando, 407-246-2620; www.leugardens.org
Harry P. Leu Gardens is 50 acres of "Old Florida" filled with fragrant blooms from the South's largest camellia collection and formal rose garden. Oaks and giant camphor trees line the miles of pathways surrounding the late-19th-century restored farmhouse, now the Leu House Museum, which depicts turn-of-the-century Florida lifestyle. The Butterfly Garden boasts more than 100 different plants designed to attract the winged insects year-round. Daily 9 a.m.-5 p.m.; Leu House Museum closed in July.

FLORIDA

★
★
★
★

ISLANDS OF ADVENTURE

1000 Universal Studios Plaza, Orlando, 407-363-8000

The 110-acre Islands of Adventure theme park boasts some of the world's most innovative and technologically advanced rides, located on five uniquely themed islands situated around a lagoon. The islands bring to life the Marvel Comics superheroes (Marvel Super Hero Island), hundreds of comic-strip heroes (Toon Lagoon), the dinosaurs of *Jurassic Park* (Jurassic Park), the greatest myths of all times (The Lost Continent) and the classic books of Dr. Seuss (Seuss Landing). Seasonal celebrations include Grinchmas, which takes place from Thanksgiving through New Year's Eve on Seuss Landing, and Halloween Horror Nights, which occur on selected nights in October. Daily from 9 a.m.; closing times vary by season.

MALL AT MILLENIA

4200 Conroy Road, Orlando, 407-363-3555; www.mallatmillenia.com

Located in southwest Orlando near the theme parks and International Drive, Orlando's newest mall has a full-service concierge and valet parking. If you need a break from shopping, check out the Grand Court, which features 12 giant LED screens airing a variety of entertainment, educational and fashion-related programs. Monday-Saturday 10 a.m.-9 p.m., Sunday noon-7 p.m.

ORANGE AVENUE

Orlando; www.orlandoonline.com

If you're into antiques and bargain hunting, you'll find plenty of antique and thrift stores punctuating the sections of Orange Avenue known as Antique and Ivanhoe Rows. Located just north of the city beyond main thoroughfare Colonial Drive, the antique district offers a tranquil alternative to the nonstop world of the theme parks. Hours vary, but generally from 9 or 10 a.m. Monday-Saturday; noon to 5 p.m. Sunday.

ORLANDO MAGIC (NBA)

Amway Arena, 600 W. Amelia St., Orlando, 407-896-2442; www.orlandomagic.com

The Orlando Magic made its NBA debut in 1989, and after acquiring Shaquille O'Neal in 1991, quickly became an annual playoff contender. The team made it to the NBA finals in 1995, led by O'Neal and then teammate Penny Hardaway. While both have moved on to other teams, the Magic now boasts some of the top names in the NBA. Home games are played at the 17,248-seat TD Waterhouse Center in downtown Orlando.

ORLANDO MUSEUM OF ART

2416 N. Mills Ave., Orlando, 407-896-4231; www.omart.org

Cited by *Newsweek* magazine as one of the best art museums in the South, the Orlando Museum of Art was founded in 1924 and presents 10 to 12 major exhibits throughout the year focusing on a broad range of artwork by both local and international artists. The museum also houses impressive collections of American, ancient American and African art. Tuesday-Friday 10 a.m.-5 p.m., Saturday-Sunday noon-4 p.m.

ORLANDO PREMIUM OUTLETS

8200 Vineland Ave., Orlando, 407-238-7787; www.premiumoutlets.com

Located near Orlando's major attractions, the Premium Outlets boast the largest collection of designer stores in the area, offering discounts of 25 to 65 percent every day for many of the hottest designers, including Dior, Burberry and Fendi. Daily.

★
★
★
★
★

ORLANDO SCIENCE CENTER

777 E. Princeton St., Orlando, 407-514-2000, 888-672-4386

Hands-on "experiential" exhibits abound in this 207,000-square-foot facility. Permanent exhibits include BodyZone, a tour inside the human body; ShowBiz Science, highlighting movie special effects; and NatureWorks, a large exhibit exploring Florida's vast ecosystem. The center also features the world's largest I-Works domed theater and planetarium shows, with combination tickets available. Tuesday-Saturday opens at 9 a.m., Sunday noon-5 p.m.

RDV SPORTSPLEX

8701 Maitland Summit Blvd., Orlando, 407-916-2442; www.rdvsportsplex.com

Offering in-line skating, skateboarding, ice skating and ice hockey, as well as a full-service athletic club and a 3,020-square-foot tennis center, the RDV Sportsplex is a 30-acre, 362,813-square-foot state-of-the-art facility owned by the same folks who own the Orlando Magic. The team trains at this facility, which offers everything from exercise equipment to juice and refreshment bars to merchandise outlets. Hours for different activities vary; call or visit Web site for information.

SEAWORLD ORLANDO

7007 SeaWorld Drive, Orlando, 407-351-3600, 800-327-2424; www.seaworld.com

A theme park with thrill rides to rival Universal and Disney, this is also the world's largest marine park (and home to the famous killer whale, Shamu). Directly across the street is its sister park, Discovery Cove, an exclusive resort that limits daily attendance to 1,000 people and provides guests the opportunity to swim with dolphins or enjoy beaching, snorkeling and swimming in a quiet and intimate setting. Recently, SeaWorld Orlando underwent its largest expansion, creating the Waterfront, a five-acre tract that is the new hub of the park. Daily from 9 a.m.; closing times vary by season.

SKYVENTURE ORLANDO

6805 Visitors Circle, Orlando, 407-903-1150, 800-759-3861;
www.skyventureorlando.com

If you've always wanted to try skydiving, but don't love the prospect of jumping out of an airplane thousands of feet in the sky, this vertical wind tunnel with 120-mph winds allows you to experience the feeling of weightlessness associated with skydiving. The experience lasts approximately one hour and includes use of a flight suit and helmet. Monday-Friday 2-11:30 p.m.; Saturday-Sunday noon-11:30 p.m.

THORNTON PARK HISTORIC DISTRICT

Thornton Park, Washington Street and Summerlin Avenue, Orlando

In this charming and eclectic neighborhood, historic homes peacefully coexist with new construction. Located directly east of downtown Orlando, the district encompasses a diverse collection of boutiques and retail shops alongside restaurants, bookstores, cafés, lofts and early Florida Craftsman-style homes on stately oak-lined brick streets. The area is also home to Dickson Azalea Park, five acres of lush Florida foliage.

UNIVERSAL CITYWALK

2000 Universal Studios Plaza, Orlando, 407-363-8000; www.universalorlando.com

Your day doesn't have to end when you've finished exploring the Universal theme parks. Check out the Universal CityWalk, which connects both theme parks to a giant parking structure. For fine dining, try Emeril's Restaurant Orlando or Jimmy Buffett's Margaritaville. A 20-screen megaplex is a great option for rainy afternoons. Live entertainment venues include Bob Marley: A Tribute to Freedom, the groove, Latin Quarter, MOTOWN Café and Pat O'Brien's. Daily 11-2 a.m.

UNIVERSAL ORLANDO RESORT
1000 Universal Studios Plaza, Orlando, 407-363-8000; www.universalorlando.com
Encompassing 840 acres, Universal Orlando combines the hip with the classic in its two theme parks, Universal Studios Florida and Islands of Adventure; three Loews hotels (Portofino Bay, Hard Rock and Royal Pacific Resort); and CityWalk, a dynamic dining, shopping and entertainment complex. Academy Award-winning director/producer Steven Spielberg serves as creative consultant to both theme parks, which feature state-of-the-art rides and attractions. All the Universal Orlando resort hotels, theme parks and CityWalk are connected by waterways, so you can give your feet a rest by hopping on one of the complimentary water taxis. Daily from 9 a.m.; closing times vary by season.

UNIVERSAL STUDIOS FLORIDA
1000 Universal Studios Plaza, Orlando, 407-363-8000; www.universalorlando.com
Universal Studios Florida, at 125 acres, is the largest working film and television production studio outside Hollywood. Drawing on its movie heritage as inspiration for its blockbuster rides and attractions, this theme park brings movies to life. Fan favorites include Back to the Future: The Ride; Men in Black Alien Attack; Jaws; E.T. Adventure; and Terminator 2: 3-D Battle Across Time. Numerous movies, television shows, commercials and music video productions routinely utilize the theme park's street sets, so visitors often get a glimpse of live moviemaking and real stars at work. Daily from 9 a.m.; closing times vary by season.

WET 'N WILD
6200 International Drive, Orlando, 407-351-1800, 800-992-9453; www.wetnwildorlando.com
The number-one water park in the world is located adjacent to its owner, Universal Orlando. (Save money with a combo ticket such as the Orlando FlexTicket.) Open year-round, the 25-acre facility features heated pools (when needed) with 12 major thrill rides, including Hydra Fighter, a swing ride that you control, and Der Stuka, a six-story speed slide. For little ones try the Kids Park, boasting a tiny wave pool, mini versions of the park's most popular rides and a life-size sand castle. Daily; hours vary by season.

WONDERWORKS
9607 International Drive, Orlando, 407-351-8800; www.wonderworksonline.com
How could you not take the time to explore an upside-down building? Interactive fun abounds in this unusual museum brimming with more than 100 hands-on exhibits focusing on the unexplainable, the amazing and the downright weird. Scale a virtual cliff or design your own roller coaster and then ride it. WonderWorks is also home of the world's largest extreme laser tag arena/arcade. Daily 9 a.m.-midnight.

SPECIAL EVENTS
ARNOLD PALMER INVITATIONAL
Bay Hill Country Club, 9000 Bay Hill Blvd., Orlando, 407-876-2888, 866-764-4843; www.bayhill.com

As long as theme parks have dominated the central Florida landscape, this tournament, held at Arnold Palmer's spectacular Bay Hill Country Club, has been a top draw on golf's PGA Tour. The tournament attracts some of the top names on the tour and is a favorite of hometown links-master Tiger Woods. Mid-March.

CAPITAL ONE BOWL
1 Citrus Bowl Place, Orlando, 407-839-3900; www.fcsports.com

Played annually and nationally televised on New Year's Day, the Capital One Bowl (formerly known as the Capital One Florida Citrus Bowl) pits the Big Ten and SEC championship teams against each other. For this game, stadium capacity is increased from 65,538 to 70,000. Parking is a mess, so if you go, take advantage of the city shuttles running from the downtown parking lot located underneath I-4 at Central Boulevard beginning at 10 a.m. The cost is just $5 and is well worth the price of avoiding the chaos. January 1.

HALLOWEEN HORROR NIGHTS AT ISLANDS OF ADVENTURE
1000 Universal Studios Plaza, Orlando, 407-363-8000; www.universalorlando.com

Halloween Horror Nights has become one of the world's premier Halloween events. Originally held at the Universal Studios theme park, the event has moved to the Islands of Adventure theme park. Featuring the best in high-tech haunted houses and live shows, the park literally crawls with hundreds of costumed actors with one goal in mind: to scare the living daylights out of unsuspecting guests. The action takes place on select nights in October and early November and separate admission is required.

MARDI GRAS AT UNIVERSAL STUDIOS FLORIDA
1000 Universal Studios Plaza, Orlando, 407-363-8000; www.universalorlando.com

Universal Studios Florida turns its back lot into the largest Mardi Gras celebration outside of the Big Easy during select nights in February, March and April. Millions of beads are tossed from 14 authentic floats during the 10-city-block-long parade. Dine on authentic New Orleans-style cuisine and enjoy real Mardi Gras-style beverages. Select Saturdays feature top acts in concert, while weekday celebrations feature the best in local music. Dates vary, so call for information.

HOTELS
★★COURTYARD BY MARRIOTT
7155 N. Frontage Road, Orlando, 407-240-7200, 800-321-2211; www.marriott.com

149 rooms. Restaurant. Fitness room. Outdoor pool, whirlpool. Airport transportation available. $

★★★CROWNE PLAZA HOTEL UNIVERSAL
7800 Universal Blvd., Orlando, 407-355-0550, 866-864-8627; www.cporlando.com

If you're traveling to Orlando to visit its theme parks, this contemporary hotel is a great choice. Within a mile of Universal and Wet 'n Wild and within three miles of SeaWorld and Discovery Cove, the Crowne Plaza offers free transportation to all the local theme parks. Guest rooms feature plush beds and amenities such as night light, sleep CD, lavender eye mask and ear plugs. 400 rooms. High-speed Internet access. Restaurant, bar. Fitness room. Outdoor pool, whirlpool. Business center. **$$**

★★CROWNE PLAZA RESORT

12120 International Drive, Orlando, 407-239-1222, 800-496-7621;
www.crowneplazaorlando.com
101 rooms. High-speed Internet access. Two restaurants, bar. Fitness room. Two outdoor pools, children's pool, whirlpool. Tennis. Business center. **$**

★★DOUBLETREE CASTLE HOTEL-ORLANDO

8629 International Drive, Orlando, 407-345-1511, 800-952-2785;
www.doubletreecastle.com
216 rooms. Pets accepted, some restrictions; fee. High-speed Internet access. Three restaurants, three bars. Fitness room. Outdoor pool, whirlpool. **$**

★★EMBASSY SUITES HOTEL ORLANDO-DOWNTOWN

191 E. Pine St., Orlando, 407-841-1000, 800-362-2779; www.embassysuites.com
167 rooms, all suites. Complimentary full breakfast. Restaurant, bar. Fitness room. Outdoor pool, whirlpool. Business center. **$**

★★EMBASSY SUITES HOTEL ORLANDO-INTERNATIONAL DRIVE SOUTH/ CONVENTION CENTER

8978 International Drive, Orlando, 407-352-1400, 800-433-7275;
www.embassysuitesorlando.com
244 rooms, all suites. Complimentary full breakfast. Restaurant, bar. Fitness room. Indoor pool, outdoor pool, children's pool, whirlpool. **$**

★FAIRFIELD INN AT LAKE BUENA VISTA

8623 Vineland Ave., Orlando, 407-938-9001, 877-682-8552; www.marriottvillage.com
312 rooms. Complimentary continental breakfast. Wireless Internet access. Fitness room. Outdoor pool, whirlpool. **$**

★FAIRFIELD INN BY MARRIOTT ORLANDO INTERNATIONAL DRIVE

7495 Canada Ave., Orlando, 407-351-7000, 800-228-2800; www.fairfieldinn.com
200 rooms. Complimentary continental breakfast. Outdoor pool, High-speed Internet access. Pets not accepted. **$**

★★★FOUR POINTS BY SHERATON ORLANDO STUDIO CITY

5905 International Drive, Orlando, 407-351-2100, 800-327-1366;
www.starwoodhotels.com
Conveniently located next to Universal Studios and near many theme parks, this circular tower hotel is a great choice for a family-oriented Orlando vacation. Hollywood is the theme here, with murals and pictures of movie stars adorning the walls of the lobby. 301 rooms. Pets accepted, some restrictions; fee. Restaurant, bar. Fitness room. Outdoor pool, children's pool. Wireless Internet access. **$**

★★★GRAND BOHEMIAN, ORLANDO

325 S. Orange Ave., Orlando, 407-313-9000, 800-228-3000;
www.grandbohemianhotel.com

Artistic interior design is the hallmark of this hotel, with rooms decorated in rich jewel tones, java wood and velvet fabrics. Distinctive artwork is a Grand Bohemian signature, from the pieces decorating the hotel to the 19th- and 20th-century European artwork displayed in the private gallery. The artistic spirit continues in the restaurant and lounge, where blues, jazz and classical music are performed nightly. 250 rooms. Pets accepted, some restrictions; fee. High-speed Internet access. Restaurant, bar. Fitness room. Outdoor pool, whirlpool. Business center. **$$$$**

★★★HARD ROCK HOTEL

5800 Universal Blvd., Orlando, 407-503-7625, 800-232-7155; www.hardrock.com

The Hard Rock Hotel at Universal Orlando sits on 14 landscaped acres and has a classic California Mission design. You'll find classic rock 'n' roll memorabilia throughout the hotel and hear music virtually everywhere, including underwater at the massive zero-entry pool with a 260-foot water slide. In-room CD sound systems keep the tunes going. Restaurants include the full-service Sunset Grill (featuring an open kitchen) and an Orlando outpost of the world-famous Palm restaurant. 650 rooms. Pets accepted, some restrictions; fee. Restaurant, bar. Fitness room. Outdoor pool, whirlpool. Airport transportation available. Business center. **$$**

★HAWTHORN SUITES

6435 Westwood Blvd., Orlando, 407-351-6600, 800-527-1133; www.hawthorn.com

150 rooms, all suites. Wireless Internet access. Fitness room. Outdoor pool, children's pool, whirlpool. **$**

★★HOLIDAY INN

5905 Kirkman Road, Orlando, 407-351-3333, 888-465-4329; www.hiuniversal.com

254 rooms. Pets accepted. Restaurant, bar. High-speed Internet access. Fitness room. Outdoor pool, children's pool. Business center. **$**

★★HOLIDAY INN SELECT

12125 High Tech Ave., Orlando, 407-275-9000, 800-465-4329; www.hiselect.com

254 rooms. Restaurant, bar. High-speed Internet access. Fitness room. Outdoor pool, whirlpool. Airport transportation available. Pool. Business center. **$**

★★★HYATT REGENCY ORLANDO INTERNATIONAL AIRPORT

9300 Airport Blvd., Orlando, 407-825-1234, 800-228-9000; www.hyatt.com

Perfect for travelers with limited time in the Orlando area, the Hyatt Regency Orlando International Airport is located inside the airport's main terminal. There are more than 30 specialty stores located within the Hyatt Atrium, as well as an outdoor pool and spa. 445 rooms. Wireless Internet access. Two restaurants, bar, Fitness room. Outdoor pool. Business center. **$$**

★★★INTERNATIONAL PLAZA RESORT AND SPA

10100 International Drive, Orlando, 407-352-1100, 800-327-0363; www.intlplazaresort.com

Located next to SeaWorld and a short drive to both Disney and Universal Studios, this resort has 28 acres of tropical landscaping. There's an onsite fitness club and spa, as well as free miniature golf. Caribbean flair sets the tone at the multilevel Blue Marlin Grille, or for a quick meal, try Max's Deli. Visiting the Disney parks is a snap with free shuttle service, and there's also a shuttle to the nearby Florida Mall. 1,102 rooms. Pets accepted, some restrictions; fee. Two restaurants, bar. Fitness room. Three outdoor pools, two children's pools, whirlpool. Business center. $$

★★★JW MARRIOTT ORLANDO GRANDE LAKES

4040 Central Florida Parkway, Orlando, 407-206-2300, 800-682-9956; www.grandelakes.com

Although this large hotel caters to business travelers, it's also a good bet for those who come to Orlando for rest and relaxation. Set on 500 landscaped acres, there are three lighted tennis courts, a heated outdoor lagoon-style pool and a 40,000-square-foot spa. Nearby is the Ritz-Carlton Golf Club, an 18-hole course designed by links legend Greg Norman, where JW Marriott guests enjoy preferred tee times and the hotel's personal golf caddie-concierge program. Guest rooms feature cozy duvets as well as laptop safes. 1,000 rooms. High-speed Internet access. Five restaurants, bar. Fitness room, spa. Outdoor pool, whirlpool. Tennis. Business center. $$

★★★MARRIOTT ORLANDO LAKE MARY

1501 International Parkway, Lake Mary, 407-995-1100, 800-380-7724; www.marriott.com

This north Orlando hotel caters to business travelers with "Rooms That Work." If you're looking for a modern hotel that isn't overrun with children wearing Mickey Mouse ears, you've found a winner. Guest rooms feature luxurious bedding, custom European furnishings and granite-and-marble baths. If you need to continue business over drinks, Cobalt's lounge specializes in martinis. If doing deals on the golf course is more your style, there are several courses in the area. 299 rooms. High-speed Internet access. Restaurant, bar. Fitness room. Outdoor pool, whirlpool. Business center. $$

★★METROPOLITAN RESORT

8444 International Drive, Orlando, 407-345-0505, 888-380-969; www.orlandometropolitanresort.com

522 rooms. Pets accepted; fee. Wireless Internet access. Restaurant, two bars. Outdoor pool, whirlpool. Business center. $

★★★ORLANDO WORLD CENTER MARRIOTT RESORT

8701 World Center Drive, Orlando, 407-239-4200, 800-228-9290; www.marriottworldcenter.com

This resort, set on 200 acres, has a spa, 18-hole championship golf course, five outdoor pools, two children's pools and a basketball court. Bar and restaurant options range from casual poolside dining to upscale Italian and Japanese restaurants. 2,000 rooms. High-speed Internet access. Five restaurants, bar. Children's activity center. Fitness room. Indoor pool, outdoor pool, children's pool, whirlpool. Golf, 18 holes. Tennis. Airport transportation available. Business center. $$

★★★★THE PEABODY ORLANDO

9801 International Drive, Orlando, 407-352-4000, 800-732-2639; www.peabodyorlando.com

Famous for the flock of ducks that parades through the hotel's lobby twice daily, this hotel is located across from the Orange Convention Center and close to Orlando's theme

135

FLORIDA

★
★
★
★
★

parks and performing and visual arts. The athletic club, pool and tennis courts lure guests away from their rooms, while top-rated golf is just a short drive away. The Peabody's restaurants have something for everyone, from a 1950s-style diner to a sophisticated steak house. 891 rooms. Wireless Internet access. Three restaurants, three bars. Fitness room (fee), spa. Outdoor pool, children's pool, whirlpool. Tennis. Business center. $$$

★★★PORTOFINO BAY HOTEL

5601 Universal Blvd., Orlando, 407-503-1000, 800-232-7827; www.loewshotels.com

The Portofino Bay Hotel at Universal Orlando re-creates the famed Italian fishing village of the same name. Guest rooms feature fluffy white duvets and warm wood furnishings. The hotel has eight different eateries, including the romantic Delfino Riviera; the full-service Trattoria del Porto; and Mama Della's, a family-style Italian restaurant. For drinks, try the Bar American or for a more casual cocktail, head to the Thirsty Fish at the water's edge. Three pools, a fitness center, a day spa and Campo Portofino for kids round out the resort experience. 750 rooms. Eight restaurants, bar. Pets accepted, some restrictions; fee. Fitness room, spa. Three outdoor pools, whirlpool. Airport transportation available. Business center. $$$

★★★RADISSON HOTEL LAKE BUENA VISTA

12799 Apopka Vineland Road, Orlando, 407-597-3400, 888-201-1718; www.radisson.com

There's sun and a whole lot of fun at this favorite family-friendly vacation spot, which is right in the middle of the Orlando action. The hotel is only a short walk to Disney World and a few minutes from SeaWorld, Universal Studios and the city's best shopping, so you'll always be close to home when you just want to crash at the end of a very long day. Plus, it helps that new rooms are outfitted with HD flat-screen TVs and Sleep Number Beds. You'll be catching Zs in no time. 196 rooms. High-speed Internet access. Restaurant, bar. Fitness center. Pool. $

★★★RENAISSANCE ORLANDO RESORT

6677 Sea Harbor Drive, Orlando, 407-351-5555, 800-327-6677;
www.renaissancehotels.com

Located across the street from SeaWorld and one mile from the Orange County Convention Center, this resort has an atrium lobby reaching 10 stories high with a free-flowing waterfall, Japanese koi pond and a Venetian free-flight aviary. Onsite activities include pingpong, basketball and volleyball, along with a playground and game room. 781 rooms. Restaurant, bar. High-speed Internet access. Children's activity center. Fitness room. Pool, children's pool, whirlpool. Lighted tennis. Airport transportation available. Business center. $$$

★★★★THE RITZ-CARLTON ORLANDO, GRANDE LAKES

4012 Central Florida Parkway, Orlando, 407-206-2400, 800-241-3333;
www.ritzcarlton.com

Architecturally, it's an homage to the Grand Palazzo of Italy. Spiritually, the Ritz-Carlton Orlando, Grande Lakes resort draws its Zen-like calm from the far east. There is the 40,000-square-foot spa which features 40 treatment rooms. Golfers reach nirvana on the Greg Norman–designed 18-hole golf course. The hotel has six onsite restaurants, including the elegant Norman's. Each guest room boasts a private balcony, spacious marble bathroom and plush robes, and parents will appreciate the Ritz Kids

Club, pool, playground and the close proximity to a certain magic kingdom. 584 rooms. High-speed Internet access. Six restaurants, bar. Children's activity center. Fitness room, fitness classes available, spa. Outdoor pool, children's pool, whirlpool. Golf, 18 holes. Tennis. Business center. **$$$**

★★★ROYAL PACIFIC RESORT

6300 Hollywood Way, Orlando, 407-503-3000, 800-235-6397; www.loewshotels.com

The 53-acre Royal Pacific Resort has a South Seas theme and features a towering bamboo forest and an authentic Balinese tower. Bamboo accents, dark woods and richly colored fabrics lend an air of the tropics to the guest rooms. There are five restaurants and six lounges to choose from, including Emeril Lagasse's Tchoup Chop, which serves South Pacific-flavored food. Have cocktails at the Bula Bar & Grille, the Orchid Court Lounge, or the massive 12,000-square-foot Lagoon pool—Orlando's largest pool. 946 rooms. Pets accepted, some restrictions; fee. Restaurant, bar. Fitness room, spa. Outdoor pool, children's pool, whirlpool. Airport transportation available. Business center. **$$**

★★★ROYAL PLAZA IN THE WALT DISNEY WORLD RESORT

1905 Hotel Plaza Blvd., Lake Buena Vista, 407-828-2828; www.royalplaza.com

Even better than staying *near* Disney World, is staying *in* Disney World. And what could top that? How about staying in style in one of the spacious rooms at the Royal Plaza, which come complete with pillow-top mattresses, plush pillows and Bath & Body Works amenities? Every family traveling to visit the Mouse wants to be close to the fun, so the hotel offers continuous transportation to all of the Disney parks. Since the hotel is in between Downtown Disney and the Crossroads Shopping Centre, it'll please the Spring Break set just as easily. Package deals offering free nights will keep everyone happy. 394 rooms. Wireless Internet access. Restaurants, bar. Fitness center. Pool. Business Center. **$**

★SPRINGHILL SUITES ORLANDO IN THE MARRIOTT VILLAGE

8601 Vineland Ave., Orlando, 407-938-9001, 877-682-8552; www.marriottvillage.com

400 rooms, all suites. Complimentary continental breakfast. High-speed Internet access. Fitness room. Outdoor pool, whirlpool. **$**

★STAYBRIDGE SUITES LAKE BUENA VISTA

8751 Suiteside Drive, Orlando, 407-238-0777, 800-866-4549; www.sborlando.com

150 rooms, all suites. Complimentary full breakfast. High-speed Internet access. Fitness room. Outdoor pool, children's pool, whirlpool. Business center. **$**

★STAYBRIDGE SUITES ORLANDO

8480 International Drive, Orlando, 407-352-2400, 800-866-4549; www.sborlando.com

146 rooms, all suites. Complimentary continental breakfast. Fitness room. Outdoor pool, children's pool, whirlpool. **$$**

★★★WYNDHAM ORLANDO RESORT

8001 International Drive, Orlando, 407-351-2420, 800-421-8001; www.wyndham.com

Offering a taste of Old Florida on the bustling International Drive, the 42-acre Wyndham Orlando Resort is a tranquil retreat from the theme parks. Indoor or outdoor entrances are available for guest rooms, which are surrounded by tropical gardens and lagoons. Amenities include Herman Miller Aeron work chairs, pillow-top mattresses and play areas for the kids. Three pools, a health club and the casual Augustine's Bar & Grille are all on the grounds of the resort. 1,275 rooms. Pets accepted; fee. Restaurant, bar. Fitness room. Three outdoor pools, children's pool, whirlpool. Tennis. Business center. $

SPECIALTY LODGINGS
COURTYARD AT LAKE LUCERNE
211 N. Lucerne Circle E., Orlando, 407-648-5188, 800-444-5289;
www.orlandohistoricinn.com
Listed on the National Register of Historic Places, the Courtyard at Lake Lucerne is a tranquil inn located within walking distance to the center of downtown Orlando. Consisting of four restored buildings from four separate eras (Victorian, Antebellum, Art Deco and Grand Victorian), the property encircles a lush, intimate garden. Guest rooms offer private baths and are tastefully decorated with unusual artwork and antiques gathered by innkeepers Sam and Eleanor Meiner during their travels around the world. 30 rooms. Children are only allowed in the Wellborn suites. Complimentary continental breakfast. $$

PERRI HOUSE BED & BREAKFAST INN
10417 Vista Oaks Court, Orlando, 407-876-4830, 800-780-4830; www.perrihouse.com
A country estate set on 16 secluded acres, this charming bed and breakfast is just minutes from Disney, but feels like it's miles away. A birdhouse museum on the property captures the interests of adults and children alike. Eight rooms. Complimentary continental breakfast. Outdoor pool. $

RESTAURANTS
★★★BERGAMO'S
5250 International Drive, Orlando, 407-352-3805; www.bergamos.com
Best known for its singing waitstaff, who take the stage throughout the night to belt out everything from Broadway tunes to opera, this restaurant has definite tourist appeal yet draws a strong local following. Sea bass served in a truffle broth with handmade semolina gnocchi is a house specialty. Italian menu. Dinner. Bar. Children's menu. Business casual attire. Reservations recommended. Outdoor seating. $$

★★CHATHAM'S PLACE
7575 Drive Phillips Blvd., Orlando, 407-345-2992; www.chathamsplace.com
American menu. Dinner. Closed Sunday. Bar. Business casual attire. Reservations recommended. Outdoor seating. $$$

★★★CHRISTINI'S
7600 Drive Phillips Blvd., Orlando, 407-345-8770; www.christinis.com
A true Italian experience is what's in store for diners at this International Drive restaurant. The menu features dishes such as linguine with fresh little neck clams, chicken marsala and veal scaloppini. Owner Chris Christini can often be seen greeting diners in the richly decorated dining room. Italian menu. Dinner. Bar. Casual attire. $$$

★★★DEL FRISCO'S

729 Lee Road, Orlando, 407-645-4443; www.delfriscosorlando.com

If you're in the mood for a good steak in a unique setting, this is the place for you. Dark wood décor creates the perfect clubby steak house atmosphere. American menu. Dinner. Closed Sunday. Bar. Business casual attire. Reservations recommended. Valet parking. $$$$

★★★DUX

9801 International Drive, Orlando, 407-345-4550, 800-732-2639; www.peabodyorlando.com

Chef de Cuisine Joseph Trevino is responsible for the menu at Dux, located within the Peabody Hotel. The dining room's ambience is elegant and regal with Travertine floors, massive columns and crystal chandeliers. The menu features dishes such as warm lobster and potato salad, sheep's milk ricotta ravioli, California halibut and Berkshire pork tenderloin. Dux derives its name from the hotels trained procession of ducks that march to and from their $100,000 Peabody duck castle, walking across the lobby's red carpet. American menu. Dinner. Closed Sunday-Monday. Bar. Business casual attire. Reservations recommended. Valet parking. $$$

★★★EMERIL'S TCHOUP CHOP

6300 Hollywood Way, Orlando, 407-503-2467; www.emerils.com

Celebrity chef Emeril Lagasse's Orlando restaurant is set in a cavernous, colorful space inside Universal Studio's Royal Pacific Resort. Though the name of the restaurant is a nod to New Orleans' Tchoupitoulas Street, the menu takes its cues from Polynesia, with Asian ingredients and preparations in most dishes. Yellowtail snapper comes steamed in lotus leaves with ginger, scallions and chilies, while New York strip steak is dressed up with homemade teriyaki sauce. New Orleans menu. Dinner. Bar. Valet parking. $$$

★GIOVANNI'S ITALIAN RESTAURANT

4441 N. Hoffner Ave., Orlando, 407-852-9818

Italian, pizza menu. Lunch, dinner. Bar. Children's menu. Casual attire. Outdoor seating. $$

★★HANAMIZUKI

8255 International Drive, Orlando, 407-363-7200, 407-363-1006; www.hanamizuki.us

Japanese, sushi menu. Lunch, dinner. Closed Sunday. Casual attire. $$$

★★HUE

626 E. Central Blvd., Downtown Orlando, 407-849-1800; www.huerestaurant.com

International menu. Lunch, dinner, Sunday brunch. Bar. Casual attire. Reservations recommended. $$$

★★ICHIBAN

19 S. Orange Ave., Orlando, 407-423-2688; www.orlandoichiban.com

Japanese, sushi menu. Lunch, dinner. Closed Sunday. Casual attire. Outdoor seating. $$

★★K RESTAURANT AND WINE BAR

2401 Edgewater Drive, Orlando, 407-872-2332; www.krestaurantwinebar.com

American menu. Lunch, dinner. Closed Sunday-Monday. Casual attire. Outdoor seating. $$

FLORIDA

★
★
★
★
☆

★★LE COQ AU VIN

4800 S. Orange Ave., Orlando, 407-851-6980; www.lecoqauvinrestaurant.com

French menu. Lunch, dinner. Closed Monday. Business casual attire. Reservations recommended. **$$$**

★★★MANUEL'S ON THE 28TH

390 N. Orange Ave., Orlando, 407-246-6580; www.manuelsonthe28th.com

Located on the 28th floor of the Barnett Bank building in downtown Orlando, this restaurant's fantastic views make it a popular place for special-occasion dining. International menu. Dinner. Closed Sunday-Monday. **$$$**

★★MING COURT

9188 International Drive, Orlando, 407-351-9988; www.ming-court.com

Chinese, sushi menu. Lunch, dinner. Bar. Children's menu. Business casual attire. Reservations recommended. **$$**

★★★★NORMAN'S

4012 Central Florida Parkway, Orlando, 407-393-4333, 800-241-3333; www.normans.com

The Ritz-Carlton Orlando, Grande Lakes Resort is home to the Orlando outpost of Norman's, owned by celebrity chef and fusion pioneer Norman Van Aken. Menu items change frequently to reflect whatever is fresh and in season. Appetizers include ahi tuna ceviche or green curry-scented lobster ravioli. Classic main dishes include whole roasted chicken with savory bread pudding. Dinner would not be complete without sampling one of the Van Aken's spice creams, such as Mexican chocolate and chipotle spice. All menu items are available with signature wine pairings. Norman's also has a private dining room and an outdoor terrace with views of the golf course. American, Caribbean menu. Dinner. Bar. Business casual attire. Reservations recommended. Valet parking. Outdoor seating. **$$$**

★★PASSAGE TO INDIA

5532 International Drive, Orlando, 407-351-3456;
www.passagetoindiarestaurant-orlando.com

Indian menu. Lunch, dinner. Bar. Children's menu. Casual attire. Reservations recommended. **$$**

★PIRATE'S DINNER ADVENTURE

6400 Carrier Drive, Orlando, 407-248-0590, 800-866-2469; www.piratesdinneradventure.com

American menu. Dinner. Bar. Children's menu. Casual attire. Reservations recommended. **$$$**

★★RAN-GETSU OF TOKYO

8400 International Drive, Orlando, 407-345-0044, 407-351-0401; www.rangetsu.com

Japanese menu. Dinner. Bar. Children's menu. Casual attire. Reservations recommended. **$$**

★★THAI THANI RESTAURANT

11025 International Drive, Orlando, 407-239-9733; www.thaithani.net

Thai menu. Lunch, dinner. Bar. Casual attire. Outdoor seating. **$$**

★★★VITO'S CHOP HOUSE

8633 International Drive, Orlando, 407-354-2467; www.vitoschophouse.com

Brick archways lead into the bar and dining areas at this classic steak house. The menu includes everything from fresh stone crab to massive steaks and meatball marinara. American menu. Dinner. Bar. Children's menu. Business casual attire. Reservations recommended. Valet parking. $$$

SPA

★★★★THE RITZ-CARLTON SPA GRANDE LAKES, ORLANDO

4012 Central Florida Parkway, Orlando, 407-206-2400, 800-241-3333;
www.ritz-carlton.com

From citrus body polishes to orange-inspired manicures and pedicures, Florida's famous fruit is the basis for many of the treatments at this 40,000-square-foot facility, which also has a lap pool, meditation room, fitness center and salon. Bindi, Thai and shiatsu massage are offered along with Shirodhara and Javanese Lulur rituals. Kids and teens have their own menu, including treatments such as the Ritz Kids fizzing manicure and pedicure or kids massage. Fitness consultations and salon services are also available.

ORMOND BEACH

John D. Rockefeller, Sr. spent his twilight years at Ormond Beach playing golf with intense seriousness until he died in 1937 at age 97. Partly on the Atlantic Ocean and the Halifax River, and with the Tomoka River at its back, Ormond Beach has a 23-mile-long, 500-foot-wide public beach. Auto racing was a popular sport here in the early 1900s, when world records were set on the sand. A Stanley Steamer went 127.66 miles per hour in January 1906. Today, 18 miles of the beach are open to cars.

Information: Chamber of Commerce, 165 W. Granada Blvd., 386-677-3454;
www.ormondchamber.com

WHAT TO SEE AND DO

BULOW PLANTATION RUINS STATE HISTORIC SITE

Old Kings Road, Flagler Beach, 386-517-2084; www.floridastateparks.org

Bulow Plantation, which flourished in the early 1800s, was destroyed by the Seminoles in 1836. Now only the ruins of its sugar mill remain on this 109-acre park. Canoe rentals, fishing, nature trails, picnicking. Interpretive center. Daily.

THE CASEMENTS

25 Riverside Drive, Ormond Beach, 386-676-3216; www.ormondbeach.com

Former winter home of John D. Rockefeller, Sr., now serves as cultural center for the city; historical exhibits include Hungarian Historic Room, Boy Scout exhibit. Monday-Friday, Saturday mornings.

ORMOND MEMORIAL ART MUSEUM AND GARDENS

78 E. Granada Blvd., Ormond Beach, 386-676-3347; www.ormondartmuseum.org

Changing exhibits include contemporary art, antiques and special collections; permanent collection of symbolic religious paintings by Malcolm Fraser; 4-acre tropical garden. Monday-Friday 10 a.m.-4 p.m., Saturday-Sunday noon-4 p.m.

HOTELS

★BEST WESTERN MAINSAIL INN & SUITES

281 S. Atlantic Ave., Ormond Beach, 386-677-2131, 800-937-8376; www.bestwestern.com
44 rooms. Complimentary continental breakfast. High-speed Internet access. Beach. Outdoor pool, children's pool. Pets not accepted. **$**

★COMFORT INN

507 S. Atlantic Ave., Ormond Beach, 386-677-8550, 800-456-8550; www.comfortinn.com
47 rooms. Pets accepted, some restrictions; fee. Complimentary continental breakfast. Beach. Outdoor pool, children's pool. **$$**

RESTAURANTS

★★JULIAN'S

88 S. Atlantic Ave., Ormond Beach, 386-677-6767; www.juliansrest.com
American menu. Dinner. Bar. Children's menu. Casual attire. Reservations recommended. **$$**

★★MARIO'S

521 S. Yonge St., Ormond Beach, 386-677-2711
Italian menu. Dinner. Bar. Children's menu. Casual attire. Reservations recommended. **$$**

PALM BEACH

One of America's most glamorous and storied resort towns, Palm Beach has been the winter haven of choice for the nation's well-heeled for more than 100 years. The Vanderbilts may have given way to the Trumps in recent years, but the town is still an exclusive, monied retreat.

Situated on the northern end of a 14-mile-long island, Palm Beach owes its resort existence to a shipwreck in 1878. The vessel's cargo of coconuts washed ashore and took root, transforming a barren ribbon of sand into a palm-shadowed haven. Railroad magnate Henry Morrison Flagler was the first to recognize the attraction of Palm Beach. He built the famous Royal Poinciana Hotel and directed major civic improvements, including extensive landscaping. The Gulf Stream at Phipps Ocean Park is closer to shore in this area (1 to 3 miles) than any other point in the United States.

These days, joining the ladies who lunch at restaurants like Boulud, a tropical outpost of the acclaimed New York boîte, or sunning oneself on the soft sandy beaches is the best way to spend a day in Palm Beach. Shopping for Lily Pulitzer frocks (the designer launched her line here in the '60s) and antiques and furnishings from regency to mid-century modern in the shops along Worth Avenue will deliver quality souvenirs worth carting home.

Information: Palm Beach County Convention and Visitors Bureau,
155 Palm Beach Lakes Blvd., 561-233-3000, 800-833-5733; www.palmbeachfl.com

WHAT TO SEE AND DO

HENRY MORRISON FLAGLER MUSEUM (WHITEHALL)

1 Whitehall Way, Palm Beach, 561-655-2833; www.flaglermuseum.us
This 55-room house was built in 1902 by Henry Morrison Flagler, developer of the Florida East Coast Railroad. An opulent monument to America's Gilded Age,

this marble palace contains paintings, silver, glass, dolls, lace, costumes and family memorabilia. Special exhibits illustrate local history and the vast enterprises of the Flagler system. On the grounds is Flagler's private railroad car, refinished and refitted with exact reproductions of the original carpeting, drapery and upholstery materials. Tuesday-Saturday 10 a.m.-5 p.m.; Sunday noon-5 p.m.

SOCIETY OF THE FOUR ARTS

2 Four Arts Plaza, Palm Beach, 561-655-7226; www.fourarts.org

Complex includes a museum, library and gardens; also lectures, films, concerts in January-March. Galleries late November-late April: Monday-Saturday 10 a.m.-5 p.m., Sunday from 2 p.m. Library November-April: Monday-Saturday 9 a.m.-1 p.m.; rest of year: Monday-Friday. Gardens November-April: Monday-Saturday 10 a.m.-5 p.m., Sunday from 2 p.m.; May-October: Monday-Friday 10 a.m.-5 p.m.

HOTELS

★★★THE BRAZILIAN COURT HOTEL

301 Australian Ave., Palm Beach, 561-655-7740, 800-552-0335; www.braziliancourt.com

Since the 1920s, the Brazilian Court Hotel has been one of Palm Beach's most dignified addresses. Just a short distance from Worth Avenue's shops, the guest rooms and suites reflect the hotel's dedication to detail. A heated outdoor pool provides a restful spot, while people on the party circuit appreciate the spa and salon services. Sophisticated palates rejoice at the dining offered here, where Manhattan's famed Daniel Boulud has opened an outpost of his award-winning Cafe Boulud restaurant. 80 rooms. Pets accepted, some restrictions; fee. Restaurant, bar. Fitness room, spa. Outdoor pool. $$$$

★★★★THE BREAKERS, PALM BEACH

1 S. County Road, Palm Beach, 561-655-6611, 888-273-2537; www.thebreakers.com

Dating back to 1896, the Breakers earned its moniker from the crashing waves on this resort's stretch of beach. Travelers have come here for more than 100 years to admire the views outside as well as the Venetian chandeliers, hand-painted ceilings and priceless antiques inside. Guest rooms feature traditional furnishings and modern treats such as CD players and Playstations. The resort includes 10 tennis courts, 36 holes of championship golf, four oceanfront pools, fine shopping, a full-service fitness center and a luxury spa. The five restaurants and four bars serve everything from beachside lobster clubs to foie gras. 560 rooms. Eight restaurants, four bars. Wireless Internet access. Children's activity center. Three fitness centers, spa. Beach. Five outdoor pools, children's pool. Golf, 36 holes. Tennis. Business center. $$$$

★★★THE CHESTERFIELD PALM BEACH

363 Cocoanut Row, Palm Beach, 561-659-5800, 877-955-1515; www.chesterfieldpb.com

Near the ocean and upscale shopping along Worth Avenue, this nicely appointed boutique hotel is set in a prime Cocoanut Row location. The atmosphere is quiet and comfortable and the interior features an island feel—tropical with and rich fabrics. Guest rooms carry the theme, but the warm tones of the lobby give way to the cool mint green, pink and coral tones. 52 rooms. Pets accepted, some restrictions. Children allowed; fee. High-speed Internet access. Restaurant, bar, fitness center. Outdoor pool, whirlpool. Business center. $$$

143

FLORIDA

★
★
★
★
★

★★★THE COLONY PALM BEACH

155 Hammon Ave., Palm Beach, 561-655-5430, 800-521-5525;
www.thecolonypalmbeach.com

This restored landmark hotel first opened in 1947 and has a prime location in the heart of Palm Beach. The elegant interior is richly decorated and furnished but with a comfortable, casual feel. The sunny guest rooms are decorated in a soft color palette, with upscale bedding and pillow-top mattresses. Bike rentals and beach kits are available to guests, and a nearby health club is complimentary. 90 rooms. Wireless Internet access. Two restaurants, two bars. Outdoor pool. Business center. **$$**

★FAIRFIELD INN AND SUITES PALM BEACH

2870 S. Ocean Blvd., Palm Beach, 561-582-2585, 800-347-5434; www.fairfieldinn.com
98 rooms. Complimentary continental breakfast. Wireless Internet access Fitness room. Outdoor pool. **$**

★★★★★FOUR SEASONS RESORT PALM BEACH

2800 S. Ocean Blvd., Palm Beach, 561-582-2800, 800-545-4000; www.fourseasons.com
This resort unites the best of Palm Beach in one spot. Just minutes from the alluring boutiques of Worth Avenue and the challenges of three championship golf courses, the hotel is set on a secluded stretch of golden beach. The guest rooms have a sophisticated tropical décor, with floral prints, pastel colors and casually elegant furnishings. Southeastern regional dishes are the specialty at the restaurant, while the patio setting of the Atlantic Bar & Grill and the canopied terrace of the Ocean Bistro are perfect for casual meals and tropical drinks. A small spa and well-equipped fitness center round out the experience. 210 rooms. Pets accepted, some restrictions. High-speed Internet access. Four restaurants, four bars. Fitness room, fitness classes available, spa. Outdoor pool, whirlpool. Children's activity center. Tennis. Airport transportation available. Business center. **$$$$**

★★★OCEAN CLUB BEACH RESORT

2842 S. Ocean Blvd., Palm Beach, 561-586-6542, 800-433-1718;
www.theocbeachresort.com

Enter under the striped awning of this oceanfront resort and experience a casual, relaxed atmosphere. Located in the center of Palm Beach Island, the hotel is approximately six miles from downtown Palm Beach. Guests can jog along the Intracoastal Waterway path, snorkel at the nearby man-made reef, rent bicycles or water sports equipment or work out at the off-site fitness center, which is complimentary to guests. Most rooms have private balconies. 134 rooms. Pets accepted; fee. Wireless Internet access. Two restaurants, bar. Beach. Outdoor pool, whirlpool. **$$**

★★★★★THE RITZ-CARLTON, PALM BEACH

100 S. Ocean Blvd., Manalapan, 561-533-6000, 800-241-3333; www.ritzcarlton.com
This luxury resort recently underwent a major renovation. Tucked away on seven oceanfront acres on the southern tip of Palm Beach Island, the hotel remains close to the area's attractions and activities. Rooms and suites artfully blend Florida style with European elegance. Two restaurants showcase the talents of the chefs; try the Ocean Cafe and Bar for lunch, or enjoy afternoon tea at the Lobby Lounge. 270 rooms. Pets accepted, some restrictions; fee. High-speed Internet access. Three restaurants, three

bars. Children's activity center. Fitness room, spa. Beach. Outdoor pool, whirlpool. Tennis. Business center. $$$$

SPECIALTY LODGING

PALM BEACH HISTORIC INN

365 S. County Road, Palm Beach, 561-832-4009, 800-918-9773; www.palmbeachhistoricinn.com

Guests can walk to the beaches, shopping and nightlife from this historic inn located in the center of downtown Palm Beach. Loaded with charm, each comfortable guest room is bright and spacious and decorated with period furnishings and accents. 12 rooms. No children allowed. Complimentary continental breakfast. $$

RESTAURANTS

★★BICE

313 1/2 Worth Ave., Palm Beach, 561-835-1600; www.bicepalmbeach.com

Italian menu. Lunch, dinner. Bar. Business casual attire. Daily. Reservations recommended. Valet parking (dinner). Outdoor seating. Credit card accepted. $$$

★★★★CAFÉ BOULUD

301 Australian Ave., Palm Beach, 561-655-6060, 212-794-2600; www.danielnyc.com

Southern France meets south Florida at the Palm Beach branch of Café Boulud. Here, Lyon-born chef Daniel Boulud offers the same pitch-perfect French cuisine as that of his New York restaurants, with deftly prepared standards like potato-leek soup and red wine-braised short ribs. While the feel of the dining room is formal, it sidesteps stuffiness by avoiding the New York outpost's mahogany and leather. Instead, Boulud uses a tropical palette of yellows and oranges, illuminated through ample windows and French doors. The restaurant boasts a prime location in the historic Brazilian Court Hotel, just steps from Worth Avenue. American, French menu. Breakfast, lunch, dinner. Saturday-Sunday brunch Bar. Business casual attire. Reservations recommended. Valet parking. Outdoor seating. $$$

★★★CAFÉ L'EUROPE

331 S. County Road, Palm Beach, 561-655-4020; www.cafeleurope.com

Three thousand bottles of wine (and about two dozen by the glass) await at Café L'Europe. The international menu takes its cues from France, Italy, Asia, Austria and Latin America. Dishes include everything from roasted rack of lamb with a goat cheese potato tart to the classic Wiener schnitzel with red cabbage. International menu. Lunch, dinner. Closed Monday. Bar. Children's menu. Jacket required. Reservations recommended. Valet parking. $$$$

★★★CHARLEY'S CRAB

456 S. Ocean Blvd., Palm Beach, 561-659-1500, 800-552-6379; www.muer.com

Located on the picturesque Intercoastal Waterway, Charley's Crab is a perfect spot to watch the sunset over the water while digging into fresh seafood, aged cuts of beef and homemade pasta dishes. A signature is Charley's Crab Platter—a mountainous plate piled high with steamed King crab legs, Dungeness clusters, fried soft-shell crab and a Maryland crab cake. Seafood menu. Lunch, dinner. Bar. Children's menu. Casual attire. Reservations recommended. Valet parking. $$$

★★★CHEZ JEAN-PIERRE

132 N. County Road, Palm Beach, 561-833-1171

Choose your preferred dining atmosphere at this many-roomed Palm Beach boîte, which range from chic and stylish to rustic Mediterranean to an intimate wine cellar. In each setting you'll experience French bistro cooking with a fine balance between traditional and more creative offerings. French menu. Dinner. Bar. Children's menu. Reservations recommended. Valet parking. Closed Sunday-Monday; Mid-July-mid-August. $$$

★★★ECHO

230A Sunrise Ave., Palm Beach, 561-802-4222; www.echopalmbeach.com

This restaurant brings a dose of contemporary flair to usually staid Palm Beach with an eclectic menu of dishes influenced by Thailand, China, Japan and Vietnam. Besides an extensive sushi bar selection, the menu includes classics like Peking duck and egg foo yung. Asian menu. Dinner. Closed Monday-Tuesday. Reservations recommended. Bar. $$$

★HAMBURGER HEAVEN

314 S. County Road, Palm Beach, 561-655-5277

American menu. Breakfast, lunch. Closed Sunday. Children's menu. Casual attire. $

★★★★L'ESCALIER

1 S. County Road, Palm Beach, 561-659-8480, 888-273-2537; www.thebreakers.com

The wine list at L'Escalier, an Old World charmer inside the Breakers resort that serves contemporary French fare, includes 1,400 bottles. The resort's collection contains 25,000 bottles, 7,800 of which are on display in the Wine Cellar adjacent to L'Escalier. In other words, if you love wine, this is the restaurant for you. The menu here is innovative yet rooted in French tradition. Seasonal ingredients are sourced from specialty purveyors, and the kitchen delicately adds layers of flavor to the plate, allowing the quality of the ingredients to shine. French menu. Dinner. Closed Sunday-Monday. Bar. Reservations recommended. Valet parking. $$$$

★★★THE LEOPARD LOUNGE

363 Cocoanut Row, Palm Beach, 561-659-5800; www.chesterfieldpb.com

Located in the landmark Chesterfield Hotel, built in 1926, the Leopard Room offers diners distinctive food served in a richly decorated, leopard-themed room featuring black and red accents, leopard skin-patterned carpet and matching menus and dishware. The menu sticks to simple classics like fat slabs of Angus beef, just-caught fish and fresh pastas. American menu. Breakfast, lunch, dinner. Bar. Children's menu. Casual attire. Reservations recommended. Valet parking. Outdoor seating. $$$

★★★RENATO'S

87 Via Mizner, Palm Beach, 561-655-9752; www.renatospalmbeach.com

Dine inside or out at this Palm Beach favorite, where Italian classics like veal Milanese with fresh arugula and tomatoes are served with panache. Italian menu. Lunch, dinner. Bar. Valet parking (dinner). Outdoor seating. $$$

★★★★THE RESTAURANT

2800 S. Ocean Blvd., Palm Beach, 561-533-3750, 800-432-2335;
www.fourseasons.com

The Four Seasons Resort in Palm Beach reopened its signature restaurant in September 2006 after a massive renovation of the décor and menu. The new contemporary and tropically inspired dining room gives every seat an ocean view. The menu melds the flavors of the South, the Caribbean and Central and South America, and comes in prix fixe versions with three, four and five courses. Appetizers include such creations as jumbo lump crab with alligator pear, golden tomato coulis and crispy potato lace, while entrées can include black duck foie gras with wild rice, passion fruit and baby root vegetables. A few Palm Beach classics remain from the previous menu, including the chateaubriand for two. American menu. Dinner. Closed Monday. Bar. Children's menu. Jacket required. Reservations recommended. Valet parking. $$$

★★★RUTH'S CHRIS STEAK HOUSE

661 Highway 1, North Palm Beach, 561-863-0660, 800-544-0808; www.ruthschris.com

Aged beef cooked to perfection has kept Ruth's Chris among America's favorite steakhouse chains. The à la carte sides are as satisfying and flavorful as the meat. Seafood, steak menu. Dinner. Bar. Reservations recommended. Valet parking. $$$

★★THE SEAFOOD BAR

1 S. County Road, Palm Beach, 561-659-8488, 888-273-2537; www.thebreakers.com

Seafood menu. Lunch, dinner. Bar. Children's menu. Casual attire. No Reservations. Valet parking. $$$

★★TA-BOO

221 Worth Ave., Palm Beach, 561-835-3500; www.taboorestaurant.com

American menu. Lunch, dinner, Sunday brunch. Daily late-night. Bar. Casual attire. Valet parking (dinner). $$

★★TESTA'S

221 Royal Poinciana Way, Palm Beach, 561-832-0992; www.testasrestaurants.com

American, Italian menu. Breakfast, lunch, dinner, Sunday brunch. Bar. Children's menu. Casual attire. Reservations recommended. Valet parking. Outdoor seating. $$

★
★
★
★
★

★TOOJAY'S GOURMET DELI & MARKET

313 Royal Poinciana Plaza, Palm Beach, 561-659-7232; www.toojays.com

American menu. Breakfast, lunch, dinner. Children's menu. Casual attire. $$

SPA

★★★★THE SPA AT THE BREAKERS

1 S. County Road, Palm Beach, 561-653-6656, 888-273-2537; www.thebreakers.com

This 20,000-square-foot facility is a pampering paradise overlooking the Atlantic Ocean. The spa features 17 treatment rooms, eight salon stations, a fitness center with ocean views, an outdoor lap pool with a whirlpool spa and an ocean terrace for outdoor massages. From marine algae body wraps to lemongrass-ginger sugar, pomegranate salt glow and honey-papaya scrubs, exfoliating and cleansing never sounded so appetizing. The salon offers a full range of beauty services, from waxing and makeup applications to hairstyling and coloring. Manicures and pedicures polish fingers and toes in regal style.

PALM BEACH GARDENS

This inland town is the home to the Professional Golfer's Association of America and its outstanding golf resort and world-class spa.

Information: www.palmbeachfl.com

HOTEL

★★★PGA NATIONAL RESORT & SPA

400 Avenue of the Champions, Palm Beach Gardens, 561-627-2000, 800-633-9150; www.pga-resorts.com

The PGA National Resort & Spa is home of the Professional Golfer's Association of America. With 90 holes of championship golf, a renowned academy, three driving ranges and six putting greens, it doesn't get much better than this. Set on 2,340 acres only 10 minutes from the beach, the resort is a paradise for outdoor enthusiasts. It features nine pools, a lavish European-style spa, a 26-acre lake, 19 tennis courts and a croquet court. Spacious and comfortable guest rooms have a country décor, while the spa soothes and reenergizes. The resort is undergoing a major renovation, which began with a complete reconstruction of the outdoor pools and addition of several restaurants last fall. 389 rooms, two cottages, high-speed Internet access. Eight restaurants, nine bars. Children's activity center. Fitness room, spa. Beach. Outdoor pool, children's pool, whirlpool. Golf, 90 holes. Tennis. Airport transportation available. Business center. $$

RESTAURANTS

★★★CAFÉ CHARDONNAY

4533 PGA Blvd., Palm Beach Gardens, 561-627-2662; www.cafechardonnay.com

Owned by husband-and-wife team Frank and Gigi Eucalitto, Café Chardonnay offers eclectic American cuisine and an extensive international wine list. The menu takes on global influences from Asia, France and Italy. Wines are offered in flights of three tastes paired with a selection of cheeses and pâté, as well as "Round-trip" flights—two half-bottles, a dessert wine, cheese and pâté. American menu. Lunch, dinner. Bar. Children's menu. Business casual attire. Reservations recommended. Outdoor seating. $$$

★★RIVER HOUSE

2373 PGA Blvd., Palm Beach Gardens, 561-694-1188; www.riverhouserestaurant.com

American menu. Dinner. Casual attire. Valet parking. Daily. Outdoor seating. Bar. $$

★★WATERWAY CAFÉ

2300 PGA Blvd., Palm Beach Gardens, 561-694-1700; www.waterwaycafe.com

American menu. Lunch, dinner. Floating Boat Bar. Casual attire. Outdoor seating. $$

PANAMA CITY

This panhandle town has earned a reputation as the spring break destination of choice for college students across the country. But Panama City and Panama City Beach have plenty of things to do for those looking for fun beyond beaches, beer and bars. To the west along the Gulf, there are 23 miles of sugar-white sand beaches. With a deepwater harbor, the city also ranks as an important coastal port. Boating is possible in the Gulf, the Intracoastal Waterway and several protected bays, and there are a number of public boat ramps and marinas.

Information: Panama City Beach Convention and Visitors Bureau, 17001 Panama City Beach Parkway, 850-233-5070, 800-722-3224; www.800pcbeach.com

WHAT TO SEE AND DO
VISUAL ARTS CENTER OF NORTHWEST FLORIDA
19 E. Fourth St., Panama City, 850-769-4451; www.vac.org.cn

The Visual Arts Center is an art museum featuring an Impressions Gallery for children and gift shop. Exhibits spotlight local, regional and national artists. Studio courses for students of all ages and skill levels, lectures, workshops, a summer youth program and other educational programs are offered. Tuesday-Saturday 10 a.m.-6 p.m.; Sunday noon-6 p.m.

SPECIAL EVENTS
BAY POINT BILLFISH TOURNAMENT
3824 Hatteras Lane, Panama City Beach, 850-235-6911; www.baypointbillfish.com

Considered by locals to be the biggest party in Bay County, the weekend's events include the Miss Billfish contest, an extravagant fireworks show, and fishing contest with weigh-in events, food and live entertainment. The parking fee is donated to local charities. Wednesday-Saturday 5:30-10 p.m., Mid-July.

INDIAN SUMMER SEAFOOD FESTIVAL
Frank Brown Park, 16200 Panama City Beach Parkway, Panama City Beach, 850-233-5070, 800-722-3224; www.visitpanamabeach.com

Tasty seafood, arts and crafts and fireworks provide for a spectacular weekend of entertainment. More than 20 different types of bands and musical acts, from jazz and blues to oldies and gospel, perform throughout the weekend. Second weekend in October.

HOTELS
★COMFORT INN
1013 E. 23rd St., Panama City, 850-769-6969, 877-424-6423; www.comfortinn.com

105 rooms. Complimentary continental breakfast. Wireless Internet access. Fitness room. Outdoor pool. $

★★EDGEWATER BEACH RESORT
11212 Front Beach Road, Panama City Beach, 850-235-4044, 850-235-4044, 800-874-8686; www.edgewaterbeachresort.com

550 rooms, all suites. Wireless Internet access. Three restaurants, two bars. Children's activity center. Fitness room, fitness classes available. Beach. Outdoor pool, whirlpool. Golf, 27 holes. Tennis. Spa. Yoga. Airport transportation available. Business center. $$$

★★HOLIDAY INN SUNSPREE RESORT

11127 Front Beach Road, Panama City Beach, 850-234-1111, 800-633-0266;
www.hipcbeach.com

340 rooms. Two restaurants, bar. Children's activity center. Fitness room. Kids 12 and under eat free at The View and The Bamboo Grill. Beach. Outdoor pool, whirlpool. Business center. **$$**

★★HOLIDAY INN SELECT PANAMA CITY

2001 Martin Luther King Jr. Blvd., Panama City, 850-769-0000, 800-633-0266;
www.hiselect.com

173 rooms. Wireless Internet access. Restaurant, bar. Fitness room. Indoor pool, whirlpool. Pets not accepted. Business center. **$**

★★★MARRIOTT BAY POINT RESORT

4200 Marriott Drive, Panama City Beach, 850-236-6000, 800-644-2650;
www.marriottbaypoint.com

Set on 1,100 acres, this resort community overlooks beautiful St. Andrews Bay and has some of the largest meeting spaces in Florida. Try one of the two 18-hole golf courses or water snorkeling, sailing and jet skiing from the white-sand beach. 320 rooms. Restaurant, bar. Children's activity center. Fitness room. Handicap-accessible rooms. One indoor pool, three outdoor pools, children's pool, whirlpool. Golf, 36 holes. Tennis. Airport transportation available. Spa. **$**

RESTAURANTS

★★★30° BLUE

3900 Marriott Drive, Panama City, 850-236-1115; www.30degreeblue.com

Overlooking the Bay Point marina and the Grand Lagoon near Panama City, this restaurant offers fine dining in a casual, comfortable atmosphere. Fresh local seafood, as well as a variety of other local food products, is used to create the menu of new-world cuisine with classic French influence. French, American menu. Dinner. Closed Sunday-Monday. Casual attire. Reservations recommended. **$$$**

★★BOAR'S HEAD

17290 Front Beach Road, Panama City Beach, 850-234-6628;
www.boarsheadrestaurant.com

Seafood menu. Dinner. Children's menu. Daily. Casual attire. Credit cards accepted. No reservation. **$$$**

★★CAPTAIN ANDERSON'S

5551 N. Lagoon Drive, Panama City Beach, 850-234-2225; www.captanderson.com

Founded by Jimmy and Johnny Patronis, this restaurant serves excellent seafood. Seafood menu. Dinner. Closed Sunday; also November-January. Bars. Children's menu. Casual attire. **$$$**

★★SWEET BASIL'S BISTRO

11208 Front Beach Road, Panama City Beach, 850-234-2855; www.sweet-basils.net

Italian menu. Lunch, dinner. Bar. Children's menu. **$$**

★TREASURE SHIP
3605 Thomas Drive, Panama City Beach, 850-234-8881; www.thetreasureship.com
Seafood menu. Dinner. Bar. Children's menu. **$$**

★UNCLE ERNIE'S BAYFRONT GRILL AND BREWHOUSE
1151 Bayview Ave., Panama City, 850-763-8427; www.uncleerniesbayfrontgrill.com
Seafood, steak menu. Lunch, dinner. Bar. Children's menu. Outdoor seating. Closed Sunday. **$$**

PENSACOLA
In Pensacola, you'll find the old South blended with a bit of modern Florida and colonial Spain. The city has 400 years of history under five flags, and Pensacola Bay, the largest natural landlocked deep-water harbor in Florida, has been the key to the city's history and development. The Spanish established a settlement here in 1559, which lasted only two years. In 1698, they reestablished the site and built a fort. After three battles in 1719, the French took over, but Spain returned in 1723. The British flew their flag in 1763 until Spain returned again in 1781. Andrew Jackson led invasions of this Spanish city in 1814 and 1818, and in 1821 returned to accept Florida as a U.S. territory. During the Civil War it was captured by Union troops and served as a base for the Union blockade of the Confederate Gulf Coast.

After an extensive study in 1914, the Navy chose Pensacola as a site for its Naval Air Station because there were more clear days for flying than at any other available place. Since then, the station has been a major factor in the city's personality and its economy.

Pensacola is the gateway to "the miracle strip," 100 miles of beach-fringed peninsulas and islands stretching to Panama City and heavily populated by sun worshipers and sport anglers. Pensacola Beach to the east and Perdido Key to the west are primarily resort communities. Beaches on both Santa Rosa Sound (Intracoastal Waterway) and the Gulf of Mexico circle the island.

Information: Pensacola Bay Area Convention & Visitors Bureau, 1401 E. Gregory St., 800-874-1234, 850-434-1234; www.visitpensacola.com

WHAT TO SEE AND DO
GULF ISLANDS NATIONAL SEASHORE
1400 Fort Pickens Road, Pensacola, 850-934-2600; www.nps.gov/guis
The 1,742 acres include old Fort Pickens, one of the largest masonry forts in the United States, where Geronimo was imprisoned. Swimming, scuba diving, fishing, picnicking, camping. No pets on beach or in historic fortifications. Santa Rosa area includes beach with pavilion, swimming, picnicking. Other areas of the national seashore include Fort Barrancas and other historical fortifications at Naval Air Station; nearly 1,400 acres of forests with picnicking and nature trails, visitor center at Naval Live Oaks off Highway 98, east of Gulf Breeze; beach recreation at Perdido Key, southwest on Highway 292; and picnic and beach areas at Okaloosa area, east of Fort Walton Beach.

HISTORIC PENSACOLA VILLAGE
205 E. Zaragoza St., Pensacola, 850-595-5985; www.historicpensacola.org
Historic park contains 20 village buildings, 10 of which are open to the public. Monday-Saturday 10 a.m.-4 p.m.

NATIONAL MUSEUM OF NAVAL AVIATION

1750 Radford Blvd., Pensacola, 850-452-3604; www.navalaviationmuseum.org

One of the largest of its kind, this museum features more than 140 historically significant aircraft on display, including the A-1 "Triad," the Navy's first biplane; the NC-4 Flying Boat, the first plane to cross the Atlantic; a vintage 1930s Marine Corps fighter; four A-4 Skyhawks (Blue Angels) suspended in a diamond formation; and full-size modern-day jets. Museum traces the history of naval aviation from the dawn of flight to space exploration; naval aviation and space memorabilia, hands-on children's exhibits, aviation art and photography. Also here is an IMAX theater (fee) and the Naval Aviation Hall of Honor. Gift shop, bookstore. Daily 9 a.m.-5 p.m.

NAVAL AIR STATION PENSACOLA

190 Radford Blvd., Pensacola; www.naspensacola.navy.mil

Home of the headquarters for the Naval Education and Training Command. Established first as the Navy Yard in 1826, the easy access to the sea made it a prime site for the construction of wooden ships. Confederate troops retreating from the Navy Yard in 1862 reduced most of the facilities to rubble. Rebuilding began but was destroyed by a great hurricane in 1906; construction was brought to a standstill once again two years later by a yellow fever epidemic. Reopened in 1914 as the first Naval Aeronautic Station, steady growth has produced such additions to the station as the Naval Aviation Depot and many other tenant commands. Sherman Field is home of the world-famous precision flying Blue Angels, the Navy's flight demonstration squadron.

OLD PENSACOLA LIGHTHOUSE

1750 Radford Blvd., Pensacola, 850-916-7864

This 176-foot structure is fully automated and remote-controlled from Santa Rosa Island. Owned by the Coast Guard; not open to the public.

PENSACOLA MUSEUM OF ART

407 S. Jefferson St., Pensacola, 850-432-6247; www.pensacolamuseumofart.org

Housed in the old city jail, the museum has changing art exhibits; library, lectures. Tuesday-Friday 10 a.m.-5 p.m., Saturday-Sunday from noon.

THE ZOO

5701 Gulf Breeze Parkway, Gulf Breeze, 850-932-2229;
www.thezoonorthwestflorida.org

A 50-acre zoo and botanical garden with more than 700 animals, including one of the largest lowland gorillas in captivity. Giraffe feeding; petting zoo. Train ride. Daily 9 a.m.-5 p.m.

SPECIAL EVENTS

GREAT GULF COAST ARTS FESTIVAL

Seville Square, Pensacola, 850-432-9906; www.ggaf.org

Music, drama, art shows, children's programs. First full weekend in November. Pets not accepted.

MARDI GRAS

21 S Tarragona St., Pensacola, 850-436-7638; www.pensacolamardigras.com

Five days of street dances, parades and musical events. Five days prior to Ash Wednesday.

HOTELS

★BEST VALUE INN AND SUITES, PENSACOLA

8240 N. Davis Highway, Pensacola, 850-479-1099, 800-962-9945

143 rooms. Pets accepted; fee. Complimentary continental breakfast. Wireless Internet access. Outdoor pool. Business center. **$**

★★CROWNE PLAZA, PENSACOLA GRAND

200 E. Gregory St., Pensacola, 850-433-3336, 877-227-6963;
www.pensacolagrandhotel.com

210 rooms. Complimentary continental breakfast. Restaurant, bar. Fitness room. Outdoor pool. Wireless Internet access. Airport transportation available. Business center. **$**

★★DAYS INN

710 N. Palafox St., Pensacola, 850-438-4922, 800-329-7466;
www.daysinn.com

102 rooms. Pets accepted; fee. Complimentary full breakfast. Restaurant, bar. Outdoor pool. **$**

★★HOLIDAY INN

7200 Plantation Road, Pensacola, 850-474-0100, 800-465-4329; www.holiday-inn.com

152 rooms. Pets accepted, some restrictions; fee. Restaurant, bar. Outdoor pool. Airport transportation available. **$**

★LA QUINTA INN

7750 N. Davis Highway, Pensacola, 850-474-0411, 800-687-6667; www.laquinta.com

130 rooms. Pets accepted. Complimentary full breakfast. Wireless Internet access. Outdoor pool. **$**

★★QUALITY INN AND SUITES

51 Gulf Breeze Parkway, Gulf Breeze, 850-932-2214, 800-424-6423;
www.choicehotels.com

168 rooms. Pets accepted; fee. Restaurant. Two outdoor pools, children's pool. **$**

★★RAMADA INN

7601 Scenic Highway, Pensacola, 850-477-7155, 800-272-6232; www.ramada.com

150 rooms. Restaurant, bar. Fitness room. Outdoor pool. High-speed Internet access. **$**

RESTAURANTS

★★ANGUS

1101 Scenic Highway, Pensacola, 850-432-0539; www.anguspensacola.com

Greek menu. Dinner. Bar. Children's menu. Closed Sunday-Monday. **$$$**

★★★JAMIE'S RESTAURANT

424 E. Zaragoza St., Pensacola, 850-434-2911

Tucked into a charming restored Victorian house from the late 1800s, this restaurant has welcomed diners since 1980. French menu. Lunch, dinner. Closed Sunday-Monday. Reservations recommended. $$$

★★MCGUIRE'S IRISH PUB AND BREWERY

600 E. Gregory St., Pensacola, 850-433-6789; www.mcguiresirishpub.com

Irish menu. Lunch, dinner. Bar food. $$

★★★SKOPELOS ON THE BAY

670 Scenic Highway, Pensacola, 850-432-6565; www.myskopelos.com

Seafood menu. Lunch (Friday), dinner, Sunday brunch. Closed Monday. Bar. Children's menu. Valet parking. Outdoor seating. Reservations recommended. $$$

POMPANO BEACH

More than three miles of this oceanfront town's seven-mile-long ocean beach remain in the public domain—the rest is fronted with motels. Situated along the Intracoastal Waterway and the Atlantic Ocean, Pompano Beach offers the full range of water sports and fishing activities.

Information: Greater Pompano Beach Chamber of Commerce, 2200 E. Atlantic Blvd., 954-941-2940; www.pompanobeachchamber.com

WHAT TO SEE AND DO

LOWRANCE ARTIFICIAL REEF

1 1/2 miles offshore of Atlantic Boulevard

The 435-foot *Lowrance* sank on March 31, 1984, to form one of the largest artificial reefs on the East Coast. This reef, in 190 feet of water, is one of the most popular fishing and diving sites in South Florida. Other ships and barges have been sunk off Pompano Beach each year to create additional artificial reefs.

SPECIAL EVENT

POMPANO BEACH SEAFOOD FESTIVAL

East Atlantic Boulevard and Highway A1A, Pompano Beach, 954-941-2940; www.pompanobeachseafoodfestival.com

Bring a blanket and spend a day in the sun enjoying music on the beach, shopping the Boardwalk Bazaar and tasting some delicious treats. Last weekend in April

HOTEL

★★BEACHCOMBER RESORT & VILLAS

1200 S. Ocean Blvd., Pompano Beach, 954-941-7830, 800-231-2423; www.beachcomberhotel.com

143 rooms. Wireless Internet access. Restaurant, two bars. Beach. Outdoor pool. Airport transportation available. $$

★★★OCEAN SANDS RESORT & SPA

1350 N. Ocean Blvd., Pompano Beach, 954-590-1000, 800-583-3500;
www.theoceansandsresortandspa.com

Suites at this ocean-front resort are contemporary and spacious, with flatscreen TVs, washers and dryers, microwaves and refrigerators. The spa offers a full range of services from massage to hydrotherapies. 89 rooms. Pool. Fitness center. Spa. Business center. Valet Parking. $$$

RESTAURANTS

★★★DARREL AND OLIVER

2601 E. Atlantic Blvd., Pompano Beach, 954-782-0606; www.cafemaxx.com

The menu at this regional Florida grill changes daily and includes a wide selection of seafoods like Florida black grouper, Key West dolphin and Nordic salmon. Meat-eaters will enjoy the lamb, Midwestern beef and free-range chicken. A variety of top-notch pastas, salads and vegetarian entrées are also on tap. The room is lively and energetic, with a partially open kitchen and a refrigerated display case at the rear that shows off the fresh fish and meats of the day. The wine collection includes more than 350 varietals. International/fusion menu. Dinner. Bar. Business casual attire. Reservations recommended. Valet parking. $$$

★★JOE'S RIVERSIDE GRILLE

125 N. Riverside Drive, Pompano Beach, 954-941-2499; www.joesriversidegrille.com

Seafood menu. Dinner. Bar. Casual attire. Outdoor seating. $$$

PORT CHARLOTTE

Charlotte County has 38 miles of natural shoreline on the Charlotte Harbor and the Peace and Myakka Rivers, in addition to more than 165 miles of man-made waterways.
Information: Charlotte County Chamber of Commerce, 2702 Tamiami Trail,
941-627-2222; www.charlottecountychamber.org

FLORIDA

★
★
★
★
☆

HOTELS

★DAYS INN

1941 Tamiami Trail, Port Charlotte, 941-627-8900, 800-329-7466;
www.daysinnportcharlotte.com

126 rooms. Pets accepted, some restrictions; fee. Fitness room. Outdoor pool. Wireless Internet access. Valet Parking. $

★HAMPTON INN

24480 Sandhill Blvd., Port Charlotte, 941-627-5600, 800-426-7866;
www.hamptoninn.com

72 rooms. Complimentary continental breakfast. Bar. Pets restricted. Outdoor pool. Business center. High-speed Internet access. $

RESTAURANT

★JOHNNY'S DINER AND PUB

1951 Tamiami Trail, Port Charlotte, 941-255-0994

American menu. Breakfast, lunch, dinner. Bar. Children's menu. $$

PUNTA GORDA

At the mouth of the Peace River on Charlotte Harbor, this is an increasingly popular resort city. Fishing, boating and water sports are particularly good here. Cattle-raising, commercial fishing, construction and land development are important industries.

Information: Punta Gorda Chamber of Commerce, 252 W. Marion Ave.,
941-639-3720; www.puntagorda-chamber.com

WHAT TO SEE AND DO

FISHERMEN'S VILLAGE

1200 W. Retta Esplanade, Punta Gorda, 941-639-8721, 800-639-0020; www.fishville.com
A 40-store specialty shopping mall built on old city fish docks 1,000 feet into Charlotte Harbor. Pool, 98-slip marina, charter fishing boats and services. Tennis. Several restaurants; lodging. Daily.

PONCE DE LEON PARK

2860 Ponce de Leon Springs Road, Ponce de Leon, 850-836-4281;
www.floridastateparks.org
Commemorates the 1513 and 1521 landings of Spaniards in the area. Boat ramp; nature trail, picnicking. Observation mound; shrine. Daily.

HOTELS

★★BEST WESTERN WATERFRONT

300 Retta Esplanade, Punta Gorda, 941-639-1165, 800-525-1022; www.bwpuntagorda.com
182 rooms. Pets accepted; fee. Restaurant, complimentary breakfast. Bar. Wireless Internet access. Outdoor pool. $

★DAYS INN

26560 N. Jones Loop Road, Punta Gorda, 941-637-7200, 800-544-8313;
www.daysinn.com
74 rooms. Complimentary continental breakfast. Outdoor pool, whirlpool. $

SANIBEL AND CAPTIVA ISLANDS

Linked to the mainland by a causeway, Sanibel Island is considered the third-best shelling site in the Western Hemisphere, with deposits on both bay and gulf beaches. North of Sanibel, only a bridge away, is Captiva. Legend has it that the pirate Jose Gaspar used the island to harbor his women captives. Together the islands comprise the Sanibel National Wildlife Refuge, a haven for more than 200 varieties of birds. The islands are a popular tourist destination and several marinas line the east pier of Sanibel.

Information: Sanibel-Captiva Islands Chamber of Commerce, 1159 Causeway Road,
Sanibel Island, 239-472-1080; www.sanibel-captiva.org

WHAT TO SEE AND DO

BAILEY-MATTHEWS SHELL MUSEUM

3075 Sanibel-Captiva Road, Sanibel Island, 239-395-2233, 888-679-6450;
www.shellmuseum.org
This is the only museum in the United States devoted entirely to the shells of the world. Major exhibits include Shells in Tribal Art, Mollusks and Medicine and Man, and Kingdom of the Land shells. Daily, 10 a.m.-5 p.m.

ISLAND HISTORICAL MUSEUM

950 Dunlop Road, Sanibel Island, 239-472-4648; www.sanibelmuseum.org

Former Cracker-style homestead restored and furnished to depict lifestyle of early settlers; antique clothing, tin-type photographs, piano. Re-created Cracker village with grocery store, tea room, post office. Wednesday-Saturday.

J. N. DING DARLING NATIONAL WILDLIFE REFUGE

1 Wildlife Drive, Sanibel Island, 239-472-1100; www.fws.gov/dingdarling

Five-mile wildlife Drive, observation tower; walking and canoe trails. Fishing is permitted; crabbing is permitted with the use of dip-nets only. Feeding alligators is strictly prohibited. Monday-Thursday, Saturday-Sunday.

SPECIAL EVENT
SANIBEL SHELL FAIR

Sanibel Community House, 2173 Periwinkle Way, Sanibel Island, 239-472-2155; www.sanibelsiesta.com

Serious shell collectors display their wares, including specimen shells and live shell exhibits; contests and prizes. First full weekend in March.

HOTELS
★★ISLAND INN

3111 W. Gulf Drive, Sanibel Island, 239-472-1561, 800-851-5088; www.islandinnsanibel.com

57 rooms. Complimentary continental breakfast. Lunch. Dinner. Sunday brunch. Restaurant. Beach. Children's menu, wireless Internet access. Business center. Outdoor pool. Tennis. $$

★★SANIBEL INN

937 E. Gulf Drive, Sanibel, 239-472-3181, 866-565-5480; www.sanibelinn.com

94 rooms. Restaurant, bar. Children's activity center. Beach. Outdoor pool. Tennis. High-speed Internet access. $$

★SONG OF THE SEA

863 E. Gulf Drive, Sanibel Island, 239-432-6718, 866-565-5101; www.songofthesea.com

30 rooms. No children allowed. Complimentary continental breakfast. Restaurant, bar. Outdoor pool, whirlpool. Tennis. Wireless Internet access. $$

★★SUNDIAL BEACH AND GOLF RESORT

1451 Middle Gulf Drive, Sanibel Island, 239-472-4151, 866-565-5093; www.sundialresort.com

270 rooms. Restaurant, bar. Children's activity center. Fitness room. Five outdoor pools, whirlpool. Tennis. Business center. Wireless Internet access. $$$$

RESTAURANTS
★JACARANDA

1223 Periwinkle Way, Sanibel Island, 239-472-1771; www.jacarandaonsanibel.com

Seafood menu. Dinner. Bar. Children's menu. Casual attire. Reservations recommended. Outdoor seating. $$

★MATZALUNA

1200 Periwinkle Way, Sanibel Island, 239-472-1998; www.prawnbroker.com
Italian menu. Dinner. Bar. Children's menu. Casual attire. $$

★★TIMBERS RESTAURANT AND FISH MARKET

703 Tarpon Bay Road, Sanibel Island, 239-395-2722; www.prawnbroker.com
Seafood menu. Dinner. Bar. Children's menu. Casual attire. $$

SARASOTA

Tourism is the main industry in Sarasota—and that has been true since the days before
a single house was built, when anglers used to pitch tents on the beach. The standard
Florida attractions of beach, fishing, golf and sunbathing are available here, and the
city has more than earned its claim as "the cradle of golf" since the first Florida
course was laid out here in 1886 by Colonel J. Hamilton Gillespie.

Ever since John Ringling selected the city of Sarasota as winter quarters for his
circus (1929-1959), the two have become synonymous. Ringling did much to develop
and beautify the area and surrounding islands.
Information: Sararsota Information Center, 701 N. Tamiami Trail, 941-957-1877,
800-522-9799; www.sarasotafl.org

WHAT TO SEE AND DO
ART GALLERY

707 N. Tamiami Trail, Sarasota, 941-365-2032; www.artsarasota.org
An Italian Renaissance-style villa created by local crafters with shiploads of columns,
doorways, roof sculptures and marble collected in Italy by John Ringling. One of the
most distinguished collections of Baroque art in the Western Hemisphere; also contemporary art, Rubens collection, sculpture garden in courtyard. Tuesday-Saturday
10 a.m.-4 p.m.

CIRCUS SARASOTA

8251 15th St. East, Sarasota, 941-355-9335; www.circussarasota.org
Professional one-ring Big Top performances at varying locations in Sarasota throughout the year.

RINGLING MUSEUM OF ART

5401 Bay Shore Road, Sarasota, 941-359-5700; www.ringling.org
The 66-acre estate of John Ringling is a cultural complex, left to the people of Florida
upon his death in 1936. On its beautifully landscaped grounds are a sculpture courtyard and a rose garden. Daily 10 a.m.-5:30 p.m.

RINGLING RESIDENCE (CA'D'ZAN)

5401 Bay Shore Road, Sarasota, 941-359-5700
An elaborate Venetian Gothic mansion patterned after the Doge's Palace in Venice,
Italy. Venetian glass windows, hand-wrought iron work, marble floors, period furnish-
ings and art objects from around the world. Daily 10 a.m.-5:30 p.m.

SARASOTA CLASSIC CAR MUSEUM

5500 N. Tamiami Trail, Sarasota, 941-355-6228; www.sarasotacarmuseum.org

Built in 1952, the museum houses more than 100 restored antique classic cars and 2,000 mechanical antique music boxes and machines; turn-of-the-century arcade; tours every half hour. Daily 9 a.m.-6 p.m.

SARASOTA JUNGLE GARDENS

3701 Bayshore Road, Sarasota, 941-355-5305, 877-861-6547;
www.sarasotajunglegardens.com

Tropical birds in a jungle paradise; more than 5,000 varieties of plants; wild jungle trails; formal gardens; flamingos, swans, peacocks and pelicans roam free. The Flamingo Café serves delicious sandwiches, ice cream and snacks and is open daily 9 a.m.-4:30 p.m. Children's playground. Daily 9 a.m.-5 p.m.

SPECIAL EVENTS

CINCINNATI REDS SPRING TRAINING

Ed Smith Sports Complex, 2700 12th St., Sarasota, 941-954-4101;
www.reds.mlb.com

Cincinnati Reds baseball spring training. Early March-early April.

SARASOTA JAZZ FESTIVAL

Van Wezel Performing Arts Hall, 777 N. Tamiami Trail, Sarasota,
941-366-1552, 941-953-3368; www.jazzclubsarasota.com

The Sarasota Jazz Festival brings together world-famous and local musicians for a week full of jazz concerts featuring an elegant buffet, wine and a beautiful setting overlooking the bay. Early April.

SARASOTA OPERA ASSOCIATION

Sarasota Opera House, 61 N. Pineapple Ave., Sarasota, 941-366-8450;
www.sarasotaopera.org

The Sarasota Opera presents 38 opera performances, plus several concerts and other special events, during its eight-week season. The opera is known for successfully producing a delightful mix of both world famous and more obscure works. Mid-February-mid-March.

HOTELS

★HAMPTON INN

5995 Cattleridge Road, Sarasota, 941-371-1900, 800-426-7866;
www.hamptoninnsarasota.com, www.hamptoninn.com

121 rooms. Complimentary continental breakfast. Fitness room. High-speed Internet access. Free stay for children with parents. Outdoor pool. **$**

★★HELMSLEY SANDCASTLE HOTEL

1540 Ben Franklin Drive, Sarasota, 941-388-2181, 800-225-2181;
www.helmsleysandcastle.com

173 rooms. Two restaurants, two bars. Fitness room. Beach. Two outdoor pools. Business center. **$$**

159

FLORIDA

★
★
★
★
★

m o b i l t r a v e l g u i d e . c o m

★★HOLIDAY INN

233 Ben Franklin Drive, Sarasota, 941-388-5555, 800-465-4329; www.lidobeach.net

135 rooms, four suites. Restaurant, two bars. Fitness room. Beach. Outdoor pool. **$$**

★HOLIDAY INN EXPRESS

6600 S. Tamiami Trail, Sarasota, 941-924-4900, 800-465-4329; www.hiexpress.com

131 rooms. Pets accepted, some restrictions; fee. Complimentary continental breakfast. Fitness room. Spa. Tennis. Outdoor pool, whirlpool. High-speed Internet access. **$**

★★★HYATT SARASOTA

1000 Boulevard of the Arts, Sarasota, 941-953-1234, 800-233-1234; www.sarasota.hyatt.com

On the Sarasota Quay waterfront and minutes from beaches and shopping at St. Armand's Circle, this property remains a popular convention site. Dine inside or out at the Boathouse, taking in views of the private Hyatt marina. 294 rooms. Pets accepted, some restrictions; fee. Two restaurants, three bars. Fitness room. Outdoor pool, whirlpool. High-speed Internet access. Business center. **$$$**

★★★★THE RITZ-CARLTON, SARASOTA

1111 Ritz-Carlton Drive, Sarasota, 941-309-2000, 800-241-3333; www.ritzcarlton.com

Located in the city's cultural district overlooking Sarasota Bay, the Ritz-Carlton is close to the boutiques and galleries of the city but maintains a resort feel. Rooms feature rich colors, sumptuous fabrics and antiques. The hotel also offers an 18-hole Tom Fazio–designed golf course. From the butlers on call to assist with computer woes to the bath drawn by the bath butlers, service is superlative. 266 rooms. Pets accepted, some restrictions; fee. Wireless Internet access. Four restaurants, two bar. Children's activity center. Fitness room, fitness classes available, spa. Beach. Outdoor pool, whirlpool. Golf, 18 holes. Tennis. Airport transportation available. Business center.

★★SARASOTA HOTEL MARINA

7150 N. Tamiami Trail, Sarasota, 941-355-2781; www.sarasotahotelmarina.com

178 rooms. High-speed Internet access. Two restaurants, two bars. Fitness room. Outdoor pool. Airport transportation available. Business center. **$**

★SIESTA BEACH RESORT HOTEL AND SUITES

5311 Ocean Blvd., Sarasota, 941-349-3211, 800-223-5786; www.siestakeyflorida.com

50 rooms. Beach. Outdoor pool, whirlpool. Wireless Internet access. **$**

SPECIALTY LODGING

THE CYPRESS

621 Gulfstream Ave. S., Sarasota, 941-955-4683; www.cypressbb.com

The rooms of this 1940 inn boast views of Sarasota Bay and the inn's historic gardens. An elaborate gourmet breakfast is included in the stay, as well as an afternoon social with hors d'oeuvres. Only a short walk away, the marina offers boat rentals and riverboat dining. Five rooms. No children allowed. Complimentary full breakfast. Wireless Internet access. **$$**

RESTAURANTS

★★★BIJOU CAFÉ

1287 First St., Sarasota, 941-366-8111; www.bijoucafe.net

This noisy, eclectic restaurant with country French décor is a converted 1930s gas station. If you're headed to the nearby Opera House, dine pre-theater on hearty options like grilled rack of lamb with roasted shallot and mint demi-glace. International menu. Lunch, dinner. Closed Sunday in summer. Bar. Business casual attire. Reservations recommended. Valet parking. Outdoor seating. $$

★★CAFÉ L'EUROPE

431 St. Armand's Circle, Sarasota, 941-388-4415; www.cafeleurope.net

Continental menu. Lunch. Dinner. Bar. Children's menu. Business casual attire. Reservations recommended. Valet parking. Outdoor seating. $$$

★★COLUMBIA

411 St. Armand's Circle, Sarasota, 941-388-3987; www.columbiarestaurant.com

Spanish menu. Lunch, dinner. Bar. Children's menu. Casual attire. Reservations recommended. Outdoor seating. $$

★★FRED'S

1917 S. Osprey Ave., Sarasota, 941-364-5811; www.epicureanlife.com

American menu. Lunch, dinner. Bar. Business casual attire. Reservations recommended. Outdoor seating. $$

★HILLVIEW GRILL

1920 Hillview St., Sarasota, 941-952-0045; www.hillviewgrill.com

American menu. Lunch, dinner. Bar. Children's menu. Casual attire. Reservations recommended. Outdoor seating. $$

★★JO-TO JAPANESE STEAKHOUSE

7971 N. Tamiami Trail, Sarasota, 941-351-4677; www.jotosteakhouse.com

Japanese menu. Dinner. Bar. Casual attire. $$

★★MARINA JACK'S

2 Marina Plaza, Sarasota, 941-365-4232; www.marinajacks.com

American menu. Lunch, dinner. Bar. Children's menu. Casual attire. Reservations recommended. Valet parking. Outdoor seating. $$

★★★MICHAEL'S ON EAST

1212 East Ave. S., Sarasota, 941-366-0007; www.bestfood.com

This contemporary restaurant showcases fresh, seasonal and organic ingredients in dishes such as local Atlantic swordfish with red potatoes and onions. The cozy, onsite piano bar offers a comfortable place to sample hors d'oeuvres such as fresh tomato bruschetta and classic cocktails. American menu. Lunch, dinner. Closed Sunday. Bar. Business casual attire. Reservations recommended. Valet parking. $$$

FLORIDA

★
★
★
★

★★PRIMO RISTORANTE

8076 N. Tamiami Trail, Sarasota, 941-359-3690, 877-774-6611;
www.primo-ristorante.com

Italian menu. Dinner. Bar. Children's menu. Casual attire. Outdoor seating. Business center. Tuesday-Saturday 4-10 p.m., Sunday 3-9 p.m. Closed Mondays for summer, until November. $$

★SUGAR AND SPICE

4000 Cattlemen Road, Sarasota, 941-342-1649

Amish menu. Lunch, dinner. Closed Sunday. Children's menu. Casual attire. $

★★★★VERNONA RESTAURANT

1111 Ritz-Carlton Drive, Sarasota, 941-309-2008, 800-241-3333;
www.ritzcarlton.com

The ambience at this restaurant inside the Ritz-Carlton, Sarasota resembles that of a Tuscan villa, complete with crystal chandeliers and elegantly arched windows. The menu, though, is contemporary American and features locally sourced organic ingredients. Signature favorites include lobster macaroni and cheese, roasted ratatouille soup, sage-orange braised veal short ribs and olive oil-poached prime beef tenderloin. Save room for the Sarasota key lime pie. American menu. Breakfast, lunch, dinner, Sunday brunch. Bar. Children's menu. Casual attire. Reservations recommended. Valet Parking. Credit cards.

SPA

★★★★THE RITZ-CARLTON MEMBERS CLUB SPA, RITZ-CARLTON, SARASOTA

1111 Ritz-Carlton Drive, Sarasota, 941-309-2000, 800-241-3333; www.rcmcsarasota.com

This exclusive spa, for use only by guests of the resort and members of the Ritz-Carlton Members Club, combines state-of-the-art design with European technique. More than 100 treatments make up the comprehensive menu, but massages, masques, scrubs and body treatments are the specialty. Ten varieties of facials cater to clients with varying skin types. Hand and foot treatments go beyond the basic manicure or pedicure to include citrus antiaging manicures and mineral powder pedicures. Salon services include hair care and styling, as well as makeup application and lessons.

SEBRING

With sandy ridge country for citrus, mucklands for vegetables and flowers and flatlands for cattle, Sebring's economy relies upon agriculture, light industry and some tourism.

Information: Chamber of Commerce, 227 U.S. Highway 27 N., 863-385-8448;
www.sebringflchamber.com

WHAT TO SEE AND DO

HIGHLANDS HAMMOCK STATE PARK

5931 Hammock Road, Sebring, 863-386-6094

An outstanding nature park with museum, foot trails, scenic drive, tours by tram. Bicycle rentals, picnic areas, camping.

SPECIAL EVENT

SEBRING 12-HOUR ENDURANCE RACE

113 Midway Drive, Sebring, 863-655-1442, 800-626-7223; www.sebringraceway.com
Oldest road race in America. Mid-March.

HOTELS

★★INN ON THE LAKES

3100 Golfview Road, Sebring, 863-471-9400, 800-531-5253;
www.innonthelakessebring.com
159 rooms. Pets accepted, some restrictions; fee. Restaurant, bar. Fitness room. Outdoor pool. **$**

★★QUALITY INN

6525 Highway 27 North, Sebring, 863-385-4500, 800-424-6423; www.qualityinn.com
149 rooms. Pets accepted, some restrictions; fee. Restaurant, bar. Fitness room. Outdoor pool, children's pool. **$**

SIESTA KEY

In 1907, Harry L. Higel and Captain Louis Roberts launched an advertising campaign to draw vacationers to what they called the prettiest spot in the world. Although the claim may be disputed, Siesta Key has been hailed as a top island destination, and Crescent Beach has been rated as one of the top three beaches in the world. Shell hunters, snorkelers and anglers usually have great success here. With close proximity to Sarasota and its attractions, Siesta Key is a good base from which to take in the sights.
Information: Siesta Key Chamber of Commerce, 5118 Ocean Blvd.,
941-349-3800, 866-831-7778; www.siestakeychamber.com

163

FLORIDA

★
★
★
★

HOTEL

★CAPTIVA BEACH RESORT

6772 Sara Sea Circle, Siesta Key, 941-349-4131, 800-349-4131;
www.captivabeachresort.com
20 rooms, all suites. Beach. Outdoor pool. **$$**

SPECIALTY LODGING

TURTLE BEACH RESORT

9049 Midnight Pass Road, Siesta Key, 941-349-4554; www.turtlebeachresort.com
10 rooms, all suites. Pets accepted; fee. Outdoor pool. **$$$**

RESTAURANTS

★★★OPHELIA'S ON THE BAY

9105 Midnight Pass Road, Siesta Key, 941-349-2212, 877-229-9601;
www.opheliasonthebay.net
You'll find worldly American offerings in an understated, tasteful atmosphere at this Sarasota Bayfront destination in the Turtle Beach Resort. Choose from two glass-walled dining rooms or the dockside patio to enjoy a splendid view. Continental menu. Dinner. Bar. Children's menu. Valet parking. Outdoor seating. **$$$**

★**TURTLES ON LITTLE SARASOTA BAY**
8875 Midnight Pass Road, Siesta Key, 941-346-2207
Seafood menu. Lunch, dinner, Sunday brunch. Bar. Children's menu. Outdoor seating. **$$**

SILVER SPRINGS

Nearly two million people come to this town each year, mostly to see the springs, one of the state's top attractions. This is lake, horse and cattle country, and a ranger district office of the Ocala National Forest is located here.

Information: Ocala/Marion County Chamber of Commerce, 110 E. Silver Springs Blvd.,
 352-629-8051; www.ocalacc.com

WHAT TO SEE AND DO
SILVER SPRINGS—SOURCE OF THE SILVER RIVER
5656 E. Silver Springs Blvd., Silver Springs, 352-236-2121
This 350-acre, multitheme nature park and national landmark includes the main spring (more than 500 million gallons of water flow every 24 hours). Estimated to be 100,000 years old, the spring has one large opening where water, filtered through limestone, surges to the surface from a 65-foot by 12-foot cavern. Four different 30-minute rides let visitors view the area: The famous glass-bottomed boats and a jungle cruise pass by 14 springs, various plant and fish species, alligators, waterfowl and exotic wildlife. The surrounding park includes the World of Bears exhibit, Kids Ahoy! Playland, entertainment on the Twin Oaks Mansion concert stage and live animal shows. Strollers, wheelchairs available. Daily.

164

ST. AUGUSTINE

Spanish towers and steeples, red-capped roofs and low, overhanging balconies are reminders of St. Augustine's four centuries of history, which began on September 8, 1565, when Don Pedro Menendez de Aviles dropped anchor and rowed ashore. As a symbol of the cultural ties between the United States and Latin nations, and in an effort to establish a Latino counterpart to Williamsburg, Virginia, St. Augustine (the oldest permanent settlement in the United States) has been restoring important historic areas to their former Spanish charm.

Ponce de Leon and his men are believed to have landed in the vicinity of what is now St. Augustine in 1513 to fill their casks with water from a local spring. However, the formal history of Spanish settlement began some 50 years later when Menendez arrived, launching St. Augustine on a history often marked by bloody violence. Following orders, Menendez wiped out the French Huguenot settlement at Fort Caroline, using such violent thoroughness that the River of Dolphins became known as the Matanzas—the Spanish word for "slaughters." To protect this strategic outpost, the Spanish built Castillo de San Marcos, a massive gray fortress that still dominates the town today. Through the centuries, St. Augustine has been attacked, counterattacked, pillaged, burned, betrayed and defended. The Spanish, British, Confederate and U.S. flags all have flown over the city.

St. Augustine began its more recent history as a fashionable resort town when in the 1880s, Henry Morrison Flagler built two large hotels here and made the city the headquarters of the Florida East Coast Railroad. The robber barons of the Gilded Age spent their winters here, building grand houses similar to those in Newport. St. Augustine occupies a peninsula with the Matanzas and North Rivers on the east and south and the San Sebastian on the west. Still a railroad crossroads, the city's industries—other than tourism—include food and seafood processing, farming, boat building, printing, bookbinding and aircraft manufacturing.

Information: St. Augustine, Ponte Vedra and The Beaches Visitors & Convention Bureau, 88 Riberia St., 904-829-1711, 800-653-2489; www.visitoldcity.com

WHAT TO SEE AND DO
CASTILLO DE SAN MARCOS NATIONAL MONUMENT
1 S. Castillo Drive, St. Augustine, 904-829-6506; www.nps.gov/casa

This massive masonry structure constructed between 1672 and 1695 was built to permanently replace a succession of nine wooden fortifications. It was made of coquina, a natural rock of shells and sand. Hispanic artisans and convicts, Native American laborers, black royal slaves and English prisoners erected walls 26 feet high, 14 feet thick at the base, 9 feet at the top and 4 feet at the parapet. Before completion in 1683, Castillo served as St. Augustine's citadel during a pirate raid. Castillo de San Marcos was never conquered. It withstood a 50-day siege when St. Augustine was captured by the South Carolinians in 1702, and another siege of 38 days in 1740. During the Revolutionary War, the British imprisoned "rebels" in the Castillo and felt confident the structure could repulse an American or a Spanish attack. The United States used the fort as a battery in the coastal defense system, as a military prison and as a magazine. Wildcat, the Seminole leader, led an escape from Castillo; Confederate and Union troops occupied it during the Civil War; and American deserters were imprisoned here during the Spanish-American War. As Fort Marion, Castillo de San Marcos was the principal fortification in a regional defense system that reached north to St. Mary's River, south to Matanzas Inlet and west to St. Mark's. A unique specimen of a vanished style of military architecture and engineering, it became a national monument in 1924.

DE MESA-SANCHEZ HOUSE
43 St. George St., St. Augustine

One of 33 original surviving colonial houses recently restored; antique furnishings from the early 1800s, when Florida was still a U.S. territory.

FLAGLER COLLEGE
74 King St., St. Augustine, 904-829-6481; www.flagler.edu

The restored main campus building is the former Ponce de Leon Hotel, built in 1887 by railroad magnate Henry Morrison Flagler. Campus tours May-mid-August, daily.

FOUNTAIN OF YOUTH
11 Magnolia Ave., St. Augustine, 904-829-3168, 800-356-8222; www.fountainofyouthflorida.com

A 15-acre tropical setting thought to be the first recorded North American landmark. Native American burial grounds; planetarium and discovery globe (both continuous shows); museum, swan pool, Ponce de Leon statue. Daily 9 a.m.-5 p.m.

GALLEGOS HOUSE
21 St. George St., St. Augustine

Reconstruction of a two-room tabby house occupied in the 1750s by a Spanish soldier and his family. Daily lifestyle and household activities of the period are depicted; demonstrations of 18th-century outdoor cooking.

GOMEZ HOUSE

27 St. George St., St. Augustine

Reconstruction of 18th-century one-room wooden dwelling occupied by a Spanish infantryman in 1763; small neighborhood shop located in a portion of the room where neighbors came to trade or barter.

GONZALES AND DE HITA HOUSES

37 St. George St., St. Augustine

The original Gonzalez House, built of native shellstone, is typical of Spanish colonial houses. The interior contains an area with demonstrations of spinning, weaving and textile arts. The de Hita residence is used for special hands-on learning activities.

LIGHTNER MUSEUM

75 King St., St. Augustine, 904-824-2874; www.lightnermuseum.org

This museum celebrating the Victorian era is set in the restored 300-room former Hotel Alcazar, a Spanish Renaissance-style structure built in 1887 by the architects who went on to build the New York Public Library and the U.S. Senate building. Natural science exhibits, a Victorian village and collections of art, porcelain, 19th-century musical instruments, needlework, ceramics, Tiffany glass, furniture and dolls. Daily 9 a.m.-5 p.m.

MISSION OF NOMBRE DE DIOS

27 Ocean Ave., St. Augustine, 904-824-2809, 800-342-6529; www.missionandshire.org

A 208-foot stainless-steel cross marks the site of the founding of St. Augustine, September 8, 1565. Also find the Shrine of Our Lady of La Leche, established in 1603 and dedicated to the Motherhood of Mary. Daily.

PENA-PECK HOUSE

143 St. George St., St. Augustine, 904-829-5064

Home of the Spanish Royal Treasurer. Original 19th-century residence; guided tours. Daily.

SPANISH QUARTER

53 St. George St., St. Augustine, 904-825-6830

Restoration of 18th-century Spanish colonial village by the Historic St. Augustine Preservation Board, a state project. The original settlement was founded in 1565. Daily.

ST. AUGUSTINE ALLIGATOR FARM

999 Anastasia Blvd., St. Augustine, 904-824-3337; www.alligatorfarm.com

This farm, established in 1893, offers views of huge alligators and crocodiles; Reptile Show, Alligator Show and Land of Crocodiles. Also on the farm are tropical birds, monkeys, deer and ducks. Daily 9 a.m.-6 p.m.

ST. AUGUSTINE LIGHTHOUSE AND MUSEUM

81 Lighthouse Ave., St. Augustine, 904-829-0745; www.staugustinelighthouse.com

Tours of restored lightkeeper's house; coastal museum with exhibits, video. Visitors can also climb to top of lighthouse tower. Daily.

THE WORLD GOLF VILLAGE

1 World Golf Place, St. Augustine Beach, 904-940-4000; www.wgv.com

World Golf Hall of Fame, interactive exhibits, IMAX golf theater, golf school, golf course, resort. Shopping, restaurants. Daily.

XIMENEZ-FATIO HOUSE

20 Aviles St., St. Augustine, 904-829-3575; www.ximenezfatiohouse.org

Originally a house and general store built of coquina; used as an inn during the 1800s. Kitchen in rear is the only original kitchen remaining in St. Augustine. Museum house of the National Society of Colonial Dames of America in the State of Florida. Tuesday-Saturday, 11 a.m.-4 p.m.

ZORAYDA CASTLE

83 King St., St. Augustine

Inspired by the Alhambra in Spain. Daily.

SPECIAL EVENT
SPANISH NIGHT WATCH

St. George Street, St. Augustine

Candlelight procession with colorful Spanish costumes commemorates the presence of the Spanish in St. Augustine. Mid-June.

HOTELS
★★AVENIDA INN

2800 N. Ponce de Leon Blvd., St. Augustine, 904-829-6581, 800-331-9995; www.avenida.com

63 rooms. Pets accepted; fee. Restaurant. Outdoor pool. $

★BAYFRONT INN

138 Avenida Menendez, St. Augustine, 904-824-1681, 800-558-3455; www.bayfrontinn.com

39 rooms. Outdoor pool, whirlpool. $

★BEACHERS LODGE

6970 A1A South, St. Augustine Beach, 904-471-8849, 800-527-8849; www.beacherslodge.com

132 rooms. Beach. Outdoor pool. $

★★★CASA MONICA HOTEL

95 Cordova St., St. Augustine, 904-827-1888, 800-648-1888; www.casamonica.com

This Spanish-style hotel dates back to 1888 but has recently been restored to its former glory. Moorish details enhance the rooms and suites, and all accommodations are outfitted with the latest amenities. The city-center location does not preclude a visit to the beach because all guests are granted privileges at the nearby Serenata Beach Club. Tee times at local courses can also be easily arranged. 138 rooms. Restaurant, bar. Fitness room. Outdoor pool, whirlpool. High-speed Internet access. Valet parking. $$

★COMFORT INN

901 A1A Beach Blvd., St. Augustine Beach, 904-471-1474, 800 228-5150;
www.comfortinn.com
70 rooms. Complimentary continental breakfast. Outdoor pool, whirlpool. $

★★★GRANDE VILLAS AT WORLD GOLF VILLAGE

100 Front Nine Drive, St. Augustine, 904-940-2000; www.wgv.com
This hotel, located at the World Golf Village complex, has one- or two-bedroom villas
with fully equipped kitchens and washers and dryers. Rooms overlook the 17th and
18th holes of the famed Slammer and Squire golf course. 104 rooms. Restaurant, bar.
Fitness room, spa. Outdoor pool, whirlpool. Business center. $

★★HOLIDAY INN

860 A1A Beach Blvd., St. Augustine Beach, 904-471-2555, 877-424-2449;
www.holidayinn.com
152 rooms. Pets accepted, some restrictions; fee. Restaurant, bar. Beach. Outdoor pool. $

★★MONTEREY INN

16 Avenida Menendez, St. Augustine, 904-824-4482; www.themontereyinn.com
59 rooms. Restaurant. Outdoor pool. $

★★★RENAISSANCE WORLD GOLF VILLAGE RESORT

500 S. Legacy Trail, St. Augustine, 904-940-8000, 888-740-7020;
www.renaissancehotels.com
Rooms at this sprawling hotel were completely renovated last fall. The only course to
be codesigned by Jack Nicklaus and Arnold Palmer is located here, as is the World
Golf Hall of Fame. 301 rooms. Restaurant, bar. Fitness room. Outdoor pool, whirl-
pool. Business center. $$

★ST. AUGUSTINE OCEAN INN

3955 Florida A1A South, St. Augustine Beach, 904-471-8010, 800-528-1234;
www.staugustineoceaninn.com
35 rooms. Complimentary continental breakfast. Outdoor pool. $

SPECIALTY LODGINGS

CASA DE LA PAZ BAYFRONT BED AND BREAKFAST

22 Avenida Menendez, St. Augustine, 904-829-2915, 800-929-2915
Built in 1915, this charming bed and breakfast has guest rooms named after
Spanish explorers. Most have views of Matanzas Bay or the Bridge of Lions. Casa de
la Paz—in conjunction with a local day spa and some of the area's better restaurants—
offers a great selection of packages for couples. Seven rooms. Complimentary full
breakfast. $

CEDAR HOUSE INN VICTORIAN BED & BREAKFAST

79 Cedar St., St. Augustine, 904-829-0079, 800-845-0012; www.cedarhouseinn.com
Restored Victorian house (1893); original floors and woodwork. Seven rooms. Chil-
dren over 10 years only. Complimentary full breakfast. $

CENTENNIAL HOUSE

26 Cordova St., St. Augustine, 904-810-2218, 800-611-2880;
www.centennialhouse.com
Eight rooms. Closed week of Christmas. Complimentary full breakfast. Whirlpool. **$$**

KENWOOD INN

38 Marine St., St. Augustine, 904-824-2116; 800-824-8151; www.thekenwoodinn.com
In historic district downtown. Restored Victorian house; courtyard. 14 rooms. Children over 8 years only. Complimentary continental breakfast. Outdoor pool. **$$**

OLD HOUSE CITY INN

115 Cordova St., St. Augustine, 904-826-0113; www.oldcityhouse.com
Colonial Revival inn built in 1873 as a stable to a mansion. Seven rooms. Complimentary full breakfast. Restaurant. **$**

OLD POWDER HOUSE INN

38 Cordova St., St. Augustine, 904-824-4149, 800-447-4149; www.oldpowderhouse.com
Built in 1899 on the site of a Spanish colonial powder house that supplied nearby fort. Nine rooms. Children over 8 years only. Complimentary full breakfast. **$$**

ST. FRANCIS INN

279 St. George St., St. Augustine, 904-824-6068, 800-824-6062; www.stfrancisinn.com
Restored inn near the oldest house in the country; library, balconies, courtyard. 14 rooms. Pets accepted, some restrictions; fee. Complimentary full breakfast. Outdoor pool. **$**

WESTCOTT HOUSE

146 Avenida Menendez, St. Augustine, 904-824-4301, 800-513-9814;
www.westcotthouse.com
This fine 1880s Victorian on the Intracoastal Waterway was originally built for Dr. John Westcott. Most of the guest rooms overlook Matanzas Bay and the Bridge of Lions. 16 rooms. Pets accepted, some restrictions; fee. Complimentary full breakfast. **$**

RESTAURANTS

★GYPSY CAB CO.

828 Anastasia Blvd., St. Augustine Beach, 904-824-8244; www.gypsycab.com
American, seafood menu. Lunch, dinner, brunch. Bar. Children's menu. **$$**

★★SALT WATER COWBOY'S

299 Dondanville Road, St. Augustine Beach, 904-471-2332; www.saltwatercowboys.com
Seafood menu. Dinner. Closed second week of December. Children's menu. Outdoor seating. **$$**

ST. PETE BEACH

This strip of islands connected by bridges and causeways is separated from the mainland by Boca Ciega Bay. Included here are Indian Rocks Beach, Indian Shores, Madeira Beach, Redington Beach, Redington Shores, St. Pete Beach and Treasure Island.
Information: City of St. Pete Beach, 155 Corey Ave., 727-367-2735, 813-360-6957;
www.stpetebeach.org

HOTELS

★★★DON CESAR BEACH RESORT, A LOEWS HOTEL

3400 Gulf Blvd., St. Pete Beach, 727-360-1881, 800-282-1116; www.loewshotels.com
Affectionately known as the pink palace, this 1920s-era resort rests on a stretch of white sand at St. Pete Beach. All guest rooms offer a Gulf view and feature crisp white bed linens and white wrought-iron headboards. Shopping is a favorite pastime here, with everything from jewelry to clothing available at the resort shops. The resort's restaurants and bars capitalize on the seaside setting and offer delectable treats. 277 rooms. Pets accepted, some restrictions; fee. Wireless Internet access. Three restaurants, two bars. Children's activity center. Fitness room, fitness classes available, spa. Beach. Two outdoor pools, two whirlpools. Business center. **$$$**

★★★DOUBLETREE BEACH RESORT

17120 Gulf Blvd., North Redington Beach, 727-391-4000, 800-678-3832;
www.doubletreebeachresort.com
This beachfront resort overlooks the Boca Ciega Intracoastal Waterway and the Gulf. Waterfront dining is available on the veranda or guests can watch the sunset from the beach bar. 125 rooms. Restaurant, bar. Beach. Outdoor pool. **$$**

★ISLAND'S END RESORT

1 Pass-A-Grille Way, St. Pete Beach, 727-360-5023; www.islandsend.com
Six rooms, all suites. Pets not accepted, some restrictions; fee. Complimentary continental breakfast. Wireless Internet access. Beach. Outdoor pool. **$$**

★★THUNDERBIRD BEACH RESORT

10700 Gulf Blvd., Treasure Island, 727-367-1961, 800-367-2473;
www.thunderbirdflorida.com
64 rooms. Restaurant, bar. Beach. Outdoor pool, whirlpool. **$**

★★★TRADEWINDS ISLAND GRAND BEACH RESORT

5500 Gulf Blvd., St. Pete Beach, 727-367-6461, 800-360-4016; www.justletgo.com
Sister to the Tradewinds Sandpiper Hotel & Suites, this 18-acre, Gulf-front resort features a Floridian-styled lobby and guest rooms decorated with white furniture, colorful artwork and shuttered windows. Many rooms also offer views of the Gulf. The property offers water sport rentals, beach cabanas and chairs, paddleboats (for use on the quarter-mile waterway that meanders through the property), nine-hole minigolf and a life-size chessboard. 585 rooms. Wireless Internet access. Five restaurants, five bars. Children's activity center. Fitness room, fitness classes available. Beach. Outdoor pool, children's pool, whirlpool. Tennis. Airport transportation available. Business center. **$$$**

★★★TRADEWINDS SANDPIPER HOTEL & SUITES

6000 Gulf Blvd., St. Pete Beach, 727-360-5551, 800-360-4016; www.justletgo.com
211 rooms. Pets not accepted, some restrictions; fee. Wireless Internet access. Restaurant, two bars. Fitness room. Beach. Two outdoor pools, whirlpool. Airport transportation available. Business center. **$$**

★TRAILS END RESORT

11500 Gulf Blvd., Treasure Island, 727-360-5541, 800-695-8284;
www.trailsendmotel.info
54 rooms. Beach. Outdoor pool. $

RESTAURANTS

★★BILLY'S STONE CRAB

1 Collany Road, Tierra Verde, 727-866-2115; www.billysstonecrab.com
Seafood menu. Lunch, dinner. Bar. Children's menu. Casual attire. Reservations recommended. Outdoor seating. $$

★DAIQUIRI DECK AND OCEANSIDE GRILL

14995 Gulf Blvd., Madeira Beach, 727-393-2706; www.daiquirideck.com
American, seafood menu. Lunch, dinner. Bar. Children's menu. $$

★HURRICANE SEAFOOD

807 Gulf Way, St. Pete Beach, 727-360-9558; www.thehurricane.com
Seafood menu. Breakfast, lunch, dinner. Closed Monday-Tuesday. Bar. Children's menu. Business casual attire. Reservations recommended. Outdoor seating. $$

★★★THE LOBSTER POT

17814 Gulf Blvd., Redington Shores, 727-391-8592; www.lobsterpotrestaurant.com
Opened in 1978, this seafood restaurant is known for its Maine lobster, Alaskan king crab and other tempting dishes from the ocean. A free cocktail or glass of wine is offered with every dinner. Seafood menu. Dinner. Children's menu. Valet parking. $$$

★★★THE MARITANA GRILLE

3400 Gulf Blvd., St. Pete Beach, 727-360-1882; www.doncesar.com
This elegant restaurant inside the historic Don Caesar resort serves a seafood menu of local favorites. Pan-seared yellow snapper is accompanied by butter poached lobster and sweet corn while pan-seared scallops come with lobster risotto. American menu. Dinner. Bar. Children's menu. Business casual attire. Reservations recommended. Valet parking. $$$

★★★PALM COURT ITALIAN GRILL

5500 Gulf Blvd., St. Pete Beach, 727-367-6461; www.justletgo.com
This intimate St. Pete Beach dining room is located at the Tradewinds Island Beach Resort and serves a traditional American and seafood menu with eclectic touches. The décor is cozy and features an outdoor patio. A great spot to celebrate a special occasion or romantic dinner, the restaurant also serves lunch and Sunday brunch. American, seafood menu. Lunch, dinner, Sunday brunch. Bar. Business casual attire. Reservations recommended. Valet parking. Outdoor seating. $$

★SKIDDER'S

5799 Gulf Blvd., St. Pete Beach, 727-360-1029
International menu. Breakfast, lunch, dinner. Children's menu. Casual attire. Outdoor seating. $

★★★WINE CELLAR
17307 Gulf Blvd., North Redington Beach, 727-393-3491; www.thewinecellar.com
More than 20 years old, this perennial favorite in a country-style house serves satisfying continental cuisine. Continental menu. Dinner. Bar. Children's menu. Valet parking. **$$$**

ST. PETERSBURG
The fourth-largest city in the state and second only to Miami as a winter resort, St. Petersburg is host to more than a million visitors each year. It draws golf and boating enthusiasts throughout the year but also has the appeal of a larger city with its service and nearby high-tech industries. St. Petersburg has a fringe of beaches, parks and yacht basins along Tampa Bay and a string of resort-occupied islands (connected to the mainland by causeways) on the Gulf side, across Boca Ciega Bay. These islands form the St. Pete Beach Area.
Information: St. Petersburg Area Chamber of Commerce, 100 Second Ave. N.,
St. Petersburg, 727-821-4069; www.stpete.com

WHAT TO SEE AND DO
MUSEUM OF FINE ARTS
255 Beach Drive N.E., St. Petersburg, 727-896-2667; www.fine-arts.org
Displays include pre-Columbian, European, American, Asian, African paintings and sculpture, decorative arts and photography, and Georgia O'Keeffe's *Poppy*. Includes galleries devoted to photography and Steuben glass. Special exhibitions; sculpture gardens. Guided tours; films, lectures, concerts. Tuesday-Saturday 10 a.m.-5 p.m., Sunday 1-5 p.m. Closed on Monday.

THE PIER
800 Second Ave. N.E., St. Petersburg, 727-821-6164; www.stpete-pier.com
A five-story inverted pyramid located at the end of this ¼-mile pier contains an observation deck with views of the city, restaurants, shops and an aquarium; special events and daily entertainment. Fishing, bait house, boating, water sports. Monday-Friday 10:30 a.m.-9:30 p.m., Saturdays 10 a.m.-9:30 a.m., Sundays 11 a.m.-6 p.m.

SALVADOR DALI MUSEUM
1000 Third St. S., St. Petersburg, 727-823-3767; www.salvadordalimuseum.org
Houses the world's largest and most highly acclaimed collection of works by famous Spanish artist Salvador Dali. Oils, drawings, watercolors, graphics and sculptures from 1914 to 1980; tours. Monday-Wednesday, Friday-Saturday 9:30 a.m.-5:30 p.m., Thursday to 8 p.m., Sunday noon-5:30 p.m.

SUNKEN GARDENS
1825 Fourth St. N., St. Petersburg, 727-551-3102; www.stpete.org/sunkengardens.htm
Butterfly garden, educational programs and more than 6,000 plants in the cool respite of a Florida ancient lake. Monday-Saturday 10 a.m.-4:30 p.m., Sunday from noon.

ST. PETERSBURG MUSEUM OF HISTORY
335 Second Ave. N.E., St. Petersburg, 727-894-1052; www.spmoh.org
Displays concentrate on the history of St. Petersburg; changing exhibits gallery. Tours available. Tuesday-Saturday 10 a.m.-5 p.m., Sunday 1-5 p.m. Closed on Monday.

HOTELS

★HAMPTON INN ST. PETERSBURG

1200 34th St. N., St. Petersburg, 727-322-0770, 800-426-7866; www.hamptoninn.com
130 rooms. Complimentary continental breakfast. High-speed Internet access. Fitness room. Outdoor pool, whirlpool. $

★★★HILTON ST. PETERSBURG BAYFRONT

333 First St. S., St. Petersburg, 727-894-5000, 866-454-8338;
www.stpetersburg.hilton.com
This downtown corporate and convention hotel is across from Progress Energy Field and Bayfront Performing Arts Center and 15 minutes from the airport. Enjoy views of the local marina from the patio deck and pool or Café 333, the hotel's American restaurant. 333 rooms. Two restaurants, bar. Fitness room, fitness classes available, spa. Outdoor pool, whirlpool. Business center, High-speed Internet access. $

★★HOLIDAY INN

6800 Sunshine Skyway Lane, St. Petersburg, 727-867-1151, 800-111-000;
www.sunspreeresorts.com
155 rooms. Wireless Internet access. Two restaurants, two bars. Fitness room. Beach. Two outdoor pools, children's pool, whirlpool. Tennis. $

★★RADISSON HOTEL AND CONFERENCE CENTER ST. PETERSBURG/ PINELLAS PARK

12600 Roosevelt Blvd., St. Petersburg, 727-572-7800, 800-333-3333;
www.radissonstpetersburg.net
205 rooms. Wireless Internet access. Restaurant, bar. Fitness room. Outdoor pool. Airport transportation available. Business center. $$

★★★RENAISSANCE VINOY RESORT AND GOLF CLUB

501 Fifth Ave. N.E., St. Petersburg, 727-894-1000, 888-303-4430;
www.renaissancehotels.com
The waterfront Vinoy Resort and Golf Club boasts an 18-hole golf course, 12 tennis courts and a private marina, all within a short distance from St. Petersburg. This historic hotel has Mediterranean Revival architecture and elegant, rich décor. Those traveling on business appreciate the full business center with secretarial services, along with in-room amenities such as large desks. Hiking and jogging trails are located right on the property. 361 rooms. High-speed Internet access. Three restaurants, two bars. Children's activity center. Fitness room, fitness classes available, spa. Outdoor pool, children's pool, whirlpool. Golf, 18 holes. Tennis. Business center. $$$

STUART

Stuart did not become part of Henry Morrison Flagler's Gold Coast development in the 1890s because the pineapple growers of this area vehemently objected to a railroad going through their land. Today, the town is being absorbed by sprawl and housing developments moving north from West Palm Beach. The St. Lucie and Indian Rivers meet in Stuart and together they flow through the St. Lucie Inlet into the ocean. The bridges and causeways around the town connect Stuart to the attractions and beaches of Hutchinson Island.
Information: Stuart/Martin County Chamber of Commerce, 1650 S. Kanner Highway,
772-287-1088; www.goodnature.org

WHAT TO SEE AND DO
ELLIOTT MUSEUM
Hutchinson Island, 825 N.E. Ocean Blvd., Stuart, 772-225-1961; www.elliottmuseumfl.org
Gracious Living wing; antique autos, shell collection, Seminole artifacts; country store, Americana shops, contemporary art gallery. Daily. Monday-Saturday 10 a.m.-4 p.m., Sunday 1-4 p.m.

HOTELS
★★BEST WESTERN DOWNTOWN STUART
1209 S. Federal Highway, Stuart, 772-287-6200, 888-932-8181; www.bestwestern.com
120 rooms. Restaurant, bar. Fitness room. Outdoor pool. Pets not accepted, complimentary full breakfast, wireless Internet access, business center. $

★★★MARRIOTT HUTCHINSON ISLAND RESORT
555 N.E. Ocean Blvd., Stuart, 772-225-3700, 800-775-5936; www.marriot.com
Set on a 200-acre island on Florida's famed Treasure Coast, this nautical resort is a great location to do business, with 22,000 square feet of meeting space. Onsite recreations include a golf course, tennis courts and a marina. 274 rooms. Pets not accepted, some restrictions; fee. Two restaurants, bar. Fitness room, spa. Beach. Outdoor pool, whirlpool. Golf. Tennis. Business center. High-speed Internet access, free phone calls. $$

★★RAMADA INN
1200 S. Federal Highway, Stuart, 772-287-6900, 800-272-6232; www.ramada.com
118 rooms. Complimentary continental breakfast. Restaurant, bar. Fitness room. Outdoor pool. Free high-speed Internet access, free local phone calls, business center. $

RESTAURANTS
★★THE ASHLEY
61 S.W. Osceola St., Stuart, 772-221-9476; www.theashleygang.com
American menu. Lunch, dinner, Sunday brunch. Bar. $$

★★CHINA STAR
1501 S. Federal Highway, Stuart, 772-283-8378
Chinese menu. Lunch, dinner. $$

★★FLAGLER GRILL
47 S.W. Flagler Ave., Stuart, 772-221-9517; www.flaglergrill.com
Steak menu. Dinner. Call for seasonal days and hours. Bar. Casual attire. $$

TALLAHASSEE
The capital of Florida, Tallahassee retains the grace of plantation days and the flavor of its rustic pioneer past. During the Civil War, this city was the only Confederate capital east of the Mississippi not captured by Union forces. The city, as well as Leon County, is now strongly oriented toward state and local government. Lumber and wood production, food production, printing and publishing help maintain Tallahassee's economy.
Information: Tallahassee Area Convention and Visitors Bureau, 106 E. Jefferson St., 850-606-2305, 800-628-2866; www.visittallahassee.com.

WHAT TO SEE AND DO

ALFRED B. MACLAY GARDENS STATE PARK

3540 Thomasville Road, Tallahassee, 850-487-4556; www.floridastateparks.com

Planted as a private estate garden; outstanding azaleas, camellias, dogwood and others, including some rare plant species, on 308 acres; donated to the state in 1953. Museum in house has an interpretive display, January-April. The Lake Hall Recreation area has swimming, fishing, boating, nature trails, biking, horsebacking riding, gardens, picnicking. Daily 8 a.m.-sunset.

THE COLUMNS

100 N. Duval St., Tallahassee, 850-224-8116

Moved from its original site in 1972, this three-story 1830 brick mansion once served as a bank, boarding house, doctor's office and restaurant. Restored and furnished with antiques, it now serves as the office of the Chamber of Commerce. Monday-Friday.

FLORIDA AGRICULTURAL AND MECHANICAL UNIVERSITY

S. Martin Luther King Jr. Boulevard and Palmer Street, Tallahassee, 850-599-3000; www.famu.edu

On campus is the Florida Black Archives, Research Center and Museum. Monday-Friday.

FLORIDA STATE UNIVERSITY

University Center between W. Tennessee and Copeland streets, Tallahassee, 850-644-3246; www.fsu.edu

On a 400-acre campus with everything from two supercomputers to its own collegiate circus. Campus tours Monday-Friday.

GOVERNOR'S MANSION

700 N. Adams St., Tallahassee, 850-488-4661; www.floridagovernorsmansion.com

Tours during regular session of legislature. March-May, Monday, Wednesday, Friday 10 a.m.-noon.

FLORIDA

★
★
★
★

TALLAHASSEE'S CANOPY ROADS

One of the Top Ten Scenic Byways in America, five routes in and around Tallahassee have been termed "canopy roads" for their umbrella of live oaks covered with Spanish moss. The Old St. Augustine Road dates back to the 1600s, when it connected colonial Spanish missions. Centerville and Miccosukee roads travel along old cotton plantations (visit Goodwood Plantation) and into the country (stop at Bradley's Country Store for homemade sausage). Meridian Route begins at the state's Prime Meridian Marker downtown and heads north to the Georgia border. Old Bainbridge Road plunges through archaeological sites of Native American villages and Spanish ranchos. For a driving tour brochure and information on accommodations, contact the Tallahassee Visitor Center at 800-628-2866. *Approximately 123 miles.*

MUSEUM OF FINE ARTS

Fine Arts Building, Copeland and W. Tennessee streets, Tallahassee, 850-644-6836;
www.mofa.fsu.edu
September-May, daily; rest of year, Monday-Friday 9 a.m.-4 p.m, Saturday and Sunday
1 p.m.-4 p.m., closed school holidays.

NATURAL BRIDGE BATTLEFIELD HISTORIC STATE PARK

7502 Natural Bridge Road, Tallahassee, 850-922-6007; www.floridastateparks.org
This 8-acre monument on the St. Marks River marks the spot where a militia of
Confederate forces stopped Union troops, barring the way to Tallahassee. The battle,
which took place on March 6, 1865, left Tallahassee as the only Confederate capital
east of the Mississippi that never fell into Union hands. Picnicking. Daily 8 a.m.-
sunset.

OLD CAPITOL MUSEUM

400 S. Monroe St., Tallahassee, 850-487-1902; www.flhistoriccapitol.gov
Restored to its 1902 grandeur, the building is now a museum, furnished with authentic
period pieces and reproductions of original furniture. Historical exhibits; architectural
tours Saturday mornings. Monday-Friday 9 a.m.-4:30 p.m., Saturday from 10 a.m.,
Sunday from noon.

SAN MARCOS DE APALACHE HISTORIC STATE PARK

148 Old Fort Road, St. Marks, 850-925-6216; www.floridastateparks.org
This site was first visited by Panfilo de Narvaez in 1527 and Hernando de Soto in
1539; ruins of a fort; museum on the site of an old federal marine hospital. Picnicking,
nature trails. Daily.

STATE CAPITOL

400 S. Monroe St., Tallahassee, 850-488-6167
At the top of Tallahassee's second-highest hill, the modern, 22-story capitol building
towers above the city; observation level on top floor.

TALLAHASSEE MUSEUM OF HISTORY & NATURAL SCIENCE

3945 Museum Drive, Tallahassee, 850-576-1636; www.tallahasseemuseum.org
Fifty-two acres with restored 1880s Big Bend farm and 1854 plantation house; grist-
mill, schoolhouse, church; hands-on Discovery Center; natural habitat zoo with wild
animals native to the area, including the endangered Florida panther; gopher nature
trail. Visitor center. Monday-Saturday 9 a.m.-5 p.m., Sunday 12:30-5 p.m.

WAKULLA SPRINGS STATE PARK

550 Wakulla Park Drive, Wakulla Springs, 850-224-5950; www.floridastateparks.org
Located in the heart of this 2,860-acre state park is one of the world's larger and deep-
est freshwater springs. Glass-bottomed boats allow visitors to see the entrance to the
cavern 120 feet below the surface. Wildlife observation boat tours encounter alligators, turtles and a variety of birds. Daily 8 a.m.-sundown.

SPECIAL EVENT

★FLYING HIGH CIRCUS

Florida State University, 269 Chieftain Way, Tallahassee, 850-644-4874; www.fsu.edu

Approximately 80 students perform in a three-ring circus. Evening and matinee performances. First two weekends in April.

HOTELS

★BEST WESTERN PRIDE INN & SUITES

2016 Apalachee Parkway, Tallahassee, 850-656-6312, 800-827-7390;
www.bestwestern.com

78 rooms. Pets accepted; fee. Complimentary continental breakfast. Outdoor pool. Business center, free wireless Internet access, free parking. $

★CABOT LODGE TALLAHASSEE NORTH MONROE

2735 N. Monroe St., Tallahassee, 850-386-8880, 800-223-1964;
www.cabotlodgenorthmonroe.com

160 rooms. Complimentary continental breakfast. Outdoor pool. Business center. Free high-speed Internet access, free news paper, free local calls. $

★★COURTYARD TALLAHASSEE CAPITAL

1018 Apalachee Parkway, Tallahassee, 850-222-8822, 800-321-2211;
www.courtyardtallahassee.com

154 rooms. High-speed Internet access. Fitness room. Outdoor pool, whirlpool. Business center. Pets not accepted, free phone calls. $

★★HILTON GARDEN INN TALLAHASSEE

3333 Thomasville Road, Tallahassee, 850-385-3553, 800-445-8667;
www.hiltongardeninn.com

99 rooms. High-speed Internet access. Restaurant, bar. Fitness room. Outdoor pool, whirlpool. Business center, pets not accepted. $$

★HOMEWOOD SUITES BY HILTON

2987 Apalachee Parkway, Tallahassee, 850-402-9400, 800-225-5466;
www.homewoodsuites.com

94 rooms, all suites. Pets accepted; fee. Complimentary full breakfast. Wireless Internet access. Fitness room. Outdoor pool. Business center. Parking free. $

★★PARK PLAZA HOTEL TALLAHASSEE

415 N. Monroe St., Tallahassee, 850-224-6000, 888-201-1803;
www.parkplaza.com/tallahasseefl

Located on the north side of downtown Tallahassee, this hotel sits five blocks away from the capitol. 119 rooms. Wireless Internet access. Restaurant, bar. Fitness room. Airport transportation available. Business center. $

★★WAKULLA SPRINGS STATE PARK & LODGE

550 Wakulla Park Drive, Wakulla Springs, 850-926-0700; www.floridastateparks.org

27 rooms. Restaurant. $

FLORIDA

★
★
★
★

RESTAURANTS

★★ANDREW'S 228

228 S. Adams St., Tallahassee, 850-222-3444; www.andrewsdowntown.com
American menu. Dinner. Closed Sunday. Casual attire. Reservations recommended.
Valet parking. **$$**

★★CHEZ PIERRE

1215 Thomasville Road, Tallahassee, 850-222-0936; www.chezpierre.com
French menu. Lunch, dinner, Sunday brunch. Bar. **$$**

TAMPA

The business and vacation hub of Florida's West Coast, Tampa is Florida's third-largest city. Within it you'll find Ybor City, a Spanish, Cuban and Italian enclave of narrow streets and cigar makers, and MacDill Air Force Base, headquarters of the 56th TT Wing, U.S. Special Operations Command and the U.S. Central Command.

Located at the mouth of the Hillsborough River at the head of Tampa Bay, the city traces its origins to Fort Brooke, established to oversee Seminole Indians who had recently moved here from Georgia and Northern Florida. An early center for Florida's cattle industry, Tampa enjoyed brisk trade with Cuba and prospered. However, subjected to hit-and-run raids during the Civil War, the city suffered a decline until 1884, when Henry Plant's narrow-gauge South Florida Railroad reached the city. Determined to outdo his East Coast rival Henry Morrison Flagler, Plant built the opulent Tampa Bay Hotel (Teddy Roosevelt trained his Rough Riders in the backyard of the hotel). In 1886, Vincente Martinez Ybor moved his cigar factory and its workers here from Key West. Most of the other cigarmakers moved with him, establishing Ybor City.

Today, the port of Tampa handles more than 50-million tons of shipping a year. Its cigar factories turn out 3 million cigars each working day. Two huge breweries are in operation in one of 33 industrial parks; two citrus plants and a variety of other factories are here.

Information: Tampa Bay Convention & Visitors Bureau, 401 E. Jackson St.,
813-223-1111, 800-448-2672; www.visittampabay.com

WHAT TO SEE AND DO

ADVENTURE ISLAND

10001 McKinley Drive, Tampa, 813-987-5660, 888-800-5447;
www.adventureisland.com
This 30-acre water theme park features four speed slides, an inner tube slide, a slow-winding tube ride, a water-sled ride, 16 water flumes, diving platforms, a pool that creates three- to five-foot waves for body and raft surfing, a large children's water play section and lifeguards. Also includes a restaurant, picnicking, games and gift shop. Open from March 14; schedule varies.

BUSCH GARDENS TAMPA

3000 E. Busch Blvd., Tampa, 813-987-5082; www.buschgardens.com
This 335-acre theme park re creates some of the sites and sounds of Africa. The area is divided into eight different regions, including the Timbuktu section that has a dolphin theater, rides, a German restaurant and an entertainment center; the Myombe Reserve

has gorillas and chimpanzees; the Serengeti Plain is home to Edge of Africa, a 15-acre animal theme park through which visitors can take a safari; and the Morocco section has shops, cafes and the 1,200-seat Moroccan Palace Theater, which features an ice-skating show. A 7-acre area named Egypt includes a museum, shopping bazaars and an inverted steel roller coaster named Montu. March-December: schedule varies.

FLORIDA AQUARIUM

701 Channelside Drive, Tampa, 813-273-4000; www.flaquarium.org
Exhibit areas replicate the state's water environments (mangrove estuary, freshwater, beach, marine and coral reef). The Swim with the Fishes attraction offers scuba diving for those ages six and older. Saltwater and freshwater tanks house species like the Bonnethead shark and the spiny lobster. Frights of the Forest contains some of the world's most dangerous wetland creatures—vampire bats, poison dart frogs, leeches and scorpions. Daily 9:30 a.m.-5 p.m.

TAMPA BAY BUCCANEERS (NFL)

Raymond James Stadium, 4201 Dale Mabry Highway North, Tampa,
813-879-2827, 800-795-2827; www.nfl.com/teams/tampabaybuccaneers
The Tampa Bay Buccaneers take the field at Raymond James Stadium, which has the look of a pirate ship, complete with realistic looking cannons that explode when the team scores a touchdown. One of the newer venues in the NFL, the outdoor stadium has ample amenities, and the temperature is almost always in the 60s or above.

TAMPA BAY DEVIL RAYS (MLB)

Tropicana Field, 1 Tropicana Drive, Tampa, 727-825-3137;
www.tampabay.devilrays.mlb.com
Professional baseball team.

TAMPA BAY LIGHTNING (NHL)

Ice Palace, 401 Channelside Drive, Tampa, 813-301-6600; www.lightning.nhl.com
Professional hockey team.

TAMPA BAY PERFORMING ARTS CENTER

1010 N.W.C. MacInnes Place, Tampa, 813-229-7827, 800-955-1045; www.tbpac.org
Includes the 2,500-seat Festival Hall, 1,000-seat Playhouse Hall, 300-seat Robert and Lorena Jaeb Theater and 100-seat Off Center Theater. The Florida Orchestra performs classical and pop concerts here September-May.

TAMPA MUSEUM OF ART

2306 N. Howard Ave., Tampa, 813-274-8130; www.tampamuseum.com
Traditional and contemporary art, children's exhibitions, Greek and Roman antiquities. Educational programs and films. Tours available by appointment only. Tuesday-Saturday 10 a.m.-5 p.m., Sunday from 11 a.m.

UNIVERSITY OF SOUTH FLORIDA

4202 E. Fowler Ave., Tampa, 813-974-2011; www.usf.edu
This 1,700-acre campus has changing art exhibits in Fine Arts Gallery (Monday-Friday), Contemporary Art Museum (Monday-Friday, also Saturday afternoons),

★
★
★
★

Visual and Performing Arts Gallery (Monday-Friday), Anthropology Museum, Social Science Building (Monday-Friday). Film, theater, music and athletic events.

UNIVERSITY OF TAMPA

401 W. Kennedy Blvd., Tampa, 813-253-3333; www.utampa.edu

Plant Hall, the main building of this 85-acre downtown campus, is the former Tampa Bay Hotel, built in 1891 by railroad magnate Henry B. Plant to compete with his East Coast rival Henry Flagler. The structure features five minarets, elaborate filigree work and interlaced gingerbread trim. The 511-room hotel hosted many famous guests, including Teddy Roosevelt. Historic walking tour leaves from lobby. Tuesday and Thursday at 1:30 p.m.

YBOR CITY

Two miles east of downtown, between I-4, 1600 E. Eighth Ave.,
Nebraska Avenue and 22nd Street; 813-242-0398; www.ybor.org

A link between the past and present, this area retains some of the atmosphere of the original Cuban settlement. Spanish and Italian are spoken as much as English. Many Spanish restaurants, coffeehouses and cigar factories are here.

SPECIAL EVENTS

NEW YORK YANKEES SPRING TRAINING

Legends Field, 1900 S. Park Road, Tampa, 813-875-7753, 800-969-2657;
www.yankees.mlb.com

Baseball spring training, exhibition games. Early March-early April. Also the home of the Gulf Coast League's Tampa Yankees.

OUTBACK BOWL

Raymond James Stadium, 4511 N. Himes Ave., Tampa, 813-874-2695;
www.outbackbowl.com

Postseason college football match up; other events. January 1.

HOTELS

★★BEST WESTERN ALL SUITES HOTEL

3001 University Center Drive, Tampa, 813-971-8930, 800-780-7234;
www.bestwestern.com

150 rooms, all suites. Pets accepted, some restrictions; fee. Complimentary full breakfast. Wireless Internet access. Restaurant, bar. Outdoor pool, whirlpool. **$**

★★EMBASSY SUITES

555 N. Westshore Blvd., Tampa, 813-875-1555, 800-362-2779; www.embassysuites.com

221 rooms, all suites. Complimentary full breakfast. Restaurant, bar. Fitness room. Outdoor pool, whirlpool. Business center. Pets not accepted. **$$**

★★★GRAND HYATT TAMPA BAY

2900 Bayport Drive, Tampa, 813-874-1234, 800-633-7313;
www.grandtampabay.hyatt.com

Situated on a 35-acre wildlife preserve on the shores of Tampa Bay, this hotel boasts the finest views in the city. The lobby is airy and decorated in pastel tones, and the guest rooms feature comfortable bedding, overstuffed chairs and work desks. Armani's, an upscale northern Italian restaurant located on the top floor of the hotel, is a sophisticated spot with exceptional views, and Oystercatcher's, the hotel's seafood dining outlet, has the best brunch in Tampa. 445 rooms. Pets accepted, some restrictions; fee. Wireless Internet access. Three restaurants, three bars. Fitness room. Two outdoor pools, whirlpool. Tennis. Airport transportation available. Business center. $$

★★★HYATT REGENCY TAMPA

211 N. Tampa St., Tampa, 813-225-1234, 888-591-1234; www.hyattregencytampa.com
This downtown hotel is just minutes from the Florida Aquarium, Ybor City and the convention center. Guest rooms are contemporary in décor and feature work desks, sitting areas and Portico bath amenities—some rooms offer views of the pool on the fifth floor. The business center is open 24 hours, and for those guests looking to work out, the fitness center located adjacent to the pool offers state-of-the-art equipment. 521 rooms. Wireless Internet access. Restaurant, bar. Fitness room. Outdoor pool, whirlpool. Airport transportation available. Business center. $$

★★★INTERCONTINENTAL TAMPA

4860 W. Kennedy Blvd., Tampa, 813-286-4400, 866-915-1557;
www.intercontampa.com
This sleek downtown hotel, with a curved glass façade, is connected to Tampa's Urban Center office complex by 11-story atriums filled with exotic foliage. The ever-popular Don Shula's restaurant is located in the lobby. 322 rooms. Restaurant, bar. Fitness room. Outdoor pool. Airport transportation available. Business center, wireless Internet access. $$$

★★★SADDLEBROOK RESORT TAMPA

5700 Saddlebrook Way, Wesley Chapel, 813-973-1111, 800-729-8383;
www.saddlebrookresort.com
This resort near Tampa is a great destination for outdoor enthusiasts. The complex includes a sports village with a state-of-the-art fitness center, volleyball courts, basketball court and sports field. Two 18-hole Arnold Palmer-designed golf courses are onsite—Saddlebrook is the world headquarters for the prestigious Arnold Palmer Golf Academy. Tennis players will love the 45-court center that offers professional instruction. 800 rooms. Restaurant, bar. Children's activity center. Fitness room, spa. Four outdoor pools, whirlpool. Golf, 36 holes. Tennis. Airport transportation available. Business center. $$

★★★WESTIN HARBOUR ISLAND HOTEL

725 S. Harbour Island Blvd., Tampa 813-229-5000, 800-937-8461; www.westin.com
The downtown Westin Harbour Island Hotel offers a location in the business district adjacent to the Tampa Convention Center. Wide hallways with nicely framed, colorful art lead guests to their comfortable rooms, which feature Heavenly beds, marble baths and Starbuck's coffee. 299 rooms. Pets accepted, some restrictions; fee. Wireless Internet access. Restaurant, bar. Fitness room. Outdoor pool. Airport transportation available. Business center. $$$

FLORIDA

★
★
★
★

RESTAURANTS

★★★ARMANI'S

2900 Bayport Drive, Tampa, 813-207-6800; www.armanisrestaurant.com

Perched high atop the Grand Hyatt Tampa Bay, Armani's offers views of the sunset over Tampa Bay as well as of planes taking off and landing at the nearby airport. The outdoor terrace is the perfect spot for a twilight cocktail, and the restaurant is formal and refined. The centerpiece of the restaurant is its antipasto bar, which features an extensive selection of grilled vegetables, smoked meats, pastas, olives, cheeses and other Italian treats. Armani's impressive Northern Italian menu includes something for everyone—poultry, lamb, beef and fish—though the kitchen is known for its veal dishes. Classico Scaloppine, Armani's, veal scaloppine sautéed with wild mushrooms and cognac in a creamy black truffle sauce, is the signature of the house. Italian menu. Dinner. Closed Sunday. Bar. Business casual attire. Reservations recommended. Valet parking. Outdoor seating. **$$$**

★ASHLEY STREET GRILLE

200 N. Ashley St., Tampa, 813-226-4400; www.starwoodhotels.com

American menu. Breakfast, lunch, dinner. Bar. Children's menu. Business casual attire. Reservations recommended. Valet parking. Outdoor seating. **$$**

★★AVANZARE

211 Tampa St., Tampa, 813-222-4975; www.tamparegency.hyatt.com

Continental menu. Breakfast, lunch, dinner, Sunday brunch. Bar. Children's menu. Casual attire. Valet parking. **$$**

★★BELLA'S ITALIAN CAFÉ

1413 S. Howard Ave., Tampa, 813-254-3355; www.bellasitaliancafe.com

Italian menu. Lunch, dinner, late-night. Bar. Children's menu. Outdoor seating. **$$**

★★★BERN'S STEAK HOUSE

1208 S. Howard Ave., Tampa, 813-251-2421; www.bernssteakhouse.com

Bern's may be the most eccentric restaurant in the world. The wine list—a five-pound document chained to the table—is the longest of any restaurant anywhere. The steak—dry-aged for two weeks more than the industry standard—is superb. The interior features an assortment of antiques displayed in several themed dining rooms. Don't miss dessert, served upstairs in private pods wired with closed-circuit TVs and jukeboxes. Steak menu. Dinner. Bar. Business casual attire. Reservations recommended. Valet parking. **$$$**

★BERNINI RESTAURANT

1702 E. Seventh Ave., Tampa, 813-248-0099; www.berniniofybor.com

Italian menu. Lunch, dinner, late-night. Bar. Business casual attire. Reservations recommended. Outdoor seating. **$$**

★COLONNADE

3401 Bayshore Blvd., Tampa, 813-839-7558; www.thenade.com

American, seafood menu. Lunch, dinner. Bar. Children's menu. Casual attire. **$$**

★★★COLUMBIA RESTAURANT

2117 E. Seventh Ave., Tampa, 813-248-4961; www.columbiarestaurant.com

Opened in 1905, this is Florida's oldest restaurant. Owned and operated by the fourth and fifth generations of the Hernandez/Gonzmart family, the extensive Spanish menu includes both tapas and full entrées. There is a $6 cover charge for the dining room when the flamenco show is performed. A jazz band in the lounge entertains Tuesday through Saturday evenings. The wine cellar features California and Spanish reds. Spanish menu. Lunch, dinner. Bar. Children's menu. Casual attire. Reservations recommended. Valet parking. **$$**

★★★DONATELLO

232 N. Dale Mabry Highway, Tampa, 813-875-6660; www.donatellorestaurant.com

Named after the famous Florentine sculptor, this authentic Italian restaurant takes its guests on a culinary tour through northern Italy. Opened in 1984, the dining room has become a favorite for business and leisure diners alike. On Monday through Saturday evenings, diners can enjoy live entertainment in the lounge area. Italian menu. Lunch, dinner. Bar. Business casual attire. Reservations recommended. Valet parking. **$$$**

★★★FLEMING'S

4322 W. Boy Scout Blvd., Tampa, 813-874-9463; www.flemingssteakhouse.com

Steak menu. Dinner. Bar. Business casual attire. Reservations recommended. Valet parking. **$$$**

★★JACKSON'S

601 S. Harbour Island Blvd., Tampa, 813-277-0112; www.jacksonsbistro.com

International menu. Lunch, dinner, late-night, Sunday brunch. Bar. Children's menu. Business casual attire. Reservations recommended. Valet parking. Outdoor seating. **$$**

★★JOTO JAPANESE RESTAURANT

310 S. Dale Mabry Highway, Tampa, 813-875-4842; www.jotosteakhouse.com

Japanese menu. Lunch, dinner. Bar. Casual attire. **$$**

★★LUNA DI MARE

725 S. Harbour Island Blvd., Tampa, 813-229-5001

Italian, American menu. Breakfast, lunch, dinner. Bar. Children's menu. Business casual attire. Reservations recommended. Valet parking. **$$**

★★★MISE EN PLACE

442 W. Kennedy Blvd., Tampa, 813-254-5373; www.miseonline.com

Across the street from the University of Tampa's historic Tampa Hotel, this downtown restaurant is a favorite date-night place to dine. New American menu. Lunch, dinner, late-night. Closed Sunday-Monday. Bar. Business casual attire. Reservations recommended. **$$$**

★★ROYAL PALACE THAI RESTAURANT

811 S. Howard Ave., Tampa, 813-258-5893; www.royalpalacethai.com

Thai menu. Lunch, dinner. Closed Monday. Casual attire. Reservations recommended. Outdoor seating. **$$**

★★★RUSTY PELICAN

2425 N. Rocky Point Drive, Tampa, 813-281-1943; www.therustypelican.com

This restaurant, which also has a location in Key Biscayne, is a favorite for fresh-from-the-water seafood. Views of Tampa Bay make for an ideal setting for enjoying fresh grilled lobster, tuna or the specialty dessert, bananas foster. American menu. Lunch, dinner. Bar. Children's menu. $$$

★★★RUTH'S CHRIS STEAK HOUSE

1700 N. Westshore Blvd., Tampa, 813-282-1118; www.ruthschris.com

This tried-and-true outpost of the national steakhouse chain is a popular choice for business travelers. The clubby interior is richly decorated and dimly lit. The restaurant offers a 40-ounce porterhouse for two, as well as seafood, chicken, veal and vegetarian dishes. Steak menu. Dinner. Bar. Business casual attire. Reservations recommended. Valet parking. $$$

★★SHULA'S STEAK HOUSE

6843 Main St., Miami Lakes., Tampa, 305-817-4072; www.donshula.com

Famous not only for its owner, University of Miami coach Don Shula, but also for its massive 48-ounce porterhouse, this restaurant attracts a large crowd every night of the week. Menus are printed on leather footballs, and there is plenty of pigskin memorabilia throughout. The atmosphere is both masculine and intimate—tables are topped with white linens, chairs are upholstered in red velvet, and French doors separate the private dining rooms from the main dining room. Steak menu. Lunch, dinner. Bar. Business casual attire. Reservations recommended. Valet parking. $$$

★★★SIDEBERN'S

1208 South Howard Ave., Tampa, 813-251-2421; www.bernssteakhouse.com

Dining in Tampa doesn't get any more creative and fun than at this contemporary offshoot of Bern's Steak House. The décor of the small, intimate dining space is modern, with brick walls, huge rice-paper pendants and mustard-colored sheers draped across parts of the room. Interesting International cuisine options complement the fresh, unique atmosphere. International menu. Dinner. Closed Sunday. Bar. Business casual attire. Reservations recommended. Valet parking. Outdoor seating. $$$

★SUKHO THAI

8201 N. Dale Mabry Highway, Tampa, 813-933-7990; www.sukhothairestaurant.net

Thai menu. Lunch, dinner. Casual attire. Reservations recommended. $$

★★TAJ

2734 E. Fowler Ave., Tampa, 813-971-8483

Indian menu. Lunch, dinner. Closed Monday. $

★WINE EXCHANGE

1609 Snow Ave., Tampa, 813-254-9463

American menu. Lunch, dinner. Bar. Business casual attire. Outdoor seating. $$

TARPON SPRINGS

Colorfully Hellenic, Tarpon Springs is famous for its sponge industry, which was most prosperous from the early 1900s to the 1940s but continues today. Greek fishermen go far out to sea in their picturesque boats and divers plunge to depths of 150 feet to pluck sponges. The city is situated between Lake Tarpon and bayous formed by the Anclote River.

Information: Tarpon Springs Chamber of Commerce, 11 E. Orange St.,
727-937-6109; www.tarponspringschamber.com

WHAT TO SEE AND DO
DODECANESE BOULEVARD
Tarpon Springs
Along the seawall of this waterfront street, anchored shrimp boats and sponge boats are decorated with Greek designs. On the other side, find restaurants, curio shops, sponge diving exhibitions, boat rides and stacks of sponges.

HOTEL
★★★INNISBROOK RESORT AND GOLF CLUB
36750 Highway 19 N., Palm Harbor, 727-942-2000, 800-456-2000;
www.innisbrookgolfresort.com
Golfers will love this resort—there are four championship golf courses. Along with golf, there are plenty of other activities offered including swimming in six pools—one of which is the Loch Ness Monster pool, complete with waterslides and waterfalls. Guest rooms include full kitchens, private balconies or patios and separate living areas. 620 rooms. Pets accepted, some restrictions; fee. Five restaurants, bars. Children's activity center. Fitness room, fitness classes available. Six outdoor pools, children's pool, whirlpool. Golf, 72 holes. Tennis. Business center. $$$

TITUSVILLE

Located on the Indian River, Titusville is known for its saltwater trout, shrimp and crab. Indian River citrus, grown along its banks, is famous the world over. The sleepy atmosphere of the area was forever changed by the nearby Kennedy Space Center where most shuttle launches and landings take place.

Information: Chamber of Commerce, 2000 S. Washington Ave., 321-267-3036;
www.spacecityflusa.com

WHAT TO SEE AND DO
CANAVERAL NATIONAL SEASHORE
212 S. Washington Ave., Titusville, 321-267-1110; www.nps.gov/cana
Area consists of 24 miles of beaches with Apollo Beach at the north (seven miles south of New Smyrna Beach on Highway A1A) and Playalinda Beach at the south (12 miles east of Titusville via Highways 406 and 402). There are no connecting roads between Apollo and Playalinda; the central portion, Klondike Beach, can be reached only by foot, by bicycle or on horseback. More than 300 species of birds have been observed within the seashore. Mosquito Lagoon, between the beach and the Intracoastal Waterway, provides a sanctuary for 14 endangered and threatened species. Recreation includes swimming, waterskiing, surfing, beachcombing, crabbing, clamming, shrimping, surf and freshwater fishing, boating (ramps), canoeing, hiking trails, picnicking, primitive camping on beach (November-April) and backcountry camping in some designated areas. Playalinda Beach and other sections may be closed periodically due to NASA launch-related activities; inquire locally. Daily.

MERRITT ISLAND NATIONAL WILDLIFE REFUGE
Highway 402, Titusville, 321-861-0667; www.fws.gov

Established in 1963, the Merritt Island National Wildlife Refuge is considered one of the top bird-watching sites in the world. Jointly owned by NASA and the U.S. Fish & Wildlife Services, it was created to provide a habitat for migratory birds, as well as numerous endangered and threatened species. More than 1,045 plant species and 500 wildlife species (16 of them on the endangered and protected lists) can be found on the 140,000 acres, including manatees, bald eagles, ospreys and Florida scrub jays. A seven-mile driving tour along Black Point Wildlife Drive exposes visitors to extensive wildlife, including alligators, various snakes, river otters, bobcats and a host of birds, many of which can be seen from the 10-foot-high Cruickshank Tower. For hikers, there are five trails ranging in length from ¼ mile to five miles long. Daily dawn-dusk; visitor center Monday-Friday 8 a.m.-4:30 p.m.; Saturday-Sunday 9 a.m.-5 p.m.

SPECIAL EVENT
VALIANT AIR COMMAND AIR SHOW
Warbird Museum, 6600 Tico Road, Titusville, 321-268-1941; www.vacwarbirds.org

World War II airshow; vintage aircraft in aerial displays of formation flying, dog-fights, aerobatics and bombing/strafing runs; pyrotechnics, special effects and current military displays. Mid-March.

HOTELS
★★BEST WESTERN SPACE SHUTTLE INN
3455 Cheney Highway, Titusville, 321-269-9100, 800-528-1234;
www.spaceshuttleinn.com

129 rooms. Pets accepted; fee. Complimentary continental breakfast. Restaurant, bar. Fitness room. Outdoor pool. Free parking. $

★★RAMADA INN & SUITES
3500 Cheney Highway, Titusville, 321-269-5510, 800-29727-6232; www.ramadaksc.com

124 rooms. Restaurant, bar. Fitness room. Outdoor pool, whirlpool, wireless Internet access. Heated pool. $$

★RIVERSIDE INN
1829 Riverside Drive, Titusville, 321-267-7900; www.riversideinnksc.com

104 rooms. Pets accepted; fee. Bar. Fitness room. Outdoor pool. $

RESTAURANT
★DIXIE CROSSROADS
1475 Garden St., Titusville, 321-268-5000; www.dixiecrossroads.com

Seafood menu. Lunch, dinner. Children's menu. Casual attire. $$

VENICE

Venice retains the spaciousness planned for it in 1924-1925 when it was transformed from an obscure fishing village into a retirement city for the Brotherhood of Locomotive Engineers. The retirement project was discontinued after the 1929 stock market crash, but a small-scale economic boom began in 1960 when the Ringling Brothers & Barnum and Bailey Circus moved its winter headquarters here from Sarasota. Three public beaches and jetties provide swimming and fishing opportunities while beach-combers can find numerous fossilized shark teeth on shore.

Information: Venice Area Chamber of Commerce, 597 Tamiami Trail South, 941-488-2236; www.venicechamber.com

WHAT TO SEE AND DO

BROHARD PARK/VENICE FISHING PIER
A 740-foot pier is the centerpiece of a beach known for its shark-tooth collecting. Beach, bait house, restaurant.

CASPERSON BEACH
Harbor Drive, Venice
Secluded beach with salt-and-pepper sands, dunes walkovers, picnicking.

OSCAR SCHERER STATE PARK
1843 S. Tamiami Trail, Osprey, 941-483-5956; www.floridastateparks.org
Approximately 1,400 acres of pine and scrubby flatwoods on the banks of a small tidal creek. Swimming, fishing, canoeing (rentals), nature trails, picnicking, camping.

WARM MINERAL SPRINGS
12200 San Servando Ave., North Port, 941-426-1692; www.warmmineralsprings.com
Springs produce nine million gallons of water at 87 degrees daily. Bathhouse and lockers (fee); Wellness center. Picnic sites. Daily.

HOTEL

★INN AT THE BEACH
725 W. Venice Ave., Venice, 941-484-8471, 800-255-8471; www.innatthebeach.com
49 rooms. Complimentary continental breakfast. Outdoor pool, whirlpool. $

RESTAURANT
★SHARKY'S ON THE PIER
1600 S. Harbor Drive, Venice, 941-488-1456; www.sharkysonthepier.com
Seafood, steak menu. Lunch, dinner. Bar. Children's menu. Outdoor seating. $$

VERO BEACH
With miles of uncrowded beaches and streets lined with tropical plants, Vero Beach is a favorite of many Florida visitors. Citrus shipping supplements tourism as a major industry.

Information: Indian River County Chamber of Commerce, 1146 21st St., Vero Beach, 772-567-3491; www.indianriverchamber.com

WHAT TO SEE AND DO

MCKEE BOTANICAL GARDEN
350 Highway 1, Vero Beach, 772-794-0601; www.mckeegarden.org
Listed on the National Register of Historic Places, this garden opened in 1932 and has recently been restored. Collection of native and exotic tropical plants, ponds and waterways, gift shop, cafe, educational building. Tours. Tuesday-Saturday 10 a.m.-5 p.m.; Sunday at noon.

MCLARTY TREASURE MUSEUM

13180 N. A1A, Vero Beach, 772-589-2147
Exhibits and artifacts of a Spanish treasure fleet downed in this area in 1715; diorama depicts salvage efforts; film on history of site. Daily 10 a.m.-4:30 p.m.

HOTELS

★★BEST WESTERN

8797 20th St., Vero Beach, 772-567-8321, 800-780-7234; www.bestwestern.com
115 rooms. Complimentary continental breakfast. Restaurant, bar. Outdoor pool, children's pool. Pets not accepted. Business center. High-speed Internet access. $

★★HOLIDAY INN

3384 Ocean Drive, Vero Beach, 772-231-2300, 800-465-4329; www.ichotelsgroup.com
104 rooms. Restaurant, bar. Fitness room. Outdoor pool, children's pool. High-speed Internet access. $

★★ISLANDER INN

3101 Ocean Drive, Vero Beach, 772-231-4431
16 rooms. Restaurant. Outdoor pool. $

RESTAURANTS

★★OCEAN GRILL

1050 Sexton Plaza, Vero Beach, 772-231-5409; www.ocean-grill.com
Seafood menu. Lunch, dinner. Bar. Children's menu. $$

★★PATIO

1103 21st St., Vero Beach, 772-567-7215; www.veropatio.com
One of the oldest eating establishments in Vero Beach; old Spanish décor. Mediterranean menu. Lunch, dinner, Sunday champagne brunch. Bar. Children's menu. Outdoor seating. $$

★
★★
★★
★★

WALT DISNEY WORLD

Since opening in 1971, Walt Disney World has received millions of visitors, making it the most popular tourist attraction in the world. From its major theme parks to its resort hotels, everything is run with a touch of make-believe in mind. It takes more than 35,000 people to keep the vacation kingdom going, and every facet of the operation is designed to keep visitors happy and content.

While the Magic Kingdom may be the best-known area of the park, it takes up only a fraction of the 28,000-acre resort complex (almost twice the size of the island of Manhattan). Combined with Epcot, Disney-MGM Studios, Animal Kingdom and a variety of new attractions, Walt Disney World is one of the most unique vacation destinations for families.

The Magic Kingdom, the first of the four major parks, offers more than 46 attractions as well as shows, shops, exhibits and special theme areas divided into seven "lands": Adventureland, Frontierland, Liberty Square, Fantasyland, Mickey's Toontown Fair, Tomorrowland and Main Street, U.S.A.

Epcot takes visitors through two distinct "worlds." Future World combines rides and attractions, technical innovations, discovery and scientific achievements, bringing to life a world of new ideas, adventures and entertainment. World Showcase unites 11 celebrated nations re-created in exact detail through architectural landmarks, shops, authentic food and entertainment.

Disney-MGM Studios explores the world of movies and television, both on-stage and off and includes a working studio. Palm-lined, Art Deco-style Hollywood Boulevard offers adventure, entertainment, shopping and dining in true Hollywood style. The park offers a mix of cinema nostalgia, sensational stunt work, television magic and backstage wizardry.

Animal Kingdom, Disney's newest theme park, unites fun with a love for animals. Seven years in the making, the park contains forests, streams and waterfalls, tropical jungles and savannahs, where many animals roam. A thousand birds and mammals representing more than 200 species are present.

In addition, Walt Disney World offers many hotels, a campground facility with a water park, a 7,500-acre conservation/wilderness area, daily parades and fireworks displays, shopping and fine dining. Activities include relaxing on more than four miles of beach, fishing, swimming, sailing, boating, waterskiing, tennis, steamboat excursions, ranch and trail rides and hiking. The five 18-hole championship golf courses are collectively referred to as the "Magic Linkdom": The Palm, Magnolia, Lake Buena Vista, Eagle Pines and Osprey Ridge, plus a nine-hole family-play course. All are open to the general public.

All of Walt Disney World is tied together by a transportation system that includes motor coaches, 19th-century ferryboats and the famous monorail. Guests at Fort Wilderness Campground and Disney-owned hotels have free use of the transporta-tion system. Special evening shows at Walt Disney World include fireworks, lasers, parades of singers and dancers, moonlight cruises and a variety of after-dark enter-tainment.

Walt Disney World is open every day of the year, with extended hours in summer and during holiday periods. Guided tours are recommended for first-time visitors. Various ticket combinations are available (inquire about details and limits at time of reservation).

WHAT TO SEE AND DO
ANIMAL KINGDOM
www.disneyworld.com
Part wildlife refuge, part theme park, part horticultural paradise—this place is home to 1,500 animals representing 250 different species. While thrill rides are featured here, the animal habitats take priority—it is a nature conservancy with an active endangered species breeding program. More than just an entrance, the Oasis is home to exotic flora and fauna. Don't miss the opportunity to smell the roses and tropi-cal gardens here. Take the bridge from the Oasis to Discovery Island to begin your adventure. Discovery Island is the central spoke of Animal Kingdom, home to Safari Village, an African-inspired area with a number of shops. At the Tree of Life, you can catch the eight-minute 3D extravaganza *It's Tough to Be a Bug!* starring Flik from *A Bug's Life*. Also check the tip boards for live entertainment schedules at the park. Take the path to the right to enter DinoLand U.S.A. Time-travel back 65 million years and come surprisingly close to some terrifying beasts on DINOSAUR, one of the most raucous rides in this kingdom. Asia, the newest land in the Animal Kingdom, is also the most exotic. Visitors are greeted by tiny but exquisite brass bells as they

enter the world of Southeast Asia, complete with rain forest, jungles and an authentic village full of artifacts. Several times daily, the 20-minute *Flights of Wonder* show can be seen at the 1,000-seat Caravan Stage outdoor amphitheater, an area that resembles an old Asian fort. Birds swoop, soar and entertain throughout, including macaws, ibis, falcons, owls and parrots. Incredibly authentic, Africa is 110 acres—larger than the entire Magic Kingdom. In addition to the village of Harambe and the Kilimanjaro Safaris, there is a walking safari along the Pangani Forest Exploration Trail, which takes you past an aviary, a giant aquarium filled with exotic fish and views of the savannah. Daily 4 p.m., check out Mickey's Jammin' Jungle Parade, a 15-minute island street party that begins at the Tusker House Gate at Harambe Village.

CIRQUE DU SOLEIL LA NOUBA

www.cirquedusoleil.com

Its name means "to party" and that's exactly what you'll do at this 90-minute (no intermission) circus that's unlike any you've ever seen. Eclectic and colorful, the show appeals to all ages. Located at Downtown Disney's West Side, *La Nouba* is performed in a 1,671-seat theater designed for the production. Shows at 6 p.m. and 9 p.m. Tuesday-Saturday.

DISNEY'S WIDE WORLD OF SPORTS COMPLEX

7491 West Highway, Kissimmee; www.disneyworldsports.com

Two hundred acres of spectator sports facilities, including a baseball stadium, cross-country course, track and field complex, martial arts venue and various sports fields. Spring training for baseball's Atlanta Braves is held here. Daily.

DISNEY-MGM STUDIOS

407-824-4321; www.disneyworld.com

Just southwest of Epcot off the main entrance road, this area houses three film and television soundstages of the Walt Disney Company, giving people a chance to watch entertainment in the making. Various rides and shows let visitors see the backlots, an animation studio, soundstages of famous films and an explanation of stunt work used in major movies. SuperStar Television and the Monster Sound Show enable guests to work with sound effects, trade quips on a sitcom and prepare for stardom in the "Green Room." Children can play on the *Honey, I Shrunk the Kids* Movie Set Adventure, with 30-foot-tall synthetic grass. Twilight Zone's Tower of Terror is a journey into a deserted hotel that ends in a 13-story plunge. Stage shows include *Beauty and the Beast, Voyage of the Little Mermaid* and *The Hunchback of Notre Dame*. Daily.

DOWNTOWN DISNEY

www.downtowndisney.com

Located on 120 acres on the north shore of the Buena Vista Lagoon, Downtown Disney is composed of three separate districts: Marketplace, Pleasure Island and West Side. It's a great place to spend an afternoon away from the theme parks. There are plenty of restaurants such as Bongo's Cuban Cafe and Wolfgang Puck Café, as well as entertainment venues such as the House of Blues, Cirque du Soleil, and for kids Disney Quest, which features video games and virtual reality experiences to please all. Daily 9 a.m.-11:30 p.m.; Pleasure Island opens at 7 p.m.

EAGLE PINES GOLF COURSE

Magic Kingdom/Disney Village, Lake Buena Vista, 407-939-4653;
www.disneyworld.com

Designed by renowned architect Pete Dye, this course features 16 holes with water, including a tee shot on number 14 that goes directly over protected wetlands. The course is laid out over a wide area and features undulating greens, like many Dye course designs do, as well as fairways that slope inward to catch some errant shots. A pine straw and sand rough waits to trap ill-placed shots, as well as help with proper drainage through the area of natural wetlands. Guests staying at Walt Disney World properties get a $10 reduction on the normal greens fee, which runs $110-$120 on most days. The courses four tee boxes (labeled "talon," "crest," "wings," and "feathers") run from a medium length of 6,772 to 4,838 yards.

EPCOT

407-939-6244; www.disneyworld.com

At 300 acres, Epcot is nearly three times the size of the Magic Kingdom. Built around a central lake, Epcot is a figure-eight-shaped park with two distinct areas. Future World features eight pavilions, including Spaceship Earth, a 16-million-pound, 180-foot-tall geosphere. Innoventions, an area that strives to present the latest in ever-changing technology; and Journey into Your Imagination, a 14-minute ride that features one of Disney's best-loved characters, Figment and his buddy Dreamfinder, who escort you through arts, literature and music. The World Showcase pavilions, surrounding a 40-acre lagoon, showcase 11 nations of the world: Canada, the United Kingdom, France, Morocco, Japan, America, Italy, Germany, China, Norway and Mexico. Each pavilion captures the international ambience of that particular corner of the world: you can buy authentic wares in shops, dine on ethnic cuisine or relax in a beer garden, pub or outdoor cafe. Street theater presentations, films and rides will entertain the kids.

ILLUMINATIONS

Epcot, Walt Disney World

A dramatic 15-minute laser, pyrotechnic and water show set to symphonic music, presented around the World Showcase Lagoon. Nightly.

MAGIC KINGDOM

Lake Buena Vista, 407-934-7639; www.disneyworld.com

The landscape of the Magic Kingdom is filled with the some of the world's most photographed sites that draw millions of families to the park every year. The most notable is Cinderella's Castle, built in 1971. Main Street, U.S.A., the first of seven "lands" that make up the Magic Kingdom, is the entrance. Stop first at City Hall, the park's main information center. Check out the board that lists expected wait times for the various rides. Moving clockwise to the left from Main Street, you'll cross an old-time wooden bridge into Adventureland, which transports you from small-town America to another place and time. Here you'll find two of the Magic Kingdom's most popular and enduring rides: Pirates of the Caribbean and the Jungle Cruise. Wild West-themed Frontierland has shooting galleries and foot-stomping hoedowns. Davy Crockett-style coonskin caps are popular but play second fiddle to some of the park's most popular rides, including Big Thunder Mountain Railroad and Splash

Mountain. Moving into Liberty Square, experience colonial America at the time of the Revolution. This is a wonderful spot for the kids to actually learn something—the Hall of Presidents offers a grand presentation of the landmarks in American history using life-like AudioAnimatronic replicas of the country's past leaders. Fantasyland is the heart and soul of the Magic Kingdom. You'll find classics including It's a Small World and Cinderella's Golden Carousel here, as well as attractions like Mickey's Philharmagic, a 3D film complete with smell-o-vision. The newest land in the Magic Kingdom, Mickey's Toontown Fair is also the best place in the park to meet and greet characters and get autographs. Last, check out Tomorrowland, originally built to showcase sci-fi at its best. The folks at Disney have done their best to update this area and make it as futuristic today as it was when it opened more than 30 years ago. It's home to some of the theme park's most popular rides, including Space Mountain and Buzz Lightyear's Space Ranger Spin.

MAGNOLIA GOLF COURSE

Magic Kingdom/Disney Village, Lake Buena Vista; www.disneyworld.com

Magnolia is the longest of the courses at Disney World, but the wide fairways make up for its length and are more forgiving for big hitters whose shots aren't always as straight as they want them to be. More than 1,500 namesake trees dot the landscape, and there are several elevated tee boxes and greens. At the edges of the greens are some 97 bunkers, including one on the 6th hole shaped like the head of the resort's famous mouse mascot.

OAK TRAIL GOLF COURSE

Magic Kingdom/Disney Village, Lake Buena Vista, 407-939-4653; www.golf.disneyworld.com

Located near the Magnolia Golf Course, Oak Trail is a family-friendly and economical option, both for playing and for simply enjoying the scenic oak-lined trails adjoining the walking course. At 2,913 yards, this Ron Garl-designed course provides a fun yet challenging quick 9 (par 36) with 15 sand bunkers and water on four holes (Daily).

OSPREY RIDGE GOLF COURSE

Magic Kingdom/Disney Village, Lake Buena Vista, 407-939-4653; www.golf.disneyworld.com

Laid out by Tom Fazio, this course features rolling fairways and high mounds that guard medium to large-sized greens. Known as the most challenging course in the area, it's also the priciest. (The twilight rate stings a little less than the normal greens fee.) Nearby is the Callaway Golf Performance Center at Bonnet Creek, which allows players to test out new clubs and have their swings evaluated via computer simulation.

PALM GOLF COURSE

Magic Kingdom/Disney Village, Lake Buena Vista, 407-939-4653; www.golf.disneyworld.com

Up-and-coming course designer Joe Lee laid out the Palm, which has 94 bunkers, 10 holes with water and several holes where sections of the fairway are separated by lengths of water. The 18th hole is a long par-four to an island green that consistently ranks among the toughest 10 holes played by golfers on the PGA Tour. Big hitters may be disappointed because they are forced to lay up to many greens due to water

FLORIDA

★
★
★
★

or elevation that makes the approach shot considerably more difficult. Still, it's a challenging and rewarding course to play. It is one of two courses that host the PGA's annual Funai Classic.

RICHARD PETTY DRIVING EXPERIENCE

Walt Disney World Speedway, Lake Buena Vista, 407-939-0130, 800-237-3889; www.1800bepetty.com

Sports fans can feel the power and speed of stock car racing. Different programs include Ride-Along (for those 16 and older) where you ride shotgun with a professional driver. The Rookie Experience, for the true stock car beginner (18 and older), is a three-hour session that goes eight laps around the track with you in charge. The more experienced can try the Kings Experience, where you race around the track for 18 laps, run in one 8-lap and one 10-lap session. And finally, for the true stock car junkie is the Experience of a Lifetime (18 and older): 30 white-knuckle laps driven in 10-lap increments. Daily; Rookie 8 a.m. and 2 p.m.; Kings and Lifetime 11 a.m.

SPECTRO MAGIC

Magic Kingdom, Walt Disney World

Musical parade of performers and floats decorated with millions of twinkling lights, covering such Disney themes as *Fantasia* and *The Little Mermaid*. Nightly, during extended hours.

TYPHOON LAGOON

A 56-acre water park located between Epcot and Disney Village Marketplace

Features world's largest wave pool, nine water slides descending from a 95-foot summit, surfing lagoon, saltwater snorkeling in Shark Reef, inner tube rides. Changing areas, lockers, showers, picnicking and restaurants.

WISHES

Magic Kingdom

Jiminy Cricket narrates this fireworks show above Cinderella's Castle (visible throughout the park). Nightly, during extended hours.

FLORIDA

★
★
★
★
★

SPECIAL EVENTS

ATLANTA BRAVES SPRING TRAINING

Cracker Jack Stadium, Walt Disney Wide World of Sports, Kissimmee, 407-934-7639; www.disneyworldsports.com

The Atlanta Braves have called the Cracker Jack Stadium at Disney's Wide World of Sports their spring training home since the complex opened to the public in March 1997. With 7,500 permanent seats and additional seating for 2,000 on a grass berm near left field, the complex is a favorite among baseball fanatics. The team normally plays 16 home games during spring training, many of them to sellout crowds. Early February-early April.

DISNEY MARATHON & HALF-MARATHON

Epcot; www.disneyworldsports.com

For the past decade, the Disney Marathon has consistently drawn huge crowds, both runners and spectators alike. The 26.2-mile race begins at Epcot, continues through the Magic Kingdom, Animal Kingdom, the Wide World of Sports complex and Disney-MGM Studios, and ends where it began. The half-marathon also begins at Epcot, but after circling the World Showcase, it continues through to the Magic Kingdom and the finish line. Runners must be able to maintain a minimum pace of 16 minutes per mile. Register early for the half-marathon, as participation is capped at 8,000 runners. Early January.

EPCOT INTERNATIONAL FLOWER AND GARDEN FESTIVAL

407-934-7639; www.disneyworld.com

Running annually between late April and early June, the International Flower and Garden Festival appeals to nature lovers of all ages. Combining incredible floral displays with interactive activities and hands-on seminars from some of America's top gardening experts, the festival also boasts a Spring Concert Series, which features some of pop music's most popular performers each weekend. Admission to the festival is included in the regular park admission fee. Late April-early June.

FUNAI GOLF CLASSIC AT WALT DISNEY WORLD

Magnolia and Palm golf course, Lake Buena Vista, 407-824-4321; www.disneyworld.com

The PGA Golf Classic at Walt Disney World has been held annually in October since 1971. The resort's Magnolia (7,190 yards) and Palm (6,957 yards) courses host the tournament, which is held near the end of the PGA season, making it a high-stakes tournament for golfers hoping to participate in the annual PGA Championship. The first two days are played as a pro-am tournament; the final round is played only on the 175-acre Magnolia course, which features 1,500 magnolia trees and 97 bunkers. Golf legends such as Jack Nicklaus, Mark O'Meara and Tiger Woods are all past champions. Late October.

HALLOWEEN

Disney Village Marketplace, Lake Buena Vista, 407-934-7639; www.disneyworld.com

Villains from Disney films, including the Evil Queen from *Snow White and the Seven Dwarfs* and Cruella DeVille from *101 Dalmatians,* make appearances after dark. Late September-late October.

WALT DISNEY WORLD INTERNATIONAL FOOD AND WINE FESTIVAL

Epcot, Lake Buena Vista, 407-939-3378; www.disneyworld.com

For almost a decade, Epcot has expanded travelers' palates with its International Food and Wine Festival, showcasing incredible creations from around the world. Appetizers are available for between $1 and $4.50. This celebration of flavor also features more than 30 brewed beers and ales. Wine-tasting seminars are offered at an additional cost, as are dinner pairings. Daily Eat to the Beat concerts by top-name artists are included in the price of admission. Call ahead for dining reservations. October-mid-November.

HOTELS

★★BEST WESTERN LAKE BUENA VISTA RESORT HOTEL

2000 Hotel Plaza Blvd., Lake Buena Vista, 407-828-2424, 800-348-3765; www.orlandoresorthotel.com

325 rooms. Wireless Internet access. Three restaurants, bar. Fitness room. Outdoor pool, children's pool. Airport transportation available. Business center. **$**

★★★CARIBE ROYALE

8101 World Center Drive, Lake Buena Vista, 407-238-8000, 800-823-8300;
www.cariberoyale.com
This hotel is a smart choice for families wanting close proximity to the theme parks. Suites are spacious and provide amenities that make guests feel pampered. The grounds include a 75-foot water slide and cascading waterfalls. 1,218 rooms, all suites. Complimentary full breakfast. Restaurant. Children's activity center. Fitness room. Two outdoor pools, children's pool, three whirlpools. Tennis. Business center. $$

★★★CELEBRATION HOTEL

700 Bloom St., Celebration, 407-566-6000, 888-499-3800; www.celebrationhotel.com
This intimate boutique hotel offers a decidedly adult experience compared to other hotels in the Disney World area. Rooms are luxurious with four-poster beds and top-quality bedding. Golf here is top notch, as is the food at the acclaimed Plantation restaurant. 115 rooms. Restaurant. Fitness room. Outdoor pool, whirlpool. Business center. $$

★★DISNEY'S ALL-STAR MOVIES RESORT

1991 W. Buena Vista Drive, Lake Buena Vista, 407-939-7000; www.disneyworld.com
1,920 rooms. Restaurant, bar. Two outdoor pools. Airport transportation available. $

★★DISNEY'S ALL-STAR MUSIC RESORT

1801 W. Buena Vista Drive, Lake Buena Vista, 407-939-6000; www.disneyworld.com
1,920 rooms. Restaurant, bar. Two outdoor pools, children's pool. Airport transportation available. $

★★DISNEY'S ALL-STAR SPORTS RESORT

1701 W. Buena Vista Drive, Lake Buena Vista, 407-939-5000; www.disneyworld.com
1,920 rooms. Restaurant, bar. Two outdoor pools, children's pool. $

★★★DISNEY'S ANIMAL KINGDOM LODGE

2901 Osceola Parkway, Lake Buena Vista, 407-938-3000; www.disneyworld.com
Disney offers the next best thing to a safari at the 75-acre Animal Kingdom Lodge, located in the middle of a lush 33-acre savannah that's home to more than 200 exotic animals. African influences permeate the property, from the handcrafted furnishings to the native cuisine served in two of the onsite restaurants. Visit the Arusha Rock Fire Pit, where outdoor events are held, and the Uzima, or "clean water" pool, which features a 67-foot-long water slide. The Hakuna Matata Playground is located next to the pool area. This resort is quite a distance (compared to the other resorts) from Downtown Disney and the Magic Kingdom, but transportation is free and frequent. 1,293 rooms. High-speed Internet access. Three restaurants, three bars. Children's activity center. Fitness room, spa. Outdoor pool, children's pool, two whirlpools. Airport transportation available. $$$

★★★DISNEY'S BOARDWALK INN

2101 N. Epcot Resorts Blvd., Lake Buena Vista, 407-939-5100; www.disneyworld.com
With the feel of the Atlantic City Boardwalk in the 1940s—complete with vintage roller coasters and period furnishings—the main hotel is a bit more luxurious in

feel than its time-share villa counterpart on the same waterfront Boardwalk. Each spacious room features a daybed, cherry-wood furniture, a classic postcard-print motif and wrought-iron bed. The Boardwalk that the hotel overlooks is chock-full of midway attractions and nightlife and is home to some of Disney's best restaurants. Children will love zipping down the 200-foot water slide or splashing in the pools. 372 rooms. High-speed Internet access. Five restaurants, four bars. Children's activity center. Fitness room, spa. Three outdoor pools, children's pool, whirlpool. Tennis. Airport transportation available. Business center. **$$$$**

★★★DISNEY'S BEACH CLUB RESORT

1800 Epcot Resorts Blvd., Lake Buena Vista, 407-934-8000; www.disneyworld.com

Architect Robert A. M. Stern has re-created a New England village with a nautical, turn-of-the-century theme. Built to look like a real seaside resort, this has waterslides and the sandy-bottomed Stormalong Bay (which holds 750,000 gallons of water). The resort also shares a full-service spa with Disney's Yacht Club Resort, its sister property. Rent boats at the marina, play a game of sand volleyball or ride bikes around the grounds. There are plenty of dining options in the hotel, and most of the park's attractions are just a short bus ride away. 854 rooms. High-speed Internet access; fee. Three restaurants, two bars. Children's activity center. Fitness room, spa. Beach. Two outdoor pools, children's pool, play ground, whirlpool. Tennis, volleyball court. Airport transportation available. Business center. **$$$$**

★★DISNEY'S CARIBBEAN BEACH RESORT

900 Cayman Way, Lake Buena Vista, 407-934-3400; www.disneyworld.com

Even in the center of Florida, you can still get a taste of the Caribbean by visiting the villages of Martinique, Barbados and Trinidad, all replicated at Disney's Caribbean Beach Resort. Located on a 42-acre lake, this resort is moderately priced but luxurious. Disney attention to detail features décor in the bright yellows and blues of Jamaica in the Victorian architecture, browns and yellows tied to the bird island of Trinidad, and the brilliant pinks and greens reminiscent of the island of Barbados. Each village has its own pool and beach area and also offers a restaurant, bar and whirlpool, as well as transportation and early admission to the Disney theme parks. 2,112 rooms. Restaurant, bar. Seven outdoor pools, children's pool. Play ground, volleyball court, water craft and bikes for rentals. High-speed Internet access; fee. **$$**

★★★DISNEY'S CONTEMPORARY RESORT

4600 N. World Drive, Lake Buena Vista, 407-824-1000; www.disneyworld.com

One of Walt Disney World's original resorts, this 14-story A-frame contemporary hotel is one of the most recognizable Disney icons, and one of the most unique. Showcasing a cavernous atrium, it is the only hotel in the world that features a monorail that travels directly through its center. The "futuristic" property, which opened with the Magic Kingdom in 1971, features modern textures and designs, as well as vibrant colors. Go to the rooftop California Grill for great views of the Magic Kingdom fireworks. 655 rooms. Five restaurants, two bars. Fitness room, spa. Beach. Two outdoor pools, two whirlpools, Volley ball. Airport transportation available. Business center. High-speed Internet access; fee. **$$$**

★★★DISNEY'S CORONADO SPRINGS RESORT

1000 W. Buena Vista Drive, Lake Buena Vista, 407-939-1000; www.disneyworld.com

The boardwalk at Disney's Coronado Springs Resort (located near Epcot, Disney-MGM Studios, and Animal Kingdom) draws its inspiration from Francisco de Coronado's travels from Mexico to the American Southwest. The hacienda-style resort is accented by mosaics, arched windows and doorways and clay-tile roofs, and even sports a five-story Mayan pyramid waterfall at the family pool. The moderately furnished guest rooms offer small refrigerators. 1,921 rooms. Disabled accessible rooms available. High-speed Internet access; fee. Six restaurants, two bars. Fitness room, spa. Beach. Three outdoor pools, children's pool, whirlpool. Airport transportation available. Business center. $$

★★DISNEY'S FORT WILDERNESS RESORT

4510 N. Fort Wilderness Trail, Lake Buena Vista, 407-824-2900; www.disneyworld.com

1,008 rooms. Restaurant, bar. Two outdoor pools, children's pool, playground Tennis, campfire sing along. $$$

★★★DISNEY'S GRAND FLORIDIAN RESORT & SPA

4401 Floridian Way, Lake Buena Vista, 407-824-3000; www.disneyworld.com

Resembling a fairy-tale castle with white towers and a red-tiled roof, Disney's Grand Floridian Resort & Spa offers a lakefront location right in the center of Walt Disney World. The Victorian lobby has an 85-foot-tall ceiling, crystal chandeliers and aviary. Cooking-themed events, Alice in Wonderland tea parties and even pirate-ship cruises are just a few of the kids programs offered here. There are also tennis courts, a fitness center and full-service spa. Dining options are plentiful, from casual, family-friendly restaurants to intimate, special-occasion spots such as Victoria and Albert's. The resort also offers monorail access. 901 rooms. High-speed Internet access; fee. Five restaurants, five bars. Children's activity center. Fitness room, spa. Beach. Two outdoor pools, children's pool, whirlpool. Tennis. Airport transportation available. Business center. $$$$

★★DISNEY'S OLD KEY WEST RESORT

1510 N. Cove Drive, Lake Buena Vista, 407-827-7700; www.disneyworld.com

709 rooms. High-speed Internet access. Two restaurants, bar. Children's activity center. Fitness room. Four outdoor pools, children's pool, whirlpool. Tennis. Airport transportation available. Volleyball and basketball courts, children's playground. $$$$

★★★DISNEY'S POLYNESIAN RESORT

1600 Seven Seas Drive, Lake Buena Vista, 407-824-2000; www.disneyworld.com

One of the original resorts at Walt Disney World, the Polynesian opened alongside the Magic Kingdom in 1971. Its tropical-themed rooms, decorated with upscale furnishings, are nestled along the shores of the Seven Seas Lagoon. The marina offers an assortment of boats to rent, and there is a large water slide in one of the pool areas. Guests can book a cruise for viewing the Magic Kingdom's nightly fireworks show. The popular Polynesian Luau Dinner Show at the Great Ceremonial House is presented twice nightly (depending on the weather). 847 rooms. High-speed Internet access. Four restaurants, two bars. Children's activity center. Fitness room. Beach. Three outdoor pools. Volleyball. Spa. Airport transportation available. $$$$

★★★DISNEY'S PORT ORLEANS RIVERSIDE RESORT

1251 Riverside Drive, Lake Buena Vista, 407-934-6000; www.disneyworld.com

The banks of Disney's re-created Sassagoula River provide a Deep South setting for the moderately priced Port Orleans Riverside Resort, reminiscent of a Southern bayou mansion. The guest rooms are rustic with birch furniture and stone accents in the bathrooms. The resort features seven pools and a three-acre Ol' Man Island great for fishing (catfish, bass and bluegill) and swimming. Port Orleans guests also have access to the water facilities at the adjacent French Quarter resort. Boat and bicycle rentals are also available, and easy access to Disney's world-class golf courses makes this resort a favorite. Boatwright's Dining Hall is the place to go for home-style cuisine. Resort-wide transportation is provided, as is early theme park admission on select days. 2,048 rooms. High-speed Internet access; fee. Seven restaurants, two bars. Five outdoor pools, children's pool, whirlpool. Airport transportation available. Horse-drawn excursion. **$$**

★★★DISNEY'S WILDERNESS LODGE

901 Timberline Drive, Lake Buena Vista, 407-824-3200; www.disneyworld.com

The Pacific Northwest and all the glory of the country's national parks are recalled in the beauty of the rustic Wilderness Lodge. Located on the south shore of the 340-acre Bay Lake, the lobby boasts a massive 82-foot-tall, three-sided quarried stone fireplace and décor inspired by Native American designs. Adding to the ambience are bubbling springs and a 12-story geyser that erupts every hour. Boat and bicycle rentals are available, as is an onsite health club and biking and jogging trails. For teens, there is the ever-popular arcade, and the Cub's Den offers supervised fun and food for children ages 4 to 12. Early theme park admission is offered on select days, and onsite transportation is complimentary. 728 rooms. High-speed Internet access. Three restaurants, two bars. Children's activity center. Fitness room, spa. Beach. Outdoor pool, children, two whirlpools. Airport transportation available, Horse dragging excursions, campfire sing along, fishing. **$$$**

★★★DISNEY'S YACHT CLUB RESORT

1700 Epcot Resort Blvd., Orlando, 407-934-7000; www.disneyworld.com

Designed by architect Robert A. M. Stern, this waterside hotel feels like a coastal New England inn, complete with a working lighthouse. Just a short walk from Disney's Boardwalk and convenient to all of the parks, the wraparound porch and sandy-bottomed pool make it feel like a retreat. Rent a bicycle for two to ride around the grounds or take a short cruise around the man-made lake. 635 rooms. Restaurant, bar. Children's activity center. Fitness room, spa. Two outdoor pools, whirlpool. Business center. Tennis. Volleyball, playground. Beach. Fishing. **$$$$**

★★DOUBLETREE GUEST SUITES

2305 Hotel Plaza Blvd., Orlando, 407-934-1000, 800-222-8733;
www.doubletreeguestsuites.com

229 rooms, all suites. Restaurant, bar. Fitness room. Outdoor pool, children's pool, whirlpool. Tennis. Pets not accepted. Restaurants open daily 7 a.m.-11 p.m. **$**

★★★HILTON IN THE WALT DISNEY WORLD RESORT

1751 Hotel Plaza Blvd., Lake Buena Vista, 407-827-4000, 800-445-8667;
www.hilton-wdw.com

A façade of pink and blue rises above the sparkling fountains and two outdoor pools. Located inside the Walt Disney World Resort, this hotel is set on 23 private acres.

It offers complimentary transportation to the parks and nine restaurant and lounge options. 814 rooms. Restaurant, bar. Children's activity center. Fitness room. Two outdoor pools, children's pool, whirlpool. Business center Pets not accepted. $$

★★HOLIDAY INN SUNSPREE RESORT LAKE BUENA VISTA

13351 State Road 535, Orlando, 407-239-4500, 800-366-6299; www.kidsuites.com
507 rooms. Restaurant, bar. Children's activity center. Fitness room. Outdoor pool, children's pool. $$

★★★HYATT REGENCY GRAND CYPRESS

1 Grand Cypress Blvd., Orlando, 407-239-1234, 800-554-9288;
www.hyattgrandcypress.com
The amenities at this hotel are spectacular, including a private lake, miles of tropical nature trails, a pool with cascading waterfalls, 12 tennis courts, an equestrian center and of course, plenty of golf, played on 45 magnificent holes designed by Jack Nicklaus. 750 rooms. Wireless Internet access. Four restaurants, five bars. Children's activity center. Fitness room, fitness classes available. Outdoor pool, children's pool, whirlpool. Golf, 45 holes. Tennis. Airport transportation available. Business center. $$$

★★STAYBRIDGE SUITES LAKE BUENA VISTA

8751 Suiteside Drive, Orlando, 407-238-0777, 800-866-4549; www.sborlando.com
150 rooms, all suites. Complimentary full breakfast. High-speed Internet access. Fitness room. Outdoor pool, children's pool, whirlpool. Business center. $

★★★VILLAS OF GRAND CYPRESS

1 N. Jacaranda, Orlando, 407-239-4700, 877-330-7377; www.grandcypress.com
Spectacular scenery sets the tone for the Villas of Grand Cypress, tucked away within the 1,500-acre Hyatt resort. Conveniently located, it is only minutes from Orlando International Airport, the Convention Center and theme parks. The villas are spacious and were designed with comfort in mind. The Golf Academy is renowned, while the resort's equestrian center, approved by the British Horse Society, offers instruction for all levels, leads trail rides and hosts special events. Retreat to the privacy of a villa for an in-room spa treatment or venture out to one of the resort's restaurants and lounges. 146 rooms, all suites. Two restaurants, two bars. Fitness room. Outdoor pool, whirlpool. Golf, 45 holes. Tennis. Business center. $$$

FLORIDA

★
★
★
★
★

★★★WALT DISNEY WORLD DOLPHIN

1500 Epcot Resorts Blvd., Lake Buena Vista, 407-934-4000, 800-227-1500;
www.swandolphin.com
Designed by Michael Graves as entertainment architecture, this hotel features a waterfall cascading down the front of the building into a pool supported by two towering dolphin statues. A great place for conventioneers and vacationers alike, the Dolphin has many dining selections, great access to the theme parks and a view of Epcot's fireworks over the lake. Guests receive free transportation to Walt Disney World by both land and water. 2,265 rooms and suites. Restaurant, bar. Children's activity center. Fitness room. Four outdoor pools, children's pool, four whirlpools. Tennis. Business center. $$$

★★★WALT DISNEY WORLD SWAN

1200 Epcot Resort Blvd., Lake Buena Vista, 407-934-3000, 800-227-1500;
www.swandolphin.com

If Walt Disney World is the vacation capital of the world, then the Walt Disney World Swan is the fantasy capital of hotels. Designed by renowned architect Michael Graves, it features two nearly five-story-tall swans that nest regally above the hotel, with multicolored waves fanning the building's outer walls. The resort has four onsite pools and a beach surrounded by lush, tranquil gardens. Aside from the theme parks, the resort offers access (and advance tee times) to Disney's top-flight golf courses, tennis courts, jogging trails and health club, as well as a miniature golf course for kids. An impressive 17 restaurants and lounges are available between the Swan and the adjoining Dolphin hotel. 1,500 rooms. Restaurant, bar. Fitness room. Four outdoor pools, children's pool, four whirlpools. Tennis. Business center. $$$

RESTAURANTS

★★★ARTIST POINT

901 W. Timberline Drive, Lake Buena Vista, 407-824-1081; www.disneyworld.com

The chef presents authentic Pacific Northwest cuisine at this delightful restaurant in Disney's Wilderness Lodge and Resort. Salmon and wild game are the specialties. Both the seven-story fireplace in the lobby and the man-made geyser that erupts several times an hour wow diners here. Pacific Northwest menu. Dinner. Children's menu. $$$

★★CALIFORNIA GRILL

4600 N. World Drive, Lake Buena Vista, 407-939-3463; www.disneyworld.com
California menu. Dinner. Bar. Children's menu. Valet parking. $$$

★★CITRICOS

4401 Floridian Way, Lake Buena Vista, 407-939-3463; www.disneyworld.com
Mediterranean menu. Dinner. Bar. Children's menu. Casual attire. Valet parking. $$$

★★FLYING FISH CAFÉ

2101 N. Epcot Resorts Blvd., Lake Buena Vista, 407-939-2359
American menu. Dinner. Bar. Children's menu. $$

★HOUSE OF BLUES

1490 E. Buena Vista Drive, Lake Buena Vista, 407-934-2583; www.hob.com
Cajun/Creole menu. Lunch, dinner. Casual attire. $$

★★★JIKO—THE COOKING PLACE

2901 Osceola Parkway, Lake Buena Vista, 407-939-3463; www.disneyworld.com
Continental menu. Dinner. Children's menu. $$$

★★OHANA

1600 Seven Seas Drive, Lake Buena Vista, 407-824-1334; www.disneyworld.com
Pacific-Rim/Pan-Asian menu. Breakfast, dinner. Bar. Children's menu. $$

★★PORTOBELLO YACHT CLUB

1650 Buena Vista Drive, Lake Buena Vista, 407-934-8888; www.levyrestaurants.com
Italian menu. Lunch, dinner. Bar. Children's menu. Valet parking. Outdoor seating. $$

★★SPOODLES
2101 Epcot Resort Blvd., Lake Buena Vista, 407-939-3463
Mediterranean menu. Breakfast, dinner. Children's menu. Valet parking. Daily. **$$**

★★★★VICTORIA AND ALBERT'S
4401 Floridian Way, Lake Buena Vista, 407-939-3463; www.disney.com
Victoria and Albert's is tailor-made for those craving sophistication. The setting is Victorian by design, with thick drapes, plush carpeting and elegant table settings. To match the regal ambience, the kitchen provides an equally impressive seven-course prix fixe menu. Dinner begins with an assortment of amuse bouche and ends with petit fours and a large selection of Madeira, ports and cognacs. The wine list is diverse and extensive, and wine pairings are offered at an extra charge. French, International menu. Dinner. Bar. Jacket required. Reservations recommended. Valet parking. **$$$$**

★★★YACHTSMAN STEAK HOUSE
1700 Epcot Resort Blvd., Lake Buena Vista, 407-939-3463; www.disneyworld.com
The feel of casual New England pervades this American steakhouse with a blue-and-khaki nautical décor. Greeted by a display of aged meats, you'll choose from beef steaks, chops, poultry and seafood. Steak menu. Dinner. Bar. Children's menu. Valet parking. **$$$**

WEST PALM BEACH
West Palm Beach has developed as a resort city because of its accessibility to nearby beaches and the Intracoastal Waterway, providing a number of boating opportunities. The downtown area was rebuilt as a planned community of shops, restaurants and housing in the 1990s and is now a popular spot for nightlife. There are more than 145 golf courses in Palm Beach County.
Information: Palm Beach County Convention & Visitors Bureau,
1555 Palm Beach Lakes Blvd., 561-233-3000, 800-833-5733; www.palmbeachfl.com

WHAT TO SEE AND DO
DOLPHIN WORLD
954-525-4441, 866-630-9868; www.dolphinworld.org
Swim with the dolphins in Southeastern Florida. Structured, natural and wild dolphin swim programs available. One-to four-day Marine Animal Vacations include dolphin swim programs, ocean snorkel trip, environmental tour, crocodile tour. Pick-up service from West Palm Beach, Fort Lauderdale and Miami to the Florida Keys. Daily.

MOUNTS BOTANICAL GARDEN
559 N. Military Trail, West Palm Beach, 561-233-1757, 561-233-1749; www.mounts.org
Oldest and largest public botanical garden in Palm Beach County. More than 13 acres of tropical and subtropical plants, including herb, palm, cactus, tropical fruit collections and more. Monday-Saturday 8:30 a.m.-4:30 p.m., Sunday noon-4 p.m.

NORTON MUSEUM OF ART
1451 S. Olive Ave., West Palm Beach, 561-832-5196; www.norton.org
Permanent collections include 19th- and 20th-century European paintings; American art from 1900 to the present; a distinguished Chinese collection; sculpture patio. Tuesday-Saturday 10 a.m.-5 p.m., Sunday 1-5 p.m.; May-October: closed Monday.

PALM BEACH ZOO AT DREHER PARK

1301 Summit Blvd., West Palm Beach, 561-547-9453; www.palmbeachzoo.org

More than 400 animals on 23 acres in natural settings. Petting zoo. Daily 9 a.m.-5 p.m.

PEANUT ISLAND

6500 Peanut Island Road, Riviera Beach, 561-845-4445, 866-383-5730

A 79-acre island where John F. Kennedy had a bomb-shelter bunker built for himself during the Cuban Missile Crisis. It is now a full-service recreational park with boat dock, fishing pier, camping, picnicking.

SOUTH FLORIDA SCIENCE MUSEUM

4801 Dreher Trail N., West Palm Beach, 561-832-1988; www.sfsm.org

Dozens of hands-on interactive exhibits, plus the expanded McGinty Aquariums. Observatory viewing and laser light shows on Friday evenings. Planetarium show daily, inquire for schedule. Museum Monday-Friday 10 a.m.-5 p.m., Saturday to 6 p.m., Sunday noon-6 p.m.

SPECIAL EVENT

BASEBALL SPRING TRAINING

Roger Dean Stadium, 4751 Main St., Jupiter, 561-775-1818

Florida Marlins and St. Louis Cardinals spring baseball training, exhibition games. March-early April.

HOTELS

★BEST WESTERN

1505 Belvedere Road, West Palm Beach, 561-471-8700, 800-937-8376; www.bestwestern.com

135 rooms. Complimentary continental breakfast. Outdoor pool. Airport transportation available. Pets not accepted. High-speed Internet access. $

★BEST WESTERN PALM BEACH LAKES

1800 Palm Beach Lakes Blvd., West Palm Beach, 561-683-8810, 800-937-8376; www.bestwestern.com

135 rooms. Complimentary continental breakfast. Outdoor pool. Airport transportation available. Pets not accepted. High-speed Internet access. $

★★COMFORT INN AND CONFERENCE CENTER

1901 Palm Beach Lakes Blvd., West Palm Beach, 561-689-6100, 877-424-6423; www.westpalm.com

160 rooms. Pets accepted, some restrictions; fee. Complimentary continental breakfast. Outdoor pool. Business center. $

★★DOUBLETREE HOTEL

4431 PGA Blvd., Palm Beach Gardens, 561-622-2260, 800-222-8733; www.doubletree.com

279 rooms. Restaurant, bar. Fitness room. Outdoor pool, whirlpool. $

★★EMBASSY SUITES

4350 PGA Blvd., Palm Beach Gardens, 561-622-1000, 800-362-2779;
www.embassysuites.com

160 rooms, all suites. Complimentary continental breakfast. Restaurants, bar. Fitness room. Outdoor pool, children's pool, whirlpool. Tennis. **$$**

★E. R. BRADLEY'S SALOON

104 Clematis St., West Palm Beach, 561-833-3520; www.erbradleys.com

American menu. Breakfast, lunch, dinner, late-night. Monday-Thursday 8 a.m.-3 p.m., Friday-Sunday 8 a.m.-4 p.m. Bar. Casual attire. Outdoor seating. **$$**

★★★HILTON SINGER ISLAND OCEANFRONT RESORT

3700 N. Ocean Drive, Singer Island, 561-848-3888, 800-445-8667; www.hilton.com

There are 210 newly decorated rooms and suites (all with private balconies overlooking the Atlantic) at this family-friendly, beachfront resort. After taking in a gorgeous sunrise walk and other ocean-side recreations, head to nearby downtown Palm Beach for shopping and dining. 210 rooms. Wireless Internet access. Restaurant, two bars. Fitness room. Beach. Outdoor pool, children's pool, whirlpool. Business center. **$$**

★★HOLIDAY INN

1301 Belvedere Road, West Palm Beach, 561-659-3880, 800-465-4329;
www.hiwestpalmbeach.com

199 rooms. Restaurant, bar. Fitness room. Outdoor pool. Airport transportation available. **$**

★★★MARRIOTT WEST PALM BEACH

1001 Okeechobee Blvd., West Palm Beach, 561-833-1234, 800-376-2292;
www.marriott.com

This hotel has 15,000 square feet of function space geared toward meeting and banquet clientele, and is located in the heart of West Palm Beach's downtown business and entertainment district. Visit the Floribbean Keys Cafe or the Cezanne bar or take in a touring Broadway show or concert at the adjacent Kravis Center. 352 rooms. Restaurant, bar. Fitness room. Outdoor pool, whirlpool. Business center. **$$**

★★★PALM BEACH GARDENS MARRIOTT

4000 RCA Blvd., Palm Beach Gardens, 407-622-8888, 800-678-9494;
www.marriott.com

Though it serves mostly business guests, this property doesn't skimp on resortlike amenities and it's just three miles from the beach. Enjoy the restaurant, bar and Club Safari nightclub, nearby championship golf courses, tennis and Gardens of the Palm Beaches shops. 279 rooms. Restaurant, bar. Fitness room. Outdoor pool, whirlpool. Business center. **$**

★★★THE RESORT AT SINGER ISLAND

3800 N. Ocean Drive, Singer Island, 561-340-1700; www.luxurycollection.com

Located on Singer Island, this property features one- and two-bedroom condos in an elegant, luxurious setting 10 miles north of Palm Beach. Floor-to-ceiling windows, contemporary art and marble and polished wood accents are showcased in an oval-shaped lobby. The condo units feature a full refrigerator, microwave, stove top, washer/dryer and Bose stereos Bathrooms are luxurious and come with Gilchrist & Soames products. 239 rooms, all suites. Wireless Internet access. Restaurants, bars. Children's activity center. Fitness room, fitness classes available, spa. Beach. Outdoor pool, whirlpool. Airport transportation available. Business center. $$$

SPECIALTY LODGING

HIBISCUS HOUSE

501 30th St., West Palm Beach, 561-863-5633, 800-203-4927; www.hibiscushouse.com
Mayor David Dunkle built this bed and breakfast in 1922 during the Florida land boom. Five rooms. Pets accepted. Complimentary full breakfast. Outdoor pool. $

RESTAURANTS

★ALEYDA'S MEXICAN RESTAURANT

1890 Okeechobee Blvd., West Palm Beach, 561-688-9033; www.aleydas.com
Mexican menu. Lunch, dinner. Children's menu. $$

★★CAFÉ DU PARC

612 N. Highway 1, Lake Park, 561-845-0529
French menu. Dinner. Closed Sunday-Monday; August-late September. Jacket required. $$$

★★★CAFE PROTÉGÉ

2400 Metrocentre Blvd., West Palm Beach, 561-687-2433; www.cafeprotege.com
Check out the stars of tomorrow at this restaurant in the Florida Culinary Institute. American menu. Lunch. Closed Saturday-Sunday. Bar. $$$

★PRONTI'S ITALIAN KITCHEN

1440 10th St., Lake Park, 561-842-3457
Italian menu. Lunch, dinner. Children's menu. $$

WINTER HAVEN

Winter Haven attracts more than 1 million visitors a year, most of whom come to see Cypress Gardens and enjoy the freshwater lakes in this area. Winter Haven is a town bolstered by tourism, citrus growing and processing and light manufacturing and distribution.
Information: Chamber of Commerce, 401 Avenue B N.W., 863-293-2138;
www.winterhavenfl.com

WHAT TO SEE AND DO

WATER-SKI MUSEUM AND HALL OF FAME

1251 Holy Cow Road, Polk City, 863-324-2472; www.waterskihalloffame.com
Museum depicts the colorful history of waterskiing; the Hall of Fame honors the pioneers of the sport. Monday-Friday 10 a.m.-5 p.m.

HOTEL

★★CLARION HOTEL

1150 S.W. Third St., Winter Haven, 863-294-4451
165 rooms. Pets accepted. Restaurant, bar. Fitness room. Outdoor pool, children's pool. $

RESTAURANT

★★CHRISTY'S SUNDOWN

1100 Third St. Southwest, Winter Haven, 863-293-0069

Seafood, steak menu. Lunch, dinner. Closed Sunday; holidays. Bar. Children's menu. $$

WINTER PARK

Winter Park is a college town, vacation retreat and artist's haven.

Information: Chamber of Commerce, 151 W. Lyman
Ave., 407-644-8281; www.winterpark.org

WHAT TO SEE AND DO

CHARLES HOSMER MORSE MUSEUM OF AMERICAN ART

445 N. Park Ave., Winter Park, 407-645-5311; www.morsemuseum.org

If you're a Tiffany glass lover, this place is a must-see. Home to the world's largest collection of Louis Comfort Tiffany artworks, the museum also houses an impressive collection of late-19th-century and early-20th-century American art including paintings, graphics, pottery and decorative arts. Make sure to check out the completely reassembled Tiffany's chapel, originally created for the 1893 World's Fair in Chicago. Tuesday-Saturday 9:30 a.m.-4 p.m., Sunday 1-4 p.m.; additional Friday hours September-May, 4-8 p.m.; closed Monday.

PARK AVENUE

150 N. New York Ave., Winter Park, 407-644-8281;
www.orlandoonline.com/parkavemer.htm

Located just six miles north of Orlando in Winter Park, Park Avenue is often called Orlando's Rodeo Drive because of its upscale shopping and unique restaurants. Far more beautiful than its Southern California counterpart, it is reminiscent of a charming New England village with its brick-lined streets and stately old-growth trees standing sentry along the route. In addition to specialty boutiques, you'll find national chains like Talbots and Crabtree & Evelyn, as well as a diverse selection of galleries. Central Park offers a relaxing spot to sit along the avenue, home to the city's famous Winter Park Sidewalk Arts Festival every March.

ROLLINS COLLEGE

1000 Holt Ave., Winter Park, 407-646-2000; www.rollins.edu

One of the best known liberal arts colleges in the country, Rollins, located in downtown Winter Park, is also Florida's oldest college, founded in 1885 by New England Congregationalists. It counts among its alumni Nobel Prize winner Donald Cram, Fred Rogers (of Mr. Rogers' Neighborhood fame), Anthony Perkins and Buddy Ebsen and has produced numerous Rhodes, Fulbright, Goldwater and Truman scholars. Of particular interest is the Walk of Fame, established in 1929 to honor significant historical figures. More than 500 separate stones can be found on the Mills Lawn in the center of campus, as well as the Annie Russell Theatre and the Cornell Fine Arts Museum.

WINTER PARK SCENIC BOAT TOUR

312 E. Morse Blvd., Winter Park, 407-644-4056; www.scenicboattours.com

Located just north of Orlando, Winter Park is where much of Florida's old money can be found. The Winter Park scenic boat tour, a narrated, one-hour-long, 12-mile

FLORIDA

★
★
★
★
★

journey that meanders through three of the town's 17 lakes, is the best way to view its stately mansions, magnificent gardens, lush foliage and tropical wildlife. Daily 10 a.m.-4 p.m. (except Christmas); tours depart on the hour.

WINTER PARK VILLAGE

500 N. Orlando Ave., Winter Park, 407-571-2502; www.shopwinterparkvillage.com
The 524,000-square-foot Winter Park Village is a new shopping oasis built on the site of the old Winter Park Mall, one of the area's first shopping centers. The Village, which resembles an old-fashioned downtown area, features everything from boutiques to restaurants to bookstores and galleries to beauty salons and a 20-screen multiplex. Daily.

SPECIAL EVENT

WINTER PARK SIDEWALK ART FESTIVAL

Park Avenue, Winter Park, 407-672-6390; www.wpsaf.org
Held annually for more than 40 years on the third weekend in March on historic Park Avenue, the Winter Park Sidewalk Art Festival is the second-largest fine arts festival in the country, boasting an impressive display of art mediums from more than 225 artists. Works span 11 categories, from photography to mixed-medium to sculpture to watercolor. Mid-March.

HOTELS

★★BEST WESTERN MOUNT VERNON INN

110 S. Orlando Ave., Winter Park, 407-647-1166, 800-992-3379;
www.bestwestern.com
143 rooms. Restaurant, bar. Outdoor pool. Fitness center. High-speed Internet access. **$**

★★★PARK PLAZA HOTEL

307 Park Ave. South, Winter Park, 407-647-1072, 800-228-7220; www.parkplazahotel.com
No two rooms are alike at this refreshing, intimate hotel just minutes from Orlando. Park Avenue shops and restaurants, beautiful woodwork, brass beds and courtyard dining at the well-recognized Park Plaza Gardens restaurant are a few reasons to visit. 28 rooms. Children over five years only. Fitness center. Complimentary continental breakfast. Restaurant. Valet Parking. **$$**

RESTAURANTS

★★PARK PLAZA GARDENS

319 Park Ave. S., Winter Park, 407-645-2475; www.parkplazagardens.com
International menu. Lunch, dinner Sunday brunch. Bar. Children's menu. Casual attire. Reservations recommended. Outdoor seating. **$$$**

★WINNIE'S ORIENTAL GARDEN

1346 Orange Ave., Winter Park, 407-629-2111; www.winniesmenu.com
Chinese and seafood menu. Lunch, dinner. Closed Monday. Casual attire. Reservations recommended. Outdoor seating. **$$**

INDEX

★
★
★
★
★

210

INDEX

★
★
★
★
★

★
★
★
★
★

★
★
★
★
★

Morton's, the Steakhouse (Boca Raton), *23*

Morton's, The Steakhouse (Jacksonville), *75*

Mounts Botanical Garden (West Palm Beach), *201*

Mr. Han (Gainesville), *67*

Mrs. Mac's Kitchen (Key Largo), *81*

Museum of Art (Fort Lauderdale), *52*

Museum of Contemporary Art (North Miami), *102*

Museum of Discovery and Science and AutoNation IMAX 3-D Theater (Fort Lauderdale), *53*

Museum of Fine Arts (St. Petersburg), *172*

Museum of Fine Arts (Tallahassee), *176*

Museum of Science and History (Jacksonville), *72*

Museums and Nature Center of Crane Point Hammock (Marathon), *95*

The Mutiny Hotel (Miami), *106*

N

Naples Beach Hotel & Golf Club (Naples), *123*

Naples Grande Beach Resort (Naples), *123*

National Hotel (Miami Beach), *114*

National Museum of Naval Aviation (Pensacola), *152*

Natural Bridge Battlefield Historic State Park (Tallahassee), *176*

Naval Air Station Pensacola (Pensacola), *152*

Nemo (Miami Beach), *117*

Neomi (Sunny Isles), *108*

News Café (Miami Beach), *117*

New York Mets Spring Training (Port St. Lucie), *64*

New York Yankees Spring Training (Tampa), *180*

Norman's (Orlando), *140*

O

Oak Trail Golf Course (Lake Buena Vista), *192*

Oasis Café (Fort Lauderdale), *60*

Ocala National Forest (Ocala), *127*

Ocean Grill (Vero Beach), *188*

Ocean Key Resort & Spa (Key West), *86*

Ocean Walk Shoppes @ the Village (Daytona Beach), *41*

Ohana (Lake Buena Vista), *200*

Old Capitol Museum (Tallahassee), *176*

Old House City Inn (St. Augustine), *169*

Old Island Day (Key West), *84*

Old Lisbon (Miami), *109*

Old Pensacola Lighthouse (Pensacola), *152*

Old Powder House Inn (St. Augustine), *169*

Old Town (Kissimmee), *90*

Old Town Manor (Key West), *88*

Omni Jacksonville Hotel (Jacksonville), *73*

Ophelia's on the Bay (Siesta Key), *163*

Orange Avenue (Orlando), *129*

Original Dolphin Encounter Cruise (Clearwater), *28*

Orlando Magic (NBA) (Orlando), *129*

Orlando Museum of Art (Orlando), *129*

Orlando Premium Outlets (Orlando), *129*

Orlando Science Center (Orlando), *130*

Orlando World Center Marriott Resort (Orlando), *135*

Ormond Memorial Art Museum and Gardens (Ormond Beach), *141*

Ortanique on the Mile (Coral Gables), *38*

Oscar Scherer State Park (Osprey), *187*

Osprey Ridge Golf Course (Lake Buena Vista), *192*

Osteria Del Teatro (Miami Beach), *117*

Outback Bowl (Tampa), *180*

P

Pablo Historical Park (Jacksonville Beach), *75*

Pacific Time (Miami Beach), *117*

Pacino's Italian Ristorante (Kissimmee), *92*

Padrino's (Boca Raton), *24*

Palm (Bay Harbor Island), *20*

Palm Beach Gardens Marriott (Palm Beach Gardens), *203*

★
★
★
★

★
★
★
★
★

223

INDEX

NOTES

INDEX